Unspun Sonnets

A Nice Finish

KAREE STARDENS

authorHOUSE®

AuthorHouse™
1663 Liberty Drive
Bloomington, IN 47403
www.authorhouse.com
Phone: 1-800-839-8640

First published by AuthorHouse 10/6/2011

ISBN: 978-1-4670-4361-8 (e)
ISBN: 978-1-4670-4362-5 (sc)

Library of Congress Control Number: 2011917706

Printed in the United States of America

Any people depicted in stock imagery provided by Thinkstock are models, and such images are being used for illustrative purposes only. Certain stock imagery © Thinkstock.

This book is printed on acid-free paper.

Because of the dynamic nature of the Internet, any web addresses or links contained in this book may have changed since publication and may no longer be valid. The views expressed in this work are solely those of the author and do not necessarily reflect the views of the publisher, and the publisher hereby disclaims any responsibility for them.

I dedicate this book to people who are afraid to change or just too afraid to take a chance. You only have one life to live and it is your choice as to how you live it; hopefully this will encourage you. I also dedicate this book to the folks who helped to make it happen. You know who you are, and I love you very much. Thanks for the support on my first book.

<u>DISCLAIMER!!!</u>

Please remember I am not bashing anyone – that is not the intent. You will see it as the book progresses. The events of this book are as told (word for word) by the girl who went through the events. They are not fictional, but the names of all the people and locations are changed for their protection. Any similar events in similar places with similar names are strictly coincidental. This book deals with mature subjects and contains some vulgar dialect.

chapter 1:

A sonnet is classified as a little song or a little poem. Since I am both a little song writer and a little poet, I decided to use that as part of my title. Sometimes you may think you are done with certain aspects of life, but then it is only a matter of time before you realize that same aspect repeats in verses three or four of the sonnet of reality. That is what I thought when I was finished writing my first book. Thinking that I was finished with writing, I threw myself into music. However, only wise old time has shown that just because I pen songs instead of books, I am still a writer. So, along with echoes of the same question, why not do both? My name is Karee Stardens and I am twenty four years old and still writing.

Life has a funny way of tabbing itself out into a song that no one can predict, transpose or rewrite. My first book, called *One Life* tells about my childhood and overcoming the trials set before me since infancy, told from memory. The little explanation is necessary since things from it will come to play a little further in this book as this short time has brought a tremendous amount of closure, thus ending that sad sonnet and beginning another one whose tune is quite unknown, but sounds much more melodically happy. So much has happened in the last four years! A lot of good tunes and a little bit of bad mixed with a dash of

…weird seventh suspended minor chords, or tri-tones, or diminished sevenths for the extreme dissonance.

Let's see…where did I leave off on the first book? Oh yes, I believe it was the first song in the studio? Yes, I had quit music entirely because absolutely EVERYONE in the world did not think that I should do it; *"you should be a cook,"* **"you should be a model,"** *"you should draw,"* **"you should write,"** and so on and so on. When something went wrong, people even said that God did not want me to sing. Well that was it; I quit. Yes sir, (or ma'am) for two years – in the car, in the shower, I also listened to music less because it hurt to not sing with it.

I had a friend who had a guitar but did not really know how to play it. One day I noticed that it was out of tune so I tuned it somehow by ear! Her eyes went wide and she said "you tuned it!" but I have no idea how it happened! I actually bought a nice keyboard and then while Sally and I were in town, said "I'm getting a guitar" (to which she responded "finally!") So we ventured into a music store and I picked out a nice sounding acoustic. Now the thing is that I bought it with my rent money, heh…so when I pulled up with Lily, later on, I was going to pretend to borrow her guitar, but lo and behold, Noella and Drew pulled up right beside my car as I was pulling both guitars out – Lily's for her car, mine for the house.

Once inside their place, I hummed and hawed and finally said "I have some good news and some bad news," with an awkward smile.

"Oh, yeah, what's that?" they asked pleasantly, shamefully widening my smirk.

"We-elllll…I got a new guitar today," I started half-guiltily.

"Really?" Noella exclaimed happily while Drew asked to see it. I showed them and all was happy…and they echoed Sally's "Finally!"

"So what's the bad news?" Noella asked, going into the kitchen to put groceries away. I trailed behind with a lively bounce…well, here goes for impulse!

"Err…um; I used this month's rent to pay for it!" I confessed, "But there's money coming in two weeks to pay you back."

"Oh, not a problem," Noella shrugged and Drew laughed.

"Really?" I asked, surprised and pleased at the lack of lecture or disappointment.

"Yeah, don't worry about it," Noella repeated – what great support! They said it was about time and they were excited because now I had good quality instruments to play and they said it would push me even more. One month later Lily and I sang in a local festival – about eight songs – where she played keyboard and I sang and then we both played guitar while I sang. It was fun and a new experience. It was after this festival that I had quit singing for some dumb reason.

Well it was not long before I picked up guitar and piano. Soon I was playing both and then it dawned on the horizon that quitting music was the stupidest idea ever! All it did was make me mopey and miserable and set me back for two years. Oh dear, no good at all! Noella's grandkids were over for the summer and they seemed to be the only ones who thought I should not quit music. We had a great chat, those kids and me. They spoke about their family life (which I had known of before) with their parents and then they told me something unexpected – that they look up to me. Perhaps the sweetest thing I have ever heard because they were so sincere. It kind of hit me, then, that I should watch what I say and do around them. So I told them about quitting music and they said "why, you love music," to which I answered "I dunno. Maybe I'm supposed to quit."

They said quitting probably wouldn't do anything, but I did anyway because all other fingers pointed in that direction. To take my mind of the woes of music, I dropped out of college and moved to Portland to work. I lived with Drew's nephew, Phil and his wife, Nancy. They owned the house and I rented the basement with a girl named Sharma. Life in Portland was a lot more miserable than I thought! If you are not where you are supposed to be then God will tell you my friends!

I got hired at a grocery store and immediately got fired for being late – having just moved to the city and not used to it at all, I didn't know my around, one would think that could be excusable at least twice. I got a cell phone and when using a public washroom was devastated to see it fall into the toilet before I flushed it. At the house Sharma was nice, but my room had spider nests in it. I awoke one night to something crawling on my face. I remember grabbing it and throwing it, hearing it hit the wall.

I forgot until the next day a big brown spider came charging angrily towards me. When I pointed out the spiders to Sharma she said she only killed one small spider in her room in the three years she had been there. One?

"I'm onto thirty two spiders and it's only two weeks here," I whined.

"Well keeping count is probably not helping the situation," she stated matter-of-factly, "and besides I'm sure if you mention it to Phil or Nancy that they would do something."

I went upstairs and told them, but Phil only said "well every basement has bugs." Okay, true, but I should not have to kill more than thirty two spiders in my first two weeks. Sometimes I would open the door of the room to find spider webs from ceiling to floor! Eventually I drowned the room in Raid before work and sealed up the windows to prevent drafts. That helped a lot! As if the spiders, losing the phone and getting fired weren't bad enough, I got so sick with strep throat that I couldn't even speak!

I went to a doctor who sounded like he couldn't speak English and when he looked in my throat he said "nothing wrong." My throat felt like it was on fire, so when I got home I stretched out my tongue and flashed a light, looking in the mirror. Sure enough, there were white sores and redness – strep throat.

I went to the store and got antibacterial lozenges, since that was the only treatment I could get, and it helped until I got it again less than a week later. I was miserable! People were so unfriendly – I smiled at an elderly lady while passing by and she scowled back. My computer also crashed with a virus, so I had absolutely *no* communication with anyone as Sharma had not moved in until a three days after all this.

I even had a casting call for the TV series, *Cornergas*, but was replaced because I was a half hour late due to wrong directions. Told to turn left at a street, I turned left and did not find the needed building so I drove the whole way of the street twice before turning right. Lo and behold, the building was right there! When I walked in, the casting director knew me by name and picture and said "sorry, you are a half hour late, you can go home now." I was crushed! All the way back I cried, so let down.

Well as it always does, things worked out – I got another phone, bought a laptop and got a job at a local Kay-Tire store as a cashier. Weaving in and out of sickness and not enjoying the job there, it was a matter of time before I got another one at a Pizzeria.

My new boss was awesome! I was a cook and cashier, and although the boys were weird, they were alright to work with. I got to make food and take it home for free.

I met a lady who notified me when extras were needed for local films and so I did do a little bit of local acting…if you can call it that. Not much skill is needed to be an extra, but it was fun nonetheless. Acting on sets is fun because you meet all sorts of artsy people and try all kinds of new things. I was a break dancer for a film, a flight attendant for another…a Muslim in another. It is neat to see how the films are made with the cameras and food and drinks were always provided. Many times, co-actors would complain if it was cold but I didn't pay attention because I was excited to be on set. The protocol is that you do not speak to main actors unless approached by them first because they are so busy with their scripts and wardrobe and make up and all that (my least favorite part about performing or acting is the hair and make up), so I was surprised when a strapping young lad (who was a main character) talked to me. He was good looking!

It was chilly on this particular set because it was outside in the late fall, so while I was looking for some tea, we ran into each other with the same mission. Finding that there was no warm water, this young man invited me to the actors' trailer and I joked around with some very interesting folks while dining and dashing. I wish I could say more happened, but sadly it didn't, ha, ha.

In Portland I started singing again near the end of my time there. There was man who heard me playing guitar in a local music store (sometimes I go just to look and play the instruments), and soon I was at his house meeting his son and wife. He was strange, but he liked the way I sang and played piano and he made promises of getting me into bands and recording. All were promises that were exciting and brought me to his house for practices, but were otherwise unfulfilled.

This man's name was Paul. He was nice enough, but he wanted to do things with me all the time and was constantly calling my phone. I thought this was unhealthy and so when he spoke of going to Nashville, I said "yeah! You should go…with your wife!"

"Yeah, but she is too scared," he said sheepishly.

"Why?" I asked.

"Because she hears all kinds of stories on the news from TV," he answered.

"So? Turn the TV off," I replied. How could they let scary stories stop them from living? Scary stuff happens all the time, even here in Portland.

"Well let's figure out this song," he interjected into my thoughts.

"Okay," I said and turned back to the piano. I had figured out most of the piano of a song by Selena Quintilla called *Where Did the Feeling Go*; a very lovely song. Paul was impressed by how I could transpose the song higher or lower, and he liked the way I sang. I decided I wanted to play guitar that day, so I told him that.

"No problem, here use mine," he offered. I took his guitar and was about to play when I heard something rattle inside. Thinking it was a pick; I rattled it again and looked at him inquisitively. It sounded big. Looking inside I saw rolled up paper stuffed inside.

"Yeah, I wrote a song about you," he said openly. I got offended. He was about 20 years older than me, and had written a song about another girl that he had helped a year or so ago. All fine and dandy, but how would his wife feel? She knew we were practicing and she was the sweetest lady ever! So how did she feel when he treated her this way?

"Here, let me read it to you," Paul said, reaching for the guitar.

"No, I don't want to hear it," I said firmly, pulling the guitar out of his reach.

"It's just a song," he scoffed lightly; "it's about how much you inspire me." I believed him, I really did, we had not done anything indecent (because he knew I was stronger than him) and I knew that he was only trying to help me out with music, but something so innocent could turn sour very quickly.

I shook my head and said "I don't think you should play it for me, write songs about your wife." To me that was the only woman he should have been writing for, but he didn't seem to appreciate her...he was nice enough, but he wasn't quite respectful to her.

"I have," he said, not making eye contact.

"Good, then leave it at that."

"You don't even want to hear it?" he wheedled.

I paused and asked myself if I did. Nope. "Nope," I confirmed aloud. I didn't need or want to hear the song. "It kind of bothers me because music is a form of worship, so I do not want you to write praise songs about me. Write about your wife or about God; please do not write about me. Tear this song up and throw it out." Thankfully Paul got the hint. I think his wife was upstairs when we were practicing so she heard or something because they both came to Kay-Tire and thanked me while I was working there.

Paul must have taken what I said seriously, because he told me that his wife said that I have a good heart because I was protecting hers. I withdrew from the family then and stopped replying to Paul's invites over to his house – whether for supper or anything. I just thought it was strange to have someone write songs after only meeting me a couple times to briefly go over songs. He called a lot, but then got the hint when I did not respond and soon I changed the number. I thought it was best for him to focus on his family, as he promised he would – and I would have distracted that.

Christmas was hard that year in Portland because I ended up alone – friends sent packages and I saved them until that day, but Noella and Drew were off somewhere and I had to stay, as I was practically the only cashier, working both Christmas Eve and Boxing Day. Sharma was with her family, Ephraim was in Perri and my friends were off to their homes and families. I grew right angry then, and wrote a bitter Christmas song. Also, to help the situation, my nice car got hit when I visited some friends in San Frisco early in the New Year.

I was with Ephraim in San Frisco, visiting Grandpa Stardens. We cooked a meal at his place and when Ephraim forgot sour cream for the perogies, I suggested that we walk down to a local store a block away. On our way out we saw police cars flashing and a big white truck being towed away.

"Uh oh, it looks like someone dinged up your car!" Ephraim said goofily.

"Ha, ha, we should see what's wrong," I said out of genuine concern. We walked over and then I saw pieces of my car scattered across the street. Ephraim just gawked at me while I internalized what happened. I was torn between laughing or crying and screaming while kicking more pieces of the car off. I did neither.

I politely addressed the police officers and they took down my information and gave me the information of the man whose truck was towed away. Perhaps part of the reason why I was able to let it go so quickly is because the man had reported it and the car was still drivable for a while, and I knew that things would work out in the end.

With that aside I made more friends and started going to church again after a couple year's absence – and by church I mean youth group once in a while. I knew some of the people attending, and so it was alright. At the start of the night was usually a sharing time for a person to share their testimonies. Maybe I just hit all the bad nights or something but one fellow got up and said "both my parents were missionaries and I grew up in the church. I had a very loving family but in grade eleven I had a friend who partied so I fell away from the Lord, but I came back…" and that was the gist of his story!

It was rather irritating because it was unfeeling and very general, but it seemed to be like that every single night I went! Of course, I was not very consistent in my attendance, so maybe I missed some heartfelt stories, but I remember walking away always shaking my head. However, I think this young man was more laying the blame on his friend. People don't "fall away" just because of one party or one drink.

"So…was that it!" I vented to Sharma on such a Tuesday evening, "I mean it is so impersonal – that's hardly a story! Why share if you're not going to share?"

"Well I think it's obvious that the people who share like that are hiding something," Sharma said, "they aren't saying what they are feeling because they are scared."

"Yes but the whole point is to open up, I mean show some heart!"

"Well," Sharma said, leaning forward, "maybe you should share your testimony then." In other words, put your money where your mouth is. If had money. I harrumphed and grumbled and mumbled and knew that she was right. All the yeah buts came running around until I spoke to Shaun and Lily, two very good friends of mine and expressed how I was feeling. The agreed with Sharma without me telling what she said. Fine.

I sucked up my pride and spoke to the pastor about sharing my story. Since he had to approve the story before it was shared, he was blown away by the things I'd been through. "So, this is true?" he asked.

"Yes it is," I said a little bit peevishly, offended at the implication.

"You would never tell by looking at you that you've been through all these things," he said sincerely. It was sweet. I looked right into his eyes and saw the honesty.

A few Tuesdays later I had friends from San Frisco and Portland all came to support me with sharing my testimony. Shaun and Lily came, Noella and Drew and Sharma were there as were Tracy, Babs, and a few other pals. When the pastor called my name to go to the front, I ate every word I vented to Sharma on the way up.

"Hello," I said tentatively, not used to using a mic, "I'm Karee, and I just want to say that I was abused." Oh, crap! All the feeling flooded forward and I couldn't speak, but the pain was evident on my face. Everyone went quiet – dead quiet.

"This is a lot harder than I thought it would be," I said emotionally and with humor. When all else fails, pull out the humor card. I sucked it up and shared with them how Joan used to hold my head under water; make Ephraim and myself kneel on cheese graters, how she threw dishes at my head. I told about how Susie and Jocelyn were treated very well and that once Ephraim was adopted I had to face everything alone, but at a young age I clung to my faith. I also shared about my drugs and drinking days in high school and that I came from life on the streets. I was in foster care technically but it did not seem like the parents really cared so I spent time roaming around and had friends who were into drugs and booze and such, so that is where I went…to my friends.

At the end I played a song by Simple Plan called *Untitled* because that song described how I felt during most of my life. People were crying right from the start – people I knew and people I didn't. After that many people came to talk to me and I spoke with some, but then it was the same old, same old.

One girl, however, shared that she had a golf ball sized cancerous cyst on her brain and the doctors, upon finding this, sent her home to die. She gave her life to God – for real (she had grown up in a Christian home), saying "God if you want to take me now, then it is in your hands." She said that after that her cyst just disappeared. She is a miracle. She is alive and well and one of the nicest young ladies ever.

Life had a few more turns for me, though, and although I should have implemented my faith, I starved it as I stopped going to church, becoming quite bitter with how uncaring and callous it was, based on experience. It was because of the distance within the church – I came, I sat and I left alone. If I sat beside someone, they either moved or sat with their backs to me. I hated church and even began to hate Christians and disassociated myself with the word. I resented the way I was treated; I'm sure many people do. It only brought back memories of how other "Christians" mistreated me.

When I stopped attending church services, I started writing again – songs – full songs or just pieces. It is like I cannot stop writing music – it always comes and drives around in my head until I have to write it down. Well work at the Pizzeria was alright – my boss was great, but soon that was not enough for me to get by.

chapter 2:

It seemed the more I searched, the less I found. I was angry, yes, because even though I had some friends, I still felt very alone. I had a little money saved up from my job and spoke to my boss. We both agreed it was best that I not work there, due to another worker's treatment. Her name was Jen and she was strange.

Upon first glance at me she smiled and said "you're cute! I'll sell you later!"

When I said "uh, no," her response was "aw, why not? I could make a pretty penny off of you!" I just think that is very inappropriate considering she was about fifty years old and I was only twenty one. It was creepy because she was also very crude and even tried to set me up with her son. When she brought him into work to see me, I spun around and flipped him the finger with a smug little grin, refusing to come to the front to meet him.

I know that my behavior was difficult but sometimes you just need to be that way in order for people to not want to try anything. Well needless to say, when Jen was hired, I was out. It was only a matter of time. Lucky for me, my boss and I had already formed a relationship – she was very motherly and took me under her wing – and so although she did "fire" me, it was a mutual decision and she was very nice about it.

I took the summer off and moved around a little bit because living at Phil and Nancy's was gross. When winter passed I had tones of wood louse eating at the backs of my ankles because the surface is hard. One day I hit a moth with a fly swatter and the blinds came crashing down. The plastic I had put over the windows was *filled* with the wood louse. I went upstairs to get Nancy.

"Yeah, that is pretty disgusting," she agreed, "I'll get Phil to come down when he's back." He was at work so I understood. When he did come downstairs all he did was tear the plastic off the window, sending bugs all over my bed, desk, and the floor and then he left, leaving my room a mess. Not cool. So I was out.

Sharma and her fiancé were getting married in the summer so they wouldn't be there anyway, as they would live together. Ben is his name and when he used to come over it was so awkward because the two of them would hole up in Sharma's room every time I came out of mine. I understand that couples do things in rooms – I had a few boyfriends, I know what it's like – but when I am not welcome in my own home, I think that is a bit unreasonable. I spoke to Sharma about it and she was quite defensive.

It wasn't until I said "if I get a boyfriend again and we get engaged, I don't want to be like you and Ben," that she really woke up and came around. After that things were still awkward, but much better.

I moved across town into a nice house close to a friend named Hailey. We hung out a lot and laughed a lot and I think it was really good. The house that I moved into was a party house full of sex addicts. I did not know that upon moving in; they also neglected to tell me that the house was only available for two months. Not cool.

My first night there they threw a big party and everyone had drinks and Miranda came over and there lots of people and booze and it was fun. One of the roommates, Lance, said that I should tell everyone that we slept together.

"Why?" I asked scornfully.

"Well because it's like I got with you on your first night here," he explained. Loser.

"No," I said firmly, "because we didn't and I wouldn't sleep with you anyway."

"Fair enough," and he let it go. His friends thought I was hot and often tried to get me to go out with them, but there is only so much partying and hitting on the one can handle. Even then it was alright until Jayne, another roommate, decided it would be fun to have sex in my bed when I was gone. I dunno, I guess I did that to Stan when I was with Josh, but it really seemed quite intrusive. What comes around goes around.

Lance was a musician and had his own piano in the house. When I played for him, he thought I was good. Trying to see what kind of pitch I had, he turned on a song I had never heard before and was trying to play it out. All I did was correct him, showing that the notes he played were too high for the girl to sing, so I played the right notes on his piano. He shut his eyes and said "hit any note on the piano and I will tell you what it is," and when I obliged, he sure did tell me those notes.

It was weird that he could do that, but not hear the key or melody of a simple song – and I could not tell the notes, but was able to locate them on the piano. Lance was going to university for psychology, and although he was interesting, he was a pig when it came to sex. He was in "yellow fever" which is a derogatory statement implying lusting after Asian women and he slept with as many as he could. It was gross.

I needed a break from the city and told Lance about my debate of whether or not to go on a hike or something. Wanting to encourage me, he showed me a film about this man who was a failed actor that was obsessed about bears. This man went on to film bears and lived with them for a portion of the year – for thirteen years. He got some beautiful footage and even touched some of the bears and got away with it. One year he was a bit foolish and hid his camp and he and his girlfriend were setting up to go about filming when they realized the bears he knew for twelve years were gone and a new group had moved in.

Determined to go out and film anyway, this man and his girlfriend were setting up cameras when a bear came behind the man and grabbed him by the head. The girl had the camera on but the lens was still on so all that could be heard were the screams as the bear ate them alive. Thanks, Lance that made it a little scarier, but not going was dumb.

I took a chance and went on a hike for a week with some college friends; we went to the mountains. It was sweet. It was bear country, so we had bear spray and I sang as loud as I could everywhere we went. Rob was the leader and he did this every year, bringing his two little daughters. The group we had was pretty good – girls in one tent, boys in the other – and the food and nature were great.

Sitting by a water fall at night by the dying fire was so peaceful; I could hear the wind changing the pitch of the waterfall, going from a minor chord to a major one. Someone told me I have relative pitch. It was so sweet and serene being out there in the mountains and forests with the clean air, so far removed from the dreary city.

On our first day we went up a mountain and some of us went down a little bit earlier than others. Emma and I were among the early ones. While waiting for everyone else to join us, we dipped our feet into a clear brook that was *freezing* by the way. Suddenly a young woman close to our age ran out of the trees and out of breath, down the path towards us.

"There is a bear off the path!" she shouted, waving her arms. We gathered up our things and got Rob's two little daughters into the van in the lot. Then Emma and I spoke to the woman. "I was preparing for a speech I'm giving at a seminar," she explained, now catching her breath, "and I heard a twig snap behind me. When I looked there was a mother black bear with two cubs." She pointed in the direction and said that she had left everything – her books, etc, where she had been sitting.

Of course, the bear was scared and had run off, and the woman collected her things, but we had to call the rangers, because half our group was still out there and black bears are the most dangerous besides grizzlies – and a mother at that! Everyone was safe and sound and it all made for some adventurous story telling.

We all chatted and shared a little bit about ourselves around the fire. I was mostly listening, when I suddenly shushed everyone. They turned to see what I was looking at. At first I thought it was the top part of the back of a bear on all fours, but soon enough, a doe raised her head to gaze at us inquisitively.

I learned from working with horses (with Noella) that if you cock your head to the side and gaze out of one eye you will not appear as a predator to them and can more easily gain their trust. I did this with the doe and she wound her way down a little path, closer, and closer, pausing every now and then to get her bearings. She was lovely. She inched her way around the fire site until she was only a few feet away from me. I looked at her out of one eye and reached out my hand slowly. She stared, blinking those big dark eyes and then calmly left, lingering for a few moments close by the trees.

For the whole week the sun was out and warm. We followed a river and went up and down a mountain in a day. At suppertime I had fun watching some playful chipmunks banter with each other, scurrying here and there and sometimes mooching for food. "It's Alvin and the Chipmunks!" someone exclaimed. I picked a dandelion and held my hand close to the ground, waiting. Soon they were eating out of my hand.

The next morning came too quickly – I was sad to feed those chipmunks dandelions for the last time and as we met in the parking lot, I was sad to drive away. Once back in Portland, Emma and I made plans to hang out and we all went our separate ways. Back in the house with Jayne and Lance was a lot more dismal…I could not stand the way they lusted after absolutely everything. That kind of environment was not healthy for me to be in – particularly with the drinking and I had drunken and driven in the city. Not good. So I left.

I responded to an ad that said "looking for mature roommate," thinking it would be a more mature place. I called Chrissie, the lady who was opening up her house to me. She had two kids, but they wouldn't be there during the days, which was good. I agreed to move in until I found another place.

Ephraim had called and was visiting Portland, so he agreed to help me move. He talked to Lance and found him interesting, too, especially when Lance said I was "a talented musician with a bit of an attitude problem." True words. We loaded up the truck that Noella and Drew lent us and then moved my things into the new house. A man named Bo was going to be moving in and when he entered the house, he stuck his hand right into our food and was kissing Chrissie and starting to pull his clothes off. He was drunk! His pupils were dilated so drugs were probably dominating his system too.

"I don't like him," Ephraim said. I could tell by his face. It was a little bit comical, the look on his face, but he was right. "Did you know he was moving in?" he asked me.

"No," I answered honestly, getting a little frightened.

Ephraim shook his head and said "how do you keep finding places like this?"

"I don't know," I said. It's not like I planned for things to happen to me.

"Well let's go and check the truck," Ephraim said in a goofy voice. He is good at making me laugh. We went to the truck and once inside he said "do you want me to move you anywhere? I don't like it, Kar, is there anywhere else you can go?"

I thought about it, but it was eleven thirty on a weekday and I did not know anyone who would help me out. I had no where to go.

When I told Ephraim this, he said "are you sure? Because I have the truck right now…"

"I know but it would be about one before we moved and where would I go?" I asked. Knowing that I was right, but still concerned, Ephraim said "okay let's pray," and then he prayed for my safety! The little bugger really cared! ☺ Even talking with him about it recently, he kept saying "I should not have left at all!" but all is well! I feel that my brother helps when he can as it is.

When he left I had no choice but to go back in. Bo looked at me and I knew from the look on his face that I was not safe. He would be working nights which meant only he would be around when Chrissie and her kids were out for the day. My mind raced, analyzing everything in about thirty seconds. I went to my room and discovering no lock, called Noella, telling her that I was scared and why.

"What you can do is build a wall of stuff going from the wall to the door and that way if he tries to get in then he can't open the door," she advised. I did that immediately. All of sudden I heard Chrissie and Bo talking downstairs and knelt by the register to hear what they were saying.

"No," Chrissie protested to whatever he was saying.

"Shhhh," he shushed loudly and sloppily because he was drunk or stoned or both.

"No," she repeated, "I don't like that you are drunk, my ad said no drinking…"

Bo shushed her again, very sloppily, and then said "it's because of the bitch upstairs isn't it? I'm going to talk to her; I'm gonna get that bitch upstairs."

He must have started towards the stairs or something, but I heard Chrissie say "no, I think she went to bed." And then I lost track of the conversation. When the house fell silent for a while I ventured out to find Chrissie in the kitchen cleaning the counter.

"I need to talk to you," I said firmly. She was kind.

"Okay," she relented.

"I don't think it is wise for you to let him live here," I cautioned.

"Well he won't do anything wrong and he said he would pay rent tomorrow," she argued.

"Well I have been through a lot and I can kind of…sense when things are going to go bad," I started. I did not even think that her children were safe because when Bo looked at me his eyes looked mad… as in crazy. I can't even imitate the look – I've tried.

"Well nothing bad has happened yet," Chrissie protested skeptically.

"The point is to avoid something bad because then something bad will have happened," I explained gently. Didn't she see that?

"I know, but who am I to judge?" Chrissie said. I felt like she was accepting something that she did not need to.

"You said you have two kids?" I inquired, having not seen them all night.

"Yes Kaya and Royden," she answered, "they are sleeping right now."

"Well then all I ask is that you think of your kids. You are allowing that man to come in and if he is walking all over you like this now, how is he going to treat me? Or the kids? It often starts small, but he is not a nice person and I don't need anymore of that," I stated very firmly, hoping that she would know that I was right. "So I have to present you with a choice," I continued, "that you either have him in long term and I will leave, or he leaves and you have someone who is safe for a month." *Noella had said to present her with this option, so here goes*, I thought.

Chrissie paused and then said "okay, then I choose him because he is long term."

Thinking my time there was done, I nodded and said "okay then I will find a place tomorrow," and went to my room. I was on my laptop, responding to an ad when I heard a tap at the door.

"Come in," I said, turning away from the email.

"Can we talk?" Chrissie poked her head in.

"Yeah, sure," I set the laptop aside and invited her in.

"I was thinking about what you said and I don't want to have him here," she blurted out, "not if he is going to be mean to my kids, I don't want him here."

"So are you going to kick him out then?" I asked for clarity.

She nodded slowly but firmly and said "yes I would rather have somebody safe for one month then somebody like that in my house." We joked about how the ad said responsible person and she told me how he had not given her rent yet. I gave her a month's rent and she declined the damage deposit because I would only be there for a month. She was very sweet.

"You know that he is going to come right back here, right?" I asked.

"Yes, maybe I will call him on his cell and tell him to get his stuff," she said, thinking out loud.

"Well you can try," I said.

"I know that you don't want to be a built in babysitter but do you mind just staying here while I get a phone card?" she asked.

"Yeah sure," I said. They were sleeping anyway. She left and was back in minutes. She called and left a message and then we closed and locked the door. She had gathered his few things – a laptop and some cords

– into a bag and put it into the living room. Sure enough it was a matter of minutes before we heard Bo pounding at the door and shouting. It was now one in the morning.

"I'll go talk to him," Chrissie said, getting up, "I'll tell him he can't live here."

"Okay. You need to be firm with him," I advised, "if you are going to kick him out, make sure he knows it and cannot get around it."

"I know, I'll tell him I advertised for someone responsible and he is drunk and high." She left to deal with him, gave him his stuff and refused to let him in the house. I heard yelling and name calling and he wanted to come after me. I sat on my bed, tired and stressed, and threw a quick prayer out there *Jesus, please make him GO AWAY!* Almost at that instant I heard a car rip away and Chrissie came back inside.

She wanted to chat, so I made a tea and then thanked her for kicking him out. She ended up unloading on me – telling me about her husband, her kids, hurts she was going through. I was a little overwhelmed, so I asked if she went to church. Hypocritical, I know, but I didn't know what else to do.

"I used to, but not so much anymore," she answered sincerely.

"Do you believe in Jesus Christ?" I asked.

"Yes," she said a little bit timidly.

"Ah, but can you declare it? Like: I, Karee Stardens, believe that Jesus Christ came for me in the flesh, died and rose again, or I, Karee Stardens, believe that Jesus Christ is my personal savior."

When Chrissie declared it the first few times she was timid and shy, but in seconds she went from weeping to laughing and saying it with ease. For the rest of my time there I tried to be as encouraging and uplifting to her as possible. She changed big time! She seemed more happy and hopeful in her demeanor.

Chrissie had said that she had prayed that someone would come into her life and help her turn around. I met her husband and encouraged them both to work through their problems because there was a lot of care even though they were separated. I discouraged the huge fights that went on because they would erupt at each other in the day and then the kids would hear and sit quietly at the table.

Seeing her love for her kids made me a little sad because I wished for it, but it also made me glad to see that she was sincere about it. She really did put her kids first. We talked a lot and her kids grew to like me over the next month. Upon leaving, I left food as well as a letter of encouragement for her to keep her head up and to stay on the path she was on. I also gave her some money and then I walked a way, a little bit sad, but happy that I had actually helped someone turn away from misery. I hope she is well right now!

While I was there I went for a little visit to San Frisco to see some good friends and visited with Noella. She came into town and we decided to cut our hair for cancer. I had always wanted to, so why not now? It was a very random decision, but we went for it. Both of us had long hair, Noella's all one length and very thick, a dirty blonde matted with gray and silver. My hair was long and auburn, cut with layers.

We went to a hair salon and they cut your hair for free if you cut it for cancer, so that was cool. The girls were sad about cutting our hair, but we were both pretty laid back about it. The girls sprayed our hair with water and then braided in into four sections. Noella brought her camera and we took pictures for fun. When my hair was braided I could see that Nicole, the girl cutting my hair did not want to cut it, but she opened the scissors and held a braid straight, she asked "are you ready?"

I nodded and waited until she was juuust about to cut the braid off before I shrieked "NO, NO, WAIT!" she jumped out of her skin and everyone laughed. As soon as the joke was over, I nodded and said "go ahead." It was funny! Neither of us felt torn about losing our hair. The minimum inches of hair we could give was eight inches and every piece we gave was as long as a ruler, some of mine were longer with the layers gathered at the ends. I took a picture pretending to eat the braids.

When we were done we looked like boys. Noella teased me, saying I looked like a cute little boy "okay, dad," I replied and we both snickered. It was so good to do something so random. My hair was now less than an inch long. Good thing it was summer! It was a nice break to give something as small. Now someone who doesn't have hair will have the same auburn waves that I did.

Back in Portland the next place I moved to was full of musicians;

Ephraim also helped me move into there. He thought it was a little better than Chrissie's. It was a metal band and I thought it was sweet. Maybe I could learn to play the drums? They were nice enough it was a couple – the girl owned the house and then a friend of theirs stayed downstairs. I went to the bar with them to sing, but looking around, I wanted more.

I went on the infamous facebook and decided to see if I could find any relatives. Whenever I asked Joan about them, she played dumb and gave little facts, but no names and not enough to go by. So I found…her brother! And many cousins! I knew it was them because when I added each one I asked if they knew a Joan from The Caribbean and they said yes. I was so excited that I called Ephraim and then Joan.

Ephraim was skeptical and Noella and Drew were cautious (because these were people related to Joan) but extremely supportive. Joan's brother that I found was Tim and he lives down south in The Caribbean, where Joan grew up. I chatted to him online first and he was pretty cool. I was thrilled! Next thing I knew, I was on the phone talking whether or not to go to The Caribbean to meet these folks.

Ephraim was very reluctant, but he was probably intrigued as well. He said yes and then I was ecstatic, and then he said no and I was disappointed. To stop the tug of war, I just told him, "Don't play with me like that, okay? If you are going to go then just say yes, and if you aren't then say no. I don't want to have high hopes only to be let down again like that." We spoke for *two hours* and then Ephraim said "okay yes I'm going, final answer." And just like that we had a trip to plan for!

I called Joan and told her about my find out of excitement…and out of plain stupidity. "I found some relatives!" I exclaimed happily.

"Oh, how?" she asked, not sounding excited at all.

"On facebook, I typed in your maiden name and a bunch of people came up!"

"Oh – they aren't related, I looked," she said with false sincerity.

"Well I sent them a message asking if they know you," I said, not adding the fact that I was talking to her brother. She would know sooner or later. She began to call my phone regularly after that and it was very odd. I was upset because after purchasing my laptop I was not told that there would be interest fees and in between moving for the summer the charges added up and then I was given a bad credit rating, which prevented me from getting a credit card.

I had to go to the store to sort all this out and the only way anyone would listen is when I pulled out the bitch card – and I **hate** doing that! I tried being nice so many times, but whatever; I got what I needed in the end. So when Joan called I quite distressed over that, but unwilling to share with her.

"Oh, come on," she wheedled, "just trust me." I did not and she continued with "you need to talk about it."

"Well it won't help very much," I said stiffly, kind of weirded out.

"Come on, let me be your sound board," she persisted. My instincts told me not to trust her, so I did not. "Is it money?" she persisted, "it is, isn't it? Tell me what's wrong." But I recognized the false security and quickly let her go.

Right away I called up my brother and he agreed that it was strange of her to all of a sudden be calling and chatty with me. She had my number for quite a while and had never bothered before. Why now? Why was she asking for my trust?

"Well it's obvious, isn't it?" Ephraim said, "She knows we're going and she is up to something." Shit. He was right.

"I'm not sure if this is a good idea," he cautioned, his voicing getting wary. I just had some feeling that I should go, so I told him that I thought it was safe to stay with our uncle and he said okay as long as I felt that way, but he was preparing for other circumstances just in case. After I told him about the phone calls with her, we both agreed to monitor the Joan situation and I agreed to ignore the phone if she called anymore. We were going to see if our big brother Jonas would come with us.

I emailed our uncle and told him that we were coming for sure, and he kindly offered his place for us to stay – to save us money, but while we agreed, we were cautious. Ephraim talked to him online as well at my house and we chatted with Skype, the three of us. I wanted to be in a place where I could think and figure things out, so I thought it would be better to move once more.

Yes, singing into a mic. was fun and great and there are some decent musicians, but I wanted to see people as far as the eye could see and I just was not okay with bar-hopping for shows. My current roommates were okay with just that, but I was tiring of bar scenes. Soon my time in Portland drew to a much anticipated close. There was more drinking near the end, though, as it seemed I could not get away from it. I had enough of Portland and so it was back to San Frisco for me.

chapter 3: _____

While I was at Noella and Drew's house for supper, they asked why I didn't just move to San Frisco as I spent plenty of time there anyway, visiting friends. That won my inner debate on if I ought to move, so I searched for a place to live and came across a kind lady whose name was Gladys. When I phoned her I mentioned that I could cover the month's rent but not the damage deposit as my place in Portland found any reason possible to keep the money. She asked to meet me first and when I went to her house, she said "I know you!"

I did not remember her from past years, but she insisted that we used to talk all the time. A few years ago, I worked in a garden center of a Kay-mart that she used to work for, and she still manages there. She remembered me from there. Small world. We went in and had a pleasant little chat.

She gestured around the house and said with a laugh "I like the house clean."

I said "I do too," and she showed me her place and it seemed like a decent fit, so in I went. Gladys helped me move in and right away we had little tiffs about small things, but when she found out I was right she was quick to say "oh yea, you were right."

"One thing you'll find is that I am always right," I said half jokingly during one of these tiffs. We got set up and then Drew left and Gladys went to bed. She said she was a Christian, so I felt that it should be a little safer here, but time would tell. She opened up her house to me and said "if you don't have money, you can eat my food until you can afford your own," and then she went on to tell how she gave her brother groceries when he couldn't afford it. I thanked her and let her eat some of my food when I bought it.

Gladys' friend Denise is married and she had some troubles with her husband because of work and money. She tried talking to him and he disappeared for a night. The police found him later on, attempting suicide. Denise and her husband were having difficulties at work – which was at the same store where Gladys managed – and so they were planning to screw over the system to get more money.

Denise left her brain at home when she told Gladys about this, because Gladys is a manger. When Denise asked if Gladys would stay quiet about this, Gladys did the right thing in saying "if Verna asks me anything about this, I have to tell the truth," and Denise got angry with Gladys for being honest. I think at least Gladys was upfront with Denise, but why would Denise go and tell her manger these things, anyway?

Well the woes of her husband dominated the evil plans, and it was a few days before Gladys got a text or a phone call from Denise. She expressed some frustration in the mean time, waving her phone and saying "she still hasn't called me or texted me!"

"Well she is going through a lot," I empathized.

"Yes, but how hard is it to pick up the phone and call someone?" she vented. When your husband almost commits suicide, very hard, I felt like saying. I stayed silent, though, because Gladys had never been married before – in a relationship on and off for twelve years – and engaged, but never married.

Gladys and I had our differences, but when she blamed me for things I didn't do and would not listen to the fact that I did not do them, something inside me warned me to be wary, but I constantly gave her the benefit of the doubt. There was a lady named Teresa who stayed with us for a few days and she would do something small like leaving toast crumbs and a dirty plate on the counter and Gladys gave me a half jokingly hard time about it, but soon it just got right annoying.

"I didn't do it," I half-kidded back, not sure if she was kidding.

"Well if you didn't do it and I didn't do it, then who did?" she guffawed, smirking and pointing at the now clean counter top.

"Whatever, it wasn't me, it was Teresa," I said, half doubting myself.

"Yeah right, blame the poor roommate who isn't even here to defend herself," Gladys scoffed. A few days later Gladys tried to pin something on me again, but I didn't do it so I said so and then Gladys said "okay I believe you, after you said it was Teresa who left the crumbs, I saw her do it the next day," and then she laughed really hard.

I thought perhaps Gladys and I clashed because of lack of empathy, so one day we were chatting in the evening and I just shared some things about my past that would enable her to understand why I react the way I do sometimes. I told about Joan's favoritism toward my sisters, Jocelyn and Susie, and the mistreatment I received in foster care. I explained that I get defensive sometimes because I have been blamed for many things that I didn't do - sometimes blamed intentionally. Gladys said she understood.

I also mentioned that I was abused physically, verbally, mentally, sexually…I told her how Joan used to cut me down with her words and that Joan also called herself a Christian. Gladys looked at me and could not fathom it. She told me pieces of her story – how her parents said things to her that hurt her, they yelled and threw things, but never hit her. She told me of her promiscuity and I related to some degree because of my high school days. She shared how her parents forced her to abort when she was fifteen under false pretenses that she was suicidal.

She also shared that she committed to twelve years of abstinence so far – all for her faith in Christ. I looked up to her because that is quite admirable! And on some level we may have connected. She worked hard to bite her tongue and I bit mine and held back my fist. So many times I wanted to leave and so many times she wanted to just kick me out, but she said that Drew, when he helped me move in "begged" her to give me a chance. Well I spoke to him and he had said he had mentioned that I had been in a rough past and to give me a chance. That does not qualify as begging, it was a simple statement.

Things got easier between us when a third person came on the scene. Teresa only needed a place for a week so she had left and in came Alana. Only in grade twelve, she was seventeen and moving in because her mother was being difficult. We welcomed her and upon meeting her for the first time, Gladys and I looked at each other and said "yup!" we liked her, so it was good that she moved in.

Gladys was awesome in that way – that before allowing someone to move in she let me have a say as to whether we liked her or not. Our opinions always aligned, so that made it quite easy. It paid off in the end because we got a great roommate out of it!

Alana moved herself in and then the fun began! Gladys was chatting with a fellow she met on a dating site, his name was Jake from New Zealand, and although he was not a romantic interest of hers, Gladys spent hours and hours talking to him almost every single day. Soon Alana and I were included in these discussions, and they were fun.

We three watched movies together and talked about the stressed of work and boys and let each other into our personal bubbles. It was great. They were a great reassurance to me when I fretted about this trip to The Caribbean which was steadily approaching. Ephraim came and visited a few times and called a LOT, but he was *wonderful* for sorting things out and getting things into order.

I worried that our aunty and uncle would be just like Joan, and I worried that Ephraim would woo everyone with his piano playing skills and leave me in the dirt even if unintentional. He is a tremendous piano player so I encourage his music playing, but we cannot do music together because he is so far ahead of me. Everyone thinks he is *amazing* – including me, and I love how open he is with teaching me knew things to play – chords, scales, etc. He is really good about it all, but sometimes I feel like I always stand in his shadow – like I am the bad twin. Perhaps I even live up to that subconsciously…I don't know.

Gladys and Alana listened with sympathetic ears and told me that I would be fine, they were praying, etc. and it was nice to hear. I had never lived with just girls before, but many of my guy friends were not around anymore. Of course we did things that irritated each other, but it never got to the point where we held a grudge. Gladys blamed me for things that Alana did and Alana was terribly messy and I felt like I was the only one cleaning all the time…things like that went on and on, but I think that's quite normal.

Gladys always said things like "love ya," when I did something for her – like the cleaning or making good food or something like that.

Something inside always blurted out "no, you like the cleaning…"

To which she would respond, "no, I love *you*," but I just could not believe those words. There was no need to say them…maybe she thought I needed to hear those words? Gladys would always tell me that I was such a great roommate and tenant and most of all a wonderful friend, and although I would thank her, I could never quite reciprocate those words to her.

We loved living with each other, though, as we laughed a lot. When Alana's parents came and stole her car and she had to get another one, we minded our business and let her work through things. We supported her events at school, and Gladys let her pay rent late a few times. She was young and needed support, so we gave it!

I was working at a tourism spot, acting as a tour guide, and also at a local spa resort, so I was doing great, loving my jobs, making friends, seeing the ones I had nearby. At work I was moseying around the little storage shed on a break off, looking for a rag to do some cleaning. Something bright caught my eye and I turned to see what it was. Poking out of a garbage bag were the sheets that were on my bed when I was still living at Joan and Daniel's house. I froze for a second, and then checked to make sure. Pulling the sheet intended for rags, I saw the exact same flower pattern on it that my sheets had; the very same flowers that I had filled in with the ink from a pen one day when I was bored in my room. I couldn't believe it! It was very peculiar to hold the material in my hands. The sheet was already cut up or I would have taken the whole thing home.

A flood of memories streamed into my mind – of all the time spent in that room, locked away; hidden from the world. My favorite place had been the bed. I had loved the sheets because they were bright and sunny and different. I held all the proof in the world that showed that Joan had given everything away. I knew in that instant that Dorothy had *not* lied when she said that my mother had sold my belongings at the end of summer, a month before I was supposed to come back if I had "changed." Now I knew without a shadow of doubt that Joan had never intended for me to come back at all.

I ripped off a tiny little chunk for a keepsake and slipped it into my pocket. It was good to have that confirmation because should the subject ever arise in the future, Joan could not convince me of anything different. Holding the material, I think I felt overwhelmed, but it was the start of many things to come. It was almost as if God was saying "*hold on a second, you're not done yet – this chapter needs to conclude before you can move on.*" Fortunately for me He already had the resolving chords in mind, so all I had to do was wait and stare in wonder and great surprise.

I mentioned finding the flowered bed sheet to Gladys later on and quite understandably, she did not have much to say. For me, having the little strip of material is a good keepsake because I do not have a lot as it is to commemorate my childhood. Life was good other than that. We even got a little puppy for one night, but upon realizing that we didn't have the schedules to take care of the little guy, we had to say goodbye. Gladys and Denise only did that because I really wanted a puppy; Gladys doesn't really like animals, even though she says she does. ☺

Gladys was also consistent in her faith, often inviting me to church... even getting me into a worship band. It was nice; at first it seemed like she was doing this because she cared. I ended up leaving the band after a short time though, because I disagreed with the way they worked. Nancy would sing the song and Evelyn would interrupt the practice to debate about whether or not it should sound like the original artist. They would hum and haw over it until I would say "okay, let's go!" but I was fresh to the band so they just laughed and said "you're new; you don't have a voice yet."

Evelyn was the band leader so she was the one who let me in, and on yet another break, she motioned me over on the first practice to come sit beside her. She asked about my faith and I admitted that I was struggling. She asked what I would like to do musically and I said "play guitar, piano, drums and sing, but I could learn more."

"I think we should get you a little more focused on something like singing and guitar," she suggested. Sure, that sounded smart. "I know what you are like," she continued, "you are just like me a few years ago." That was weird. How could she say that? She didn't even know me. When she left practice angry later on, because she and Nancy could not agree on how to play the song, I stayed and jammed with the band.

Davey, Evelyn's husband, was on guitar and I was playing beside him. He said I could "really rock out," ha, ha. It was fun and being in a band felt *right*. At the end of the practice on my way out, Evelyn called me into her office. I went in and sat down.

"So, what do you think?" she asked, swiveling around on her chair.

"It's okay," I commented evasively. I didn't want to say that they spent too much time bickering…I had different work ethics than they did.

She smiled. "That's it?"

"You left angry," I pointed out.

"Yes," she admitted, "I left rather than saying what was bothering me, you would do the same if you were in my shoes, right?" she asked knowingly.

"No, I wouldn't," I said honestly, "I would have worked it out instead of leaving like that." Especially in a band. After that the term 'worship team' seemed false because they were fighting over who did what and who to sound like. When I vented to Gladys, she just said that they needed to work things out and that Evelyn may have seen something spiritually, but it was probably too soon to say so.

After that I only went to a few more practices because nobody notified me when there weren't practices. After the first time this happened I made sure that Evelyn had my phone number and email and she told me that she had Gladys' number. I knew Evelyn and Gladys spoke regularly because Gladys told me that Evelyn checked in to see if I was going to church and how I was doing. Even after that I went to four more practices that were cancelled without me knowing. I left angry and did not bother anymore. Obviously I was not part of the band.

Lucky for me that was not all I had musically. I started vocal lessons in Portland with a fellow named Rick. He wrote music that was performed here and there and he was supposed to be really good. He was quirky *and* he liked the way I sounded! He was willing to work with me to see what I liked about my voice.

"You do have a good range," he assessed as I sang up and down the scales, "how about you breathe?" I took a deep breath and was surprised when the whole musical phrase of a song became ten times easier! "Ha, whaddaya know! Breathing helps singing!" he scoffed lightly. He was funny, but I had to quit lessons because I couldn't afford them and my car got hit – yes, another time! Both times parked…both times Chrysler New Yorkers - talk about frustrating!

I started teaching guitar and piano and was surprised that Gladys offered to allow the house to be open for Monday night lessons. She was pretty adamant about her TV shows, so that was a real sign that she liked me. One of my students was a lady named Trudy. She wanted to learn how to read notes, but to play like I could. Well, I told her that I actually don't read very well, but I had some books to start her through if she wanted. She had heard me play – as I played for all the students before agreeing to lessons – and I just explained that someone had shown me from C to C was a major scale and from A to A was a minor scale, staying only on the white keys for these two scales.

I showed her how I learned the other scales by closing my eyes, so I closed my eyes and played them all for her. I also did double octaves and things like that, so I asked what she wanted to learn and started her off on those easier scales. I thought she was catching on quickly and I wrote them out for her.

Another student was my friend Rachel who worked with me at the local resort, and had went to college with me for a while. Rachel is a little bit troubled, but she is a wonderful singer and we have always found common grounds there. When I started lessons with her, I was a little bit frustrated that she was not picking it up as quickly as I was. I know it sounds petty shallow, but it seems like I just picked up the guitar and played it – I do not remember practicing that much and have never taken lessons.

I showed her a C to Em chord change on guitar and when she went into her zone, I asked what she wanted to learn. "How do I get to where you are?" she asked with a smile. That was a bit flattering because Rachel is a wonderful singer and I see her as a raw vocal talent. Seeing that she perked up a bit, I just told her to start simple – that's what I did and I still consider myself beginner in everything. We played along and she got the chords when I played with her, but on her own she needed to work on it.

She was very supportive, but a little bit peculiar. Sometimes I would be explaining things to her and she would zone out.

"Rachel?" I would call, "Rachel, Rachel!" and I would have to work for her attention and then she would go "hm?" and then not listen to what I said. Whatever.

Another student ended up being the girl who had cut my hair for cancer. A lovely young lady – she was the most promising student! It was funny when she first started because she couldn't hold the strings down due to long nails. I went into the bathroom and came out with nail clippers. I keep my nails right short…well below my finger tips.

"Do you know what time is it?" I asked her.

"No…" she said, oblivious to the clippers in my hand.

"Time to cut your nails," I said firmly but nicely because I wasn't sure if she would. She did! And then we played and she was catching on really quickly, too! I was looking forward to playing with her at the end. However, life took a turn for the worst for her and she ended up having her baby and moving out of town.

Trudy and I had a good time playing together and she was an older lady in her late thirties, so it may have been embarrassing to be taught by someone so much younger - I don't know. She got really discouraged, saying that she wasn't as talented as me. I got discouraged at that because she wasn't giving herself a try…well lessons were pretty consistent and I was grateful because I had been seeking to play with other musicians.

Lessons were a great learning tool as well, but having never taught before; it was a little bit frustrating that not everyone caught on as quickly as I did. Something a little weird was how much I cared for the well being of my students. I cared if they had a good or bad day and

I wanted to see what each of their goals were and help them begin to achieve it. I knew that to be a better teacher I had to keep learning, so I looked for more.

It was not long before I hopped into a local studio with Angie's friend Dylan. He was awesome to work with! He is very knowledgeable, patient and experienced. My first time going in, I was nervous and said I would like to do a quick cover of a song.

"Okay, what song do you want to do?" he asked.

"Uh, I dunno - something quick?" I said uncertainly.

"Well hurry up and pick one!" he said with hints of laughter. I picked Bob Dylan's *Knocking on Heaven's Door* because that song is simple. In the studio, Dylan had me play guitar to the metronome, something I had never done before. It was hard! And then I sang the song. Most of my mistakes were forgetting the words, but he was really good about it. I loved being in there and wished that I was better.

We talked about the sound we wanted to go for and he kind of... let me wear the pants. It was neat because he knows how to put a song together, but he let me say my ideas and change things he had done... and we worked well together.

When I was recalling the experience later, I realized that I was flat for the singing, and when I told him, he said "well at least you can hear it." after an awkward pause (and I'm sure to lighten things up), he said "that means there's hope for you." And I was encouraged. We agreed to take it one song at a time at a set rate. Hearing my voice singing through the speakers was great – Dylan knows what he is doing and how to bring out the best in the recording artist. I learned a lot just from the one song.

Gladys listened as I ranted and raved excitedly about this one little recording experience. She slowly started getting strange – always asking where I was going or what I was doing when I left so she wouldn't "worry," constantly telling me what to do...it was peculiar because I never noticed her doing this to Alana, who also noticed and felt bad, saying "there shouldn't be any favorites." When I lent Gladys a hand, say with the water jugs for her to water her horses, she always said I had "roommate points" because apparently her other tenants did not lift a finger to help. She said they were miserable and that she dreaded coming home when they were there, but with Alana and me there, she looked forward to coming home.

The first snow of the season was an interesting experience, as I tend to get a tad bit dramatic. I had opened the kitchen blinds in the evening and all three of us were in the kitchen when I suddenly shrieked and said "oh, noooooooo!" Big white flakes were drifting down, clinging to the ones already hiding the green of the fern bushes outside.

Alana almost dropped her cup of tea and asked "what?" as Gladys also peered out the window. Her face lit up when she saw the snow and Alana laughed at my mock horror. I sighed heavily and turned back to the window sadly.

"Goodbye green, green grass," I said dramatically waving, "goodbye skies of blue that filled my days with hope, goodbye warm sunshine that keeps me alive!"

"Can we say drama queen?" Gladys declared, poking light fun at me.

"Yeah, no kidding!" Alana chimed in, now looking on with amusement.

"I need to wear black!" I rushed on, ignoring them and running to my room, grabbing a black hoodie, then running back to the kitchen.

"Why?" Alana asked, puzzled.

"Um, that's not going to stop the snow," Gladys said.

"I'm wearing it to mourn – to mourn the loss of my good friend summertime," I carried on. Both were bemused and Gladys asked if I would join her for a walk in it. I usually went for walks – plenty in the summer and fall – but not on this day! I stayed inside and she went out for a short while. When she got back we watched a movie and stayed up late, chatting. Things were good for a while.

Gladys kindly turned her front porch into a bedroom that she lived in – and she made it quite cozy, too. The three of us used to pile onto her bed and chat with her and her online friend, Jake. Even though we all had early mornings, we always stayed up late and chatted until we were falling asleep. I told them that this whole chick thing was new to me as I had hung out with guys a lot in my high school and college days.

I ended up getting sick with the infamous H1N1 virus – it was horrible! I hummed and hawed and slept for days with fever and migraines and heaving. After a solid week of this, I could not hack it, so I called up Sally. Sally and I were pretty good friends – if it wasn't for her, I would not be recording in the studio with Dylan because he was a friend of hers. Well I called her up…

"Hello?" she answered.

"Hey Sally?" I croaked.

"Hey are you okay? You sound sick," she said right away.

"Would you mind taking me to the hospital?" I asked.

"Sure, what do you have?" she questioned.

"Not sure," I fibbed, not wanting to tell her it was the H1N1. Well she came and then I told her on the way to the hospital. She was a bit irritated because I could have exposed her to the sickness. Oh, well. At the hospital they confirmed what I was thinking and gave me Tylenol and Advil and quarantined me for two lonely weeks. Work had no choice but to be fine with it and in due time I was better. I had to go without medication, though, because although I asked Gladys to pick me up some jello and Tylenol or Advil, she forgot. But what doesn't kill you makes you stronger and I was up in no time!

Work was going good for all of us and before we knew it I was singing Christmas tunes and Alana was on holidays from school. Alana played piano so there was a bit of musicality in the house. Gladys said that she used to play instruments, too, so she at least appreciated music. She had a drum set that I nagged her to set up, but she never got around to it. For a person twenty – something years older than Alana and me, Gladys was pretty cool. We teased her about her age and she kidded that we were her kids.

All three of us shared food and worked our way around each other for the bathroom. I took long showers, singing at the top of my lungs, so before I went, out of courtesy, I always checked if anyone needed the washroom. When I first moved in, before Teresa and Alana, Gladys and I had a squabble about me cutting a tomato on the counter without a cutting board – I was not using my head, I'll give her that.

Instead of just pointing it out and handing me the cutting board,

Gladys went on and on and just made me feel stupid. "Look, at what you did!" she squawked, pointing at several cut marks on the counter.... uhhh...no way. I was not there for two weeks yet and all I had cut before the tomato was an apple; I was not taking the blame. Especially when she was harping about how it would cost twelve hundred dollars to fix...

I got indignant and denied it, but she would hear none of it. So, like I did to Noella many times, I bit my tongue and waited until she ran out of words. Then I stuck my hand out and lifted my eyebrows pointedly. After that I used the cutting board, but all she had to do was ask, not blame and not make me feel like shit. Gladys and I went from being so frustrated with each other – she was so *annoying* (and she probably says the same of me) – to learning how to communicate and really actually enjoying each other's company. I think Alana played a big part in that.

Now one thing about Christmas is that I love the season. On the actual day I am a bitter mouse. I wanted to set up decorations as soon as it snowed, but we put it off and then it was hard to find times that we were all there, so when December rolled around, I pulled up the decorations from downstairs and waited. A few more missed days – we were all working different times – and then I decorated a bit by myself.

I hung garlands up in the living room, put out some candles and ornaments and strung some lights in the kitchen. Then I brought out my Christmas tree as well as Gladys' tree because I figured she would want it up there. When she came home from work with her friend, Travis, who lived a few hours away and stayed over when he was on business trips, she wanted to decorate my tree.

"No way, man!" I argued.

"I'm not saying to cover the tree, I'm just saying a few here and there," she explained, gesturing with her hands.

"Come on, a few decorations would be nice," Travis piped in.

"Uh, no, decorations on trees are so overrated," I said stubbornly.

"Well what about this one?" Travis asked, putting one on there. I thought it looked dumb. My tree was white fiber-optic – it didn't need decorations...it was given to me by Noella and Drew. After they came back from their trip last year and found me all bitter in Portland, they offered to buy me a Christmas tree. They said it could be a hundred dollars, and this one came to ninety-nine, ninety-eight. It was a Boxing Day sale.

"Oh, fine," I relented begrudgingly because Gladys and Travis had already put some decorations on the tree, "but I'm not putting any on."

"That's fine," Gladys said quickly. I realized that this is what families do; argue over decorations – where to put what and all that. It was nice, and our arguing was all in good fun. Alana came home and was slightly sad that we didn't wait for her. We tried to though, and we all made excuses to playfully blame each other, and then she was fine.

I remember one night in Gladys' room, the three of us piled on her bed, and we shared about Christmases. When I said that Joan used to have extravagant Christmases and it was the one time of year she dropped her troubles with me, then Gladys "well that's where you get it from," meaning my zest for the decorations. Alana talked about her Christmases and the family feuds that started and the gifts and food, and Gladys shared about her suppers. She did not have very much family left, actually and did not have kids of her own; only two brothers, a nephew that she adored, and an aunty. But she always celebrated with a turkey supper.

When I told them that in foster care I had to do all the cleaning and cooking and sit at different tables than everyone one Christmas they were displeased. "That would suck," Gladys said, clearing her throat like she does when she's upset.

I got sick a few times that winter and moaned and groaned about it, moping around the house saying "I'm gonna *die*" because that's how I felt.

"Power of the spoken word!" Gladys jumped in quickly, along with a spiel about how what you say can affect your life and blah, blah, blah. When I got really sick I slept for days, but soon enough I got better was back to bouncing around and playing pranks. Alana and I pulled a few pranks of Gladys and she took them very well!

One night when we were up and chatting, she was falling asleep because she had work the next day and so we said "good night Gladys, good night Gladys, goodnight Gladys," a few times and the Alana recorded it onto her phone and hid her phone under Gladys' bed. We left and then I called her phone from my phone and we *killed* ourselves laughing because we could hear it through the door.

We could also hear Gladys saying "what the heck? Where is it?" when she opened the door she was laughing, so we took the phone and everyone went off to bed. There were stacks of National Geographic magazines on the kitchen, so one day I put them all in Alana's bed. Gladys is very jumpy so we often startled her on purpose, thus getting the reaction we were after.

I wanted to do something nice for my lovely roommates, so I bought eggnog, and at my job (at the local resort), they gave their staff a huge turkey – which I found out through Rachel who also worked there and brought it over. I tried to find days that they would both be here over supper time, but it was nearing impossible, and they were wondering why I was so interested in their schedules all of a sudden.

"Fine, I wanted to make you guys a turkey meal!" I blurted out.

"Oh, well, why didn't you just say so?" they asked

"Well it was supposed to be a surprise," I said, "but so much for that idea!"

I ended up making it shortly before Christmas day, with Noella's help, and it was quite tasty. Christmas day was good – my eyes opened at six in the morning – like any other kid who wants to dig into their stockings…except that we didn't have stockings this year. I sleepily picked up my acoustic guitar and stood with it outside Gladys' door, strumming as loud as possible. "Wake up! Time to get up!" I half sang, half shouted. When Gladys turned her light on in her room, I did the same to Alana.

Alana is more like me in the mornings – I am a light sleeper, but it is hard to pull me out of bed. Alana has the best of both worlds – a heavy sleeper and hard to get out of bed! When my musical awakening did not wake her, I wandered into her room and jumped on the bed, and then I lay down, stealing all her blankets, wrapping myself in them so she couldn't just tug them back. And then I wiggled for more room – not to get comfortable so I could sleep, but to wake her up. It worked…until I left the room.

Well Gladys was up and soon Alana joined us in the living room. We had a playful tiff because Alana was super grumpy and I was fighting the bitterness inside. Gladys laughed and said we were "just like one big happy family..." with a big smile on her face. When I looked into her blue eyes, they looked really happy – actually happy for the first time in probably a long time. Good. She deserved it.

We read a note that Gladys wrote to us from herself (pretending to be Santa) about how sad it was that no one left cookies or milk, but because of our great roommate Gladys, Santa decided to leave some presents after all. Our stockings were FULL of candy. After Alana and I traded our candy and I "ooo"ed and "aaaah"ed over the soft socks (I love socks!!), we opened presents, with Gladys tossing them at us and then us telling her which one she should open next.

Alana had the funniest gift ever – it was in a box so huge that it was almost as big as the couch it sat on!! I had tried lifting it and it was sooooo heavy! When I asked for a hint she said six words and nine syllables.

"Is it something to do with music?" I quizzed. Ha, I'm so predictable!

"Yup. You as a musician should know all about it!" I thought and guessed and thought, but I could not guess! She enjoyed it, and rightfully so! Well on Christmas day I opened it to find....bricks? And old bottles? And newspapers? But then there was something in a bag, so I opened it to find a long tube of something wrapped up. Hm, A violin bow? Yeah, right! I opened that to find two little tiny wrapped up balls. A guitar pick holder and some picks! I definitely told her I loved it! That was a good prank! Very well thought out and very well delivered. I appreciated it!

The best was yet to come. I thought all the present opening was done, and was flipping the puck Gladys bought me in my hand, watching it spin in the air. It had been a while since I had skated or played...I started cleaning up the wrapping paper and putting boxes in boxes and tidying up. Then I noticed that Alana and Gladys were downstairs... and they were whispering quietly...hm...

I hopped down the stairs to ask if they needed anything and Alana shoed me up the stairs. "Okay..." I said slowly turning and going up.

Not thinking anything more of it, I looked at a little tiny hockey stick Gladys got for my uncle in the Caribbean. It was only days until that trip now – *four days to be exact*, I thought, turning it over in my hands. I heard a commotion in the kitchen and went to look.

To my utter and complete delight, Gladys and Alana were playing hockey in the house with two mini sticks and the tiny plastic pucks that they came with! Okay. We have to pause here and I need to tell you something, dear reader. I have this…addiction to playing hockey in the house. Yes, it is true. Ever since I stopped skating – which has been many years – I have taken to playing inside. I would play outside but it's really lame when you're by yourself. Inside you have closer walls to knock it back and hallways to run down…okay. I forgot to tell Gladys of this problem before I moved in.

Funny story; on one of my first days living in her house, I pulled out my mini hockey stick and cheap plastic puck and was shooting quietly in the house, playing music on the TV. Soon I got into the "game" and did an open slap shot that went sailing into the air. While the puck was in the air, Gladys opened the door and came in from work.

The puck whizzed past her nose and hit the wall inches from her head. I froze because I had no idea she was coming! "What the heck?" she turned to me. I am a horrible liar, so I'm sure my face was red, so I immediately went to put my little hockey stick away. "What was that?" she asked.

"What was what?" I asked nonchalantly, stifling gales of laughter.

"The puck that went flying past my head!" she exclaimed, making the motion with her hand. "No hockey in the house!" she said loudly.

Another rule. "Fine," I sighed. It was her house. I still laughed at it.

"No seriously, you could break something," she continued.

"No I couldn't," I argued with a smirk despite my effort, "I don't hit it that hard."

"Yes you do. You break it you buy it…" and she went on. I got it. So no hockey in the house…I was much more careful after that – to know if she was coming or not. I did not break anything and as long as it wasn't hurting anyone, what's the harm? Well I tell you, on this Christmas day it surprised the *pants* off of me to see Gladys and Alana playing hockey in the kitchen with **two** pucks!! That was dynamite! I had broken my mini stick from a hard slap shot, so I started playing with the tiny little stick Gladys bought for my family in The Caribbean.

It was a short game, but fun. They gave me the sticks and pucks "oh, but right, no hockey in the house!" Gladys joked. I blushed...aahhh, what the heck? So she knew...I thought she knew but I wasn't sure. "No slap-shots," she insisted, "but around the corner is what you *really* can't do in the house."

"What?" I didn't get what she said.

"Just go look around the corner," Alana said impatiently. My eyes lit up when I saw the good ole hockey stick – an actual stick – resting against the wall. That was **awesome!** I couldn't believe it because Gladys had been so set against hockey in the house! I loved it! We had been in a store together a few weeks ago on our way to get ice cream, when I stopped to look at the sports stuff – mainly hockey. Shhhh...don't tell anyone, but that is what I do sometimes; look at the sports stuff after the music section.

Anyway, we ran into a friend of hers who used to play and next thing I knew we were playing hockey in the aisle around Gladys! And then she went and bought a stick. She had even mentioned that she had a present for me in her car, and I had said "what is it, a hockey stick?" but I was just kidding because she didn't like hockey in the house. It is absolutely hilarious that she had bought me one. Tasteful humor right there!

We all went our separate ways on Christmas day, then; I went to visit with Noella and Drew and some of Drew's family. They were having a dinner at his brother's house and we played games and had a little gift opening. I gave Noella and Drew the starting papers of legal parental adoption – to show them that I consider them my parents.

It was all very good. As soon as Christmas was over, though, I was more worried about this trip. Everything was in order, so it seemed like God wanted us to go. We were going on the twenty-ninth of December and Jonas would meet us there in the first week of January. We planned and worked and I was fretting because I had no extra money. I had to cover my bills for when I was gone and then the rest of my money went to the flight and insurance – I didn't even have enough for medical insurance.

What was I going to do if we got into a rut? I did not think that Ephraim would cover me; he said he would if he had to, but I always wondered if bark came to bite, if he would. I actually prayed about it and had a few friends pray as well. Well the day before I left my credit card came in the mail and I activated it so I did not leave the country empty handed. That was a surprise, given the fact that when I applied for it I was not approved. Some other friends had a little parting party for me and I ended up getting sloshed. I had told Gladys about my struggle with alcohol (earlier on) and she did not like it in her house. Well I had two Mickey's and I was not about to dump it out unless it was straight into my mouth; a learned behavior.

I will admit that maybe not all of my friends have a good influence on me. Gladys took it well. When we got back at three in the morning, two friends crashed on the couches in the living room and I puked in the bathroom. Well unfortunately, Emma needed to puke as well and so she aimed for outside. She had just caught the door on her way out and it was all liquid – no food, so she didn't notice the door. Neither did I on my last day of work before the big trip. Gladys did not mention a thing.

Alana and Gladys were supportive and were already missing me, ☺ and Noella and Drew and many people were praying and Ephraim made overly sure that I had everything packed up. Next thing I knew, we were off, with Monika from Perri, driving us there. There was always dissonance between the two of us because when I was sixteen to eighteen and trying to establish a relationship with Ephraim, Monika tried to not allow it to happen. Ephraim didn't get phone messages and was not allowed to spend much time with me; I had only to talk to Monika to know of her distaste. Part of that stemmed from things she had heard and seen of the lifestyle that I lived in high school.

When Ephraim had told me that she had offered to drive us to Winnipeg for free, I had said a flat out "no."

"Are you saying no?" Ephraim checked again.

"That's correct," I stated without hesitation.

"Well she is offering us a free ride which means we don't have to pay for gas, and she would pay for our hotel room," he explained. I could see the logic, but I wanted to stay with Jonas' adoptive parents. "I am taking the ride," he said firmly.

I knew that Ephraim is his mother's boy (by his mother I mean Monika, not Joan), and after humming and hawing with Noella, I decided to go for it. Just because Monika was driving us didn't mean that I had to bond with her and sometimes it is good to stretch boundaries. So off we went on this great big adventurous trip of unknowns. It was like listening to a new song for the first time – you never know what could come next (well, actually most songs these days are quite predictable). I like adventure and claim to be a "fly-by-the-seat-of-my-pants" type of gal, well, now it was time to put the money where the mouth was! Which I could do at this point because of that new credit card! Funny how it all worked out!

chapter 4:

Well, the ride to Winnipeg was long and boring. Ephraim had a connection with his mother and his foster sister Daisy was young and shy. I texted people like crazy and they humored me. We stopped for a meal and Monika bought, which I was not expecting. At dinner she was civil and carried a decent conversation. Sometimes I thought her topics were getting a little bit too personal, so I closed the doors.

"So tell me what you went through after you left us," she implored, leaning forward. She had finished eating and I was nibbling on some fries. I looked at Ephraim. He was going to let me do the talking. I was slightly taken aback and did not feel at ease with the abrupt question coming from her.

"No." I said curtly, but not rudely.

"That's it?" she asked, slightly taken aback. I nodded and that was it. She did not judge me for that and did not push the issue. I thought the whole thing was odd and dismissed it. I think it was good for Monika to see the interactions between Ephraim and me. Perhaps she would let us be when she saw that it was his choice to have his sis in his life. I was surprised that she was letting him go to The Caribbean, but it was his choice and I had a feeling that she had advised him not to go.

Ephraim later told me she did; but he went anyway. That's it. Good for him because now we have some good memories.

I respect Monika and truly believe that she is Ephraim's mother, so I did not protest when she checked us into the hotel or wanted to go shopping. I went along with everything, bored out of my mind. Ephraim knows these folks and I can know them to a certain degree, but I have more experience than not that their doors were closed to me, so on this trip I expected nothing less. They were waaay nicer than I thought they would be…and perhaps things may have been more fun if I hadn't shut the door on them myself that evening. I just wandered off to do my own thing because it felt so weird but they were chill…they didn't mind.

At the mall I was in a bookstore reading a manga because I look to those books for ways to draw and paint anime, and they just texted to know where I was. I ended up meeting with Jonas' adoptive mother. I call her by name but for now we will call her Mrs. Krieger.

She is one of the nicest ladies I know and has taken quite a liking to me. Jonas is lucky to have been adopted into such a good caring home! They always send gifts over Christmas and they call and I am welcome at anytime to their place in Winnipeg. The whole family is like that. Anyway, we had touched base and met up at a local court in the mall and it was so good to see her friendly face!

"How are you?" she asked as I awkwardly side-hugged her.

"Pretty good," I said with a deep breath and a little grin.

"Are you nervous about your trip? Are you excited?" she asked, being a little goofy but sincere at the same time. She was so good at that! It was good to see her face before the trip!

"Both," I admitted, "but I think it will be fun." She asked where Ephraim was and I said that I didn't know as they were shopping.

"Okay, well, where do you want to eat?" she asked with her familiar kind smile.

"I don't know," I said with a wave of my hand. We picked a place close by and I was texting Ephraim when he showed up right behind us; excellent timing because my phone battery died right then. We met up with everyone and figured things out. Monika did not look too happy, but I was happy to see a familiar face – a kind face. We ate our dinner and then decided to go back to the hotel for some rest. I left my jacket and phone with Mrs. Krieger since Ephraim and I had different routes back, I would be seeing her after the trip.

That night was the worst sleep ever! Daisy and I could not sleep because of Monika's snoring. At first it was funny, but when four in the morning rolled around and we hadn't slept a wink, we just whispered to each other. Ephraim wore ear plugs and slept like a baby beside his momma. I thought about pulling a prank or two on them, but decided against it and listened to music instead.

Morning came as soon as I closed my eyes. Monika bought us breakfast at the hotel restaurant and we ate heartily. She checked with us to make sure we had everything and cautioned us. It was rather nice to hear a reassuring word from her because she had traveled quite a bit so it was experience talking. She made some comment about wanting to talk to me or something like that and I did what I always do – I spoke my mind.

"Why now?" I asked suddenly.

"Why now what?" she asked.

"Well you never liked me before," I stated very bluntly but not emotional.

She kind of laughed, and said "who said that? I've always liked you." Right – insert a roll of the eyes right here. "I wish I would have taken you in," she said just as suddenly, "when pastor Harry called, I knew it was bad, but I didn't know how bad it was." I just looked at her skeptically wondering where this was all coming from. I didn't know that he had called her…or maybe I did and forgot. I think she was glad to know of my whereabouts so that she could navigate the situation and protect Ephraim.

"Honestly, I saw this girl in a hospital one time and she was crying – really crying – and I wanted to help her so badly," Monika continued. Well I could see that she was genuine, but still had no idea as to where this was going…or coming from.

"Why didn't you?" I asked, keenly observing her.

She shrugged her shoulders and said an honest "pride." Hm. It was interesting that she chose now to be open with me. Maybe she was trying to patch up a broken road? I didn't pass any kind of judgments on the fact that she did not help me out when I was younger or the other girl recently; I just didn't really didn't think anything at all about it. Even now I still don't know. I just let it go right away, but I do commend her honesty. Her honesty mirrors the honesty of another lady who could have helped but didn't. It takes guts to be open like that. Somehow the topic of Joan came up – and I know I did *not* bring that up!

"I think she was raped," Monika said, "to make her turn against men like that."

I kind of frowned and said "well we shouldn't speculate." And that was that. Ephraim went for the *longest* turd in human history, and then we were at the airport, passports in hand. Monika was **great**, then, supporting us both, hugging her little boy and then turning to hug me, which I pushed away. I am not affectionate to many people at all, but it was all kept very light, and then we were in the plane flying away. We mostly kept to ourselves, and I think Ephraim was distant because Monika had probably told him to be careful around me or maybe he was already homesick or nervous or all of the above. I think it was great to see the interaction between Ephraim and his mom as I never got to be part of that, but it's really cool because there is no envy when I see it. I like seeing it and want to meet people in his life just to know them.

A little surge of excitement at the unknown spurted within me and I was wide awake. We had two flight transfers and then a long flight. All together it was 14 hours of flight. Noella had told me that traveling "makes or breaks a relationship" so I was actually prepared for it to break the relationship between Ephraim and myself because I did not think it was strong.

I am so glad that Ephraim was there, though, as he really pulled out the papa bear card – he watched my back and found the way around the airports and covered our bases. It was probably annoying for him at times, but I was glad that he was well informed because he had a bit of experience traveling, too. We caught our flights and luggage was taken care of. We kept all of our paper work ready and close by. Four days prior to leaving, (so on Christmas day), a man in Germany had tried to get into the United States with a liquid bomb.

He would have gotten through, too, but his father had noticed differences in his son's behavior and out of concern for the man and people around him, found out about his plans and turned him in. Because of the high security, we were allowed only one technological device and maybe a book or something. I had my music. It was a long trip, but we stuck it out in good nature and at night we saw the shape of the Caribbean island form right before our eyes. I had the window seat so I was gawking.

It was gorgeous and I wish I had my camera! The lights from the cities looked like jewels and the ocean was black with night. We were ten thousand miles high, so it took time for us to descend. When we saw the islands in the sky, they were bejeweled in the night. When we landed, it was 9 am their time. Right away I noticed the vegetation and moisture. Ephraim noticed a shipwreck. We were getting quite excited.

The airport was definitely a contrast to our American ones, but poverty is a lot more common as well as weather wear and tear. Right away we were noticed because we look different – not necessarily American, but just different. Ephraim had to give up his army hat because if he walked out wearing it then he could be shot. He gave it up with a cute little pout, and I teased him about his hat hair to keep it light.

I think that Ephraim really did his homework before going, but I jumped in with both feet. We worked well together, and at the airport is when I realized that things were seriously different than Canada or the United States. Crime was so much more scary and serious and common here.

Luckily for us, our uncle Tim had talked to us on Skype because he was waiting with our cousin Steve (very American names for The Caribbean), and they were able to recognize us from the video as well as facebook pictures. They were waiting at the gates for us. I told Ephraim that I was going to take things easy at first – I thought it would be hard talking to them.

"So you're not going to talk?" he had asked, disagreement in his voice.

"Well yes, but not as much," I had to explain, "I would like it if you start it off because you are better at handling people."

"Okay," he said. Well at first I couldn't look at them, the same way as when I met Jonas for the first time, I pulled out the shy card, but when Ephraim started chatting with them I could feel their good nature, so I joined and soon the awkward silence dissipated.

"So much for the shy card," Ephraim said quietly to me and then "no, it's good."

Okay so the first thing we learned the hard way is that Caribbean people drive like crazy! Not only do they drive on the "wrong" side of the road (the left side), but they speed and crowd each other and do not even stop for emergency vehicles. In America if an ambulance or police car has siren bellowing, we get out of the way. One time when we were driving with out uncle, we saw a wailing ambulance stuck in traffic. Crazy!

Another thing is the cars are so clean. No dust, no bugs, lots of dents though. Lots of new rims, stereos, tires, lights, paint, tints, etc., it's like their cars are their pride. Then the vegetation – there is so much of it and it is very healthy. Moisture, lots of fruit, but *huge* fruits and flowers and trees and bushes…the leaves seem more wide and tall.

Our uncle is fantastic and so in our aunty Beth. They opened up their house to us and Steve and I got along fantastically. They quite enjoyed my humor and in a short time I was comfortable enough to be myself around them. Ephraim advised me to be careful, but soon enough his goofy side came out too and we shared a lot of snickers and giggles.

Their house was brightly painted – like most other houses there – each room was a bright vivid color and the rooms were a lot more open and inviting with less walls and more color. No two houses looked the same – it was sweet. The only thing is that each house also had tall fences with iron gates and huge locks. Security. Our uncle had four dogs. Dogs were common there – I think we only saw two cats when we were there.

Ephraim and I got bit by some crazy bugs after new blood. We had bites the size of loonies and we could not sleep. If I drifted off and Ephraim couldn't sleep, he sat up, put his head on his hand and stared with a goofy expression so that I laughed when I saw him. We talked all the time about everything and nothing. Our aunty and uncle teased us about the bites, saying like bugs were greeting us or that they liked Americans. It was fun, but they were also very hospitable in providing bug spray and cream. We eventually wore long sleeved shirts and sweats and socks to bed – insufferable in the heat!

So by now you have probably gathered that we shared a room. I thought it would be awkward, but it really wasn't. I had the bed with a big net coming down; Ephraim had a mattress on the floor. My side was messy – clothes popping out of my tiny suitcase and backpack, books and things thrown everywhere; his side was organized into his huge suitcase…with shelves in it. Ah, the joys of being a twin. I liked it.

We saw parrots and parakeets and lizards. Uncle Tim came up to me with something in his hand and wanting to scare me, he put a lizard in it. I was fascinated. We went shopping for clothes and souvenirs and again the difference between Ephraim and I flared up. I am a look, see, touch, or go person – in and out – usually only shopping for a very short time or with a definite purpose; I rarely dawdle.

Ephraim…well he is quite different. I joke that he is more girly than I am. With our cousin Steve, Tim's boy, we went shopping around. I looked at the stuff in the store and was done in a matter of minutes. In Ephraim's defense it was a men's clothing store. He went upstairs to look at some clothes and Steve and I joined him. **Three hours later** we finally left the store. Ephraim had been in the upstairs section for most of that time. Well Steve and I got to know each other pretty well. We teased Ephraim about it a lot.

When we went to the street market, it reminded me a lot of Mexico. There were shops set up and people bustling all out and about. It was busy. Everyone there looked angry or tired…and brown or black. In Canada there are a lot of mixed races and that is what I grew up seeing, right? So it was different to be in a country where that was not so – and it was not too welcomed either. I think during our duration we saw one white woman there.

When we were on the street market, my uncle would come and stand right by me. When we were walking I was usually in the middle of the line somehow. I started thinking I was paranoid, so I tested my theory by walking over to look at a nice shirt when Steve and Ephraim stopped to look at pants. Sure enough, uncle came and stood close by, keeping his eyes open and watching. Wow. He was protecting me. It was weird! I didn't know what to make of it, so I stuck close to the group and didn't say anything about it.

When we got back from our adventures of the street market, Ephraim and I were catching up on what we thought of things. I told him how uncle stood watch over me every time I stopped. He knew and said "well you got a lot of male attention out there."

"I did?" I said, surprised. I was in no way asking for it...I was decently clothed, I didn't comb my hair, no make up, no perfume...

"Yeah, well you did" Ephraim stated.

"How do you know?" I chided gently.

"Because I stared them down, I was like this," and then he showed me a face that made me laugh. He said when a guy checked me out he eyeballed them and then the guy looked away quickly. Ephraim being intimidating? Huh. Wonders never cease. But I felt special, you know, for the first time in my life people were looking out to protect me. I have had people help once something bad had happened, but here were family members working to keep me safe. It was cool.

My brother and I slept a lot, and we figured it was the sudden heat and humidity because it was snowy and cold and very dry when we left our home land, going from minus thirties to plus thirties is quite a weather change. Part of it was probably jet lag, too. We ate dinner with our aunty and uncle at their kitchen table, sometimes with Cousin Steve and his wife, all crowding each other, eating off each other's plates and teasing one another. It was great. This is what it was like to be a part of a family – and these were all my blood relatives; sweet.

I remember when I was fourteen and at the Swazie's farm in foster care, how I vowed to be reunited with my family. At the time I had meant the only family I knew – Joan, Daniel, Susie, Jocelyn and Ephraim. I had not bet on finding Jonas two years later, or my aunties and uncles a few years down the road. In that moment of eating roti and curried chicken and mango massala, laughing and taunting each other, my fourteen year old dream was fulfilled.

Aunty Beth is a *terrific* cook, making roti, mango massala, chutney, curried chicken, fruit bread…other dishes that I can't remember…all very good. She was always checking to see what we liked or didn't and was so accommodating. We jokingly call her the "Iron chef" and my uncle and I are the "Iron eaters." Ephraim and I helped out in the kitchen, cleaning a little bit with the cooking, or just even watching to learn the secrets. It was so cool too that we drank coconut juice from real huge green coconuts off the trees, ate mangoes grown in their back yard, saw sugar cane (it wasn't ripe yet) and bananas (they weren't ripe yet either).

When we were seeing where uncle worked, he said "let's go for doubles," and I thought he meant shots, right? That's what we say, "ya, bartender, I'd like a double…"

So I was like "really? Okay!"

Weeeelll, he definitely meant something else. It is a roti wrapped around Dahl puree and some other good stuff. So we joked about that too. It was neat because they really opened up and let us in – they made our stay safe and as best as it could possibly be and it has not gone unnoticed. We are blessed to call them family. I think God wanted me to see the good side of my family, and it was indeed good.

We also went around on a beach and it was gorgeous out the whole time we were there. Our uncle and aunty centered around safety first, so when uncle said to us "go ahead, go take a walk," we thought he meant *take a walk*. So we walked how we walk – fast and far. We walked on the shore and took pictures and talked and joked. There were these weird bubbles popping up on the sand – thousands of them and we wondered what they were. Ephraim was strutting around, popping them loudly in his sandals. One washed ashore and as it did I bent to look. They were jelly fish! Blue and purple tentacles stretched all the way down to shore from the top of the beach.

"Don't touch them or I'll have to pee on you," Ephraim half-joked.

"Ew…why?"

"Because urine cures the sting," he explained. Gross. I bent down and picked one up anyway, careful not to let the fluctuating tentacles touch me, and Ephraim snapped a quick picture. When I had stooped to see what they were, I noticed that the jelly fish had heaved a long, sad sigh as it slowly died in the heat. I felt bad and so after taking the picture, tossed it into the waves to end its misery. We collected shells and found these weird little pots and started collecting those too. We saw that the holes in the shells – these tiny, perfect holes, right on the edge of the shells (perfect for necklaces) were made by birds. We had found what type of bird in a bird book, but I forget the name. The purple shells scattered across the beach as beautiful as they were are a mark of torture. The birds peck and beat the clams until they open and then they eat them live.

We walked and wandered and let the water lap at our feet. The sunlight shone like broken jewels and the warm wind played with our hair. It was so peaceful and I felt like we were in a movie. While we strolled along, we suddenly saw a man with a long machete in the trees. He looked at us and we avoided eye contact with him and then we walked a little bit faster. We had walked for quite some time before we realized that we should probably head back. On our way back I picked up a sand dollar – it was whole and it was beautiful. I kept trying to put jellyfish back into the ocean to make it live, but they kept washing ashore. They were destined to die.

"Do you really think that'll make a difference," Ephraim asked, walking ahead.

"It might in this one's life," I said tossing it into the water. Sadly, it washed right up shore again, so I stopped trying because it was prolonging their anguish. When we looked up we saw our uncle and grandpa running toward us, worried looks on their faces.

"Where were you?" Uncle Tim asked, his voice matching his worried face.

"Walking," we answered ignorantly.

"Why did you go so far?" he asked while grandpa just looked on.

"You said to go for a walk," I replied, shrugging. What's the big deal?

"Yes, I said a walk, I meant where we could see you," he pointed to a big fallen tree that we had passed at the start of our little journey, and said "nobody goes past this tree here because it is not safe."

"Okay," I said, slightly exasperated. Ephraim was quiet, but neither of us felt angry or anything. We just hadn't known better, but now we did. This is what happens in families.

"I'll tell you," uncle continued, "about two weeks before you came here, a young couple from England on their honeymoon and they were walking just like the two of you, but at dusk. At night some robbers came and axed them to pieces, stealing their money." He gestured down the beach "it was right on this same beach, so when I look up and didn't see you, I thought something happen to you."

"Karee," Ephraim said suddenly and came over to me, handing me a rock.

"Yeah?" I asked, thinking he had something funny to say. I tossed the rock into the ocean and looked over at him, ready to listen or joke back if necessary.

"Nothing," he said with a little smirk, and I noticed a man looking at us as he walked past. "I thought that man was following you," Ephraim admitted. Uncle decided it was too dangerous for us because we looked American and Ephraim looked like he had lots of money in his nice clothes, so we left without tension. I thought it was still fun.

It was sweet that they were so concerned. We were careful after that. We soon learned about how everyone lived in fear. Every house had iron gates or stone walls, all with large locks and usually a few big dogs to stop theft. Crimes were so high because of drinking. One night we were having another tasty supper when we all fell silent because a vehicle was driving down the street announcing that a man had been shot twice in his home and the wife and kids were safe because they were not there at the time. Killer and robber still at large. They drove up and down the street saying that through a giant megaphone so all could hear from inside their houses.

"They do that so you know to go inside," uncle explained, seeing my face grow serious. We continued eating quietly, the kitchen radio playing some chutney tunes. Well that night Ephraim and I agreed to be more careful. At night we stayed in and read books, watched movies, went online and Ephraim kept saying that we should tell them about my past, how Joan treated me. "No," I would decline, "I did not come to talk about her," but Ephraim thought I should still prepared to share my testimony. I did not.

I think Ephraim tried a couple times to bring it up, but I always changed the topic very abruptly or decided to have a shower or eat or somehow evade the conversation. Whenever the topic of Joan came up, my face always fell because I just did not want to hear her name on this trip. I was here to meet my family, and I knew that they love her because to Tim she is a sweet little sister who made it into America, so I did not want to tarnish their view of her. Grandpa tried to talk to me about her as well, but I always steered the conversation away, as usual. Well one time he got me good because Ephraim was in the shower so I couldn't really make an excuse to leave.

I had just poured myself a nice glass of auntie's wonderful sorrel juice and wandered into the living room to join uncle and grandpa watching a show. Grandpa turned to me and said "I wish I could have brought you here." Right away, that old familiar wall slid into place so I didn't say anything and suddenly the TV was so interesting. He carried on, even though he knew I was purposely ignoring him, "I don't like the way she treated you," of course he knew that I could hear him.

Sensing a serious conversation, uncle turned the TV volume down low and went into the kitchen to join aunty. Thanks a lot! That was my distraction...finally I looked at grandpa resting on the floor and said "just don't. You don't even know," and I was going to say "anything," but he interrupted. I guess I had to listen.

"I know," he insisted, "I know the way she treated you and your brothers."

Okay. "How?" I asked, skeptically. I did not want to partake of this dialogue because they had a positive outlook of Joan and it was not up to me to wreck it.

"The Holy Spirit showed me," he stated, looking right into my face. Oh boy.

"What did it show you?" I asked mostly to humor him.

"I know that you have seen dark times because of Joan." Hm. Well, he got that right. I was still quite reluctant to be in this moment, so silence was best.

"I wanted to have you kids, you know," grandpa said again, determined to be heard, "but the government wouldn't let me have you. Joan said the government wouldn't let me have you."

"Well she lied," I said quickly, anger rising to the surface, "the first place the government looks is for family to take them in." I had taken some law classes in high school; we had covered this.

"All I needed was money and I would have come and got you myself," grandpa said. What does one say to that?

"Uh, look, I don't think we should ta -"

"I wanted you kids, but the son of a bitch wouldn't let me have you kids!" he shouted, pounding his fists on the couch. "I may have had your mother, but I am not a fool." I disliked the reference of Joan being my mother and almost cringed at it.

Okay I finally believed him. I couldn't help but grin – I was so surprised that he swore and that he called Joan a son of a bitch, but maybe he meant the government by "son of a bitch". I knew he was a Christian so it was kind of funny to see him pound his fists and swear, but maybe it shouldn't have been. I didn't know what to make of it all.

"I wanted to take you away from there," he continued now that he had my attention, "I prayed for you to be released. And when you went away, the Holy Spirit showed me that wasn't the right place either so I prayed you get out of there." What? Lucky for me Ephraim was now out of the shower, uncle came into the living room and aunty asked every one if they wanted fruit cake. I got up and offered to help, mostly to do something, but there wasn't much to do.

Grandpa looked on, still resting on the floor, and said "don't play me for a fool; I know," with a knowing look in his eyes. Okayyyy...well soon it was over and we all piled into the living room watching a movie. That night Ephraim asked what that was all about and I re-iterated the conversation back to him and he thought it was cool. I could tell that these folks had a soft spot for me; grandpa had bought me some jewelry and aunty and uncle were always looking out for me and stuff, so that was good enough for me – more than I had expected or thought about. They knew that Joan had hurt me despite her many efforts to make me the grinch, and so they were making up for it by loving me.

I really, honestly had felt no need to hash things out, but they had a need to show their love and support, so it was up to me to accept it. "I told uncle and aunty that you went through a lot because of Joan, so maybe that's why" Ephraim admitted.

"When - why would you do that?" I asked defensively.

"I think they need to know," he said. Well there was nothing I could do, so I let it go. What the heck. I was here now and determined to enjoy this time with my family. Ephraim also told aunty and uncle that I was an alcoholic because I had spotted some rum and had a shot...so what? It was only a shot. And then when we were drinking out of coconuts I was going to pour some of the rum in there, just to taste, but it was gone.

One night, walking over to the computer, I noticed the absence of the rum again and gasped dramatically. "What?" Ephraim queried with a tiny little grin.

"Where's the rum?" I asked, dramatically pointing.

"Oh, I told uncle that you are an alcoholic," he snickered. What?! "Well I told them that you drink a lot," he corrected, "but I said that you had been through a lot."

"But – the rum is gone!" I repeated, reminding myself of Jack Sparrow off of *Pirates of the Caribbean*. Oh, man! So they had removed the alcohol. Eehhh...whatever. We heard many drunkards at night anyway, shooting firecrackers and speeding and hooting and hollering. I thought it was very annoying but it wasn't the end of the world. Ephraim thought my reaction was funny...or at least he acted like he did.

On New Year's Eve we headed to church – I was the only non-church-goer, so majority ruled. I thought it would be neat to see church half-way across the world anyway. Uncle was proud of us and told everyone that we were his niece and nephew, and then service began. There was singing – quite a bit more heartfelt and energetic than in America – and I tried to sing along, but didn't know many of the songs. I did notice that Ephraim and I play piano on the side of our legs...same leg too...but I also did guitar strums and emphasized drums. Never thought about it; just do it. He noticed, too.

The service was alright although I don't recall what it was about. The pastor was adamant and very passionate. Steve's wife, Isabel, is a very lovely little lady and she went and shared some praise items. Ephraim really appreciated what she said – I think he appreciated the whole service. I did too, but it was a little out of my league. As the service ended there was worship until midnight countdown, and I heard fireworks at the stroke of midnight. Wanting to go see them, I told uncle excitedly and he said "by the time we get there they'll be over," which was a very nice "no."

Well if there is one thing new, it's fire works on New Year's Day, (in north America, the fireworks come on Canada Day or Independence Day, both in summer) so I peered out the perforated walls, catching some greens, reds and yellows splashing against the night sky. I did not have a very good view, but at least I could see them shooting and whizzing up in the dark evening. When they were over, I sighed in relief and went up to the front with Cousin Steve and Ephraim who were going to jam with the instruments. I played on the drums while a man played piano and Steve played bass.

When I was done with the drums, I went to play guitar, but Steve had it, so I picked up bass for the first time ever and was able to play along to some simple chords. Ephraim chatted with the fellow at the keyboard. The pastor came and greeted us individually and then when it was time to go, but I was not quite ready to leave yet because the music was a blast. Grandpa had been observing and when I came down from the front of the church; he smiled proudly and said "you know music real well, huh?"

I smiled shyly and said "well sort of," and back home we went. They spoke of this uncle, Tim's brother, who was in BC by the name of Vinny. I had chatted to his son on msn, and we had swapped music. Vinny is a musician and that explains where it comes from because neither Joan nor Daniel is musical. He is a singer, so they liked that I could sing. Steve even left his guitar at the house there so we could play on it, but I pulled out the shy card when they asked me to sing because I did not think that they would like my choice of songs since it is not worship. They were alright with that, teasing me and then just listening when I did my own thing. They were encouraging and supportive anyway.

We also went to visit our auntie's aunty (whom she was raised by), and what a lovely house! We tried new juices and foods of all kinds. She was very loud and boisterous and comical in her stern way. I helped set the table and take dishes away and she was eager to show me rooms and let us look around. Ephraim and I both appreciated her hospitality. After our visit to the beach close by her house, Ephraim and I reclined with books. I was stretched outside and reading when all of a sudden a drunken man walked right into her yard and started jabbering at me with his strong accent.

That was weird, so I went into the house and told Tandy (auntie's aunt; that's what they called her). She came out and shooed the man away. He was a drunkard that came to her because she felt compassion and gave him food or money when he asked. She said he wouldn't stop coming now. We had a delightful time there. We also ventured over to uncle's neighbor's house for a feast. It was a religious one offered to Buddha or something like that, so we were cautioned for what to say and what not to say. I minded my manners. The neighbor's son's name was "Bighead," no lie – or it was a nickname; so funny. Jonas got to meet him (when he came later on) and look at his shiny new car. Ephraim and I jokingly call him Jonas bighead.

We ate lots of hand foods there, and on leaves instead of plates. I thought the leaves were plastic, but upon leaving saw the plant standing tall outside. The food was delicious, as always, and the people were very welcoming and generous. We also got to meet some more people later on – I am not even sure if they are cousins or friends or what, but we saw the sorrel plant and had some juice. I believe they were the family of Aunty Beth's – her cousin, so their sons were Steve's second cousins. The sorrel plant is like a flower, with the seeds taken out and the petal part dried. The petals are not like rose petals, but very rich in color with waxy texture.

The juice was not as good as our auntie's but it was tasty and refreshing. There was the *cutest* little puppy ever and I played with it while everyone visited. When I joined, I saw that Ephraim had struck a chord with one of the boys our age named Zack, because they were both in school for biochemistry. They all treated us very well, Ephraim and me; the two peas in a pod. Well the third little pea was very warmly welcomed, too.

chapter 5: _____

A few days later Jonas showed up on the island and we were thrilled to see him. He was staying at another place with his fiancée, Eve, because her uncle owned the place. They came over for supper and we joked and talked and crammed ourselves around the table and ate. It was so cool, because this was my real family and I was a real part of it.

I loved it because they enjoyed my quirky sense of humor and made me laugh a LOT, which I love to do. There were no prejudices despite things that Joan may have said and they told us that they were worried about us kids because we disappeared and they had no idea what happened. They said that it was Joan's personal affairs and so they thought it best to not push her, but they knew something was wrong. We had become the "question marks" of the family, just like they were to us. Well now they knew about us and now we knew about them.

Jonas, Ephraim, Uncle, Aunty, Eve, and I piled into the living room to look at pictures. Jonas' face sparkled and he looked at the pictures. Uncle Tim pointed here and there, describing what he knew and we saw pictures of grandpa Stardens' farm, and Daniel with Tim loading bales and pictures of Joan. Tim turned the album to me and said "whose face is that, looking at you?" it was Joan when she was young. Well we looked alike, that's for sure. She was beautiful and her brother was beaming proudly.

We passed by a precious picture of Daniel holding Jonas when he was a baby. In the picture baby Jonas' hand reached toward Daniel and they both wore grins. Jonas' cute little baby grin was matched by a tender and proud fatherly smile. Seeing that picture gave me a heart for Daniel. Seeing how Jonas liked the picture, they generously gave him a couple of them, so that he could treasure them. Jonas was happy as a lark and it was very monumental for the three of us to be there like that. We were blessed.

Soon we just relaxed and Ephraim busied himself taking pictures and we asked questions, but mostly I just happily observed. Ephraim and I decided to spend a couple days with Jonas and his fiancée at her uncle's place. We cruised town and battered each other and set up camp in his nice place; a sweet to ourselves. There were local stores near by and so we went shopping, walking together and Jonas was so funny. He would pretend not to care (just like I do) and then buy us all meals.

"Aw, thanks, buddy bro," I teased, clapping him lightly on the back. A big grin spread across his face and he ducked behind a wall, but I knew he was pleased. We took the food and went back to our little place. Stopping at the local store, Ephraim and I were able to pick up some spices and things to take back home. I got some coconut rum and Jonas advised on what he thought we should get. Sometimes we listened, other times we didn't. He bought some shark and I am glad I turned it down because Ephraim said it was disgusting; he couldn't even finish his plate.

We later learned that one is supposed to boil the shark three times over before cooking it as it is a salt water animal with salt added for preservation. We all teased Jonas and he grinned goofily. We went to visit grandpa at his house where Joan had grown up. I briefly remembered pictures from a long time ago. The house was now so old that it was falling apart and there were holes in the roof. I was worried about grandpa living there! The furniture was comfortable but covered in sheets and the stairs were so rickety that I just jumped down. Grandpa said he would not give the house up because of the history – his parents had built it and he had grown up there as well as his kids. There were lots of fruit trees various kinds of vegetation in the back yard. A lot of the leaves had a waxy substance that made one think it was plastic and there were various shades of green mixed with bright spots of vibrant color.

The whole island is covered with lots of vegetation – large, waxy leafs; long, smooth, shiny leaves with deliberate lines on them; bright batched of beautiful flowers; shrubs and tall palm trees or fruit trees, bordering the yards or beaches of roads. The air was fresh and warm and humid, immediately creating a laid back atmosphere. The people lived a laid back lifestyle – more about "liming" (relaxing) with family and friends than being busy and going to work. The roads were smooth and not as marked up as in America – in the cities there were white markings to direct the immense flow of traffic, but the highways were narrow due to the smaller vehicles and had little markings.

The stores were not elaborate, but they carried what you needed – there was a mixture of street shops and city malls. The pace was much slower that the American consumer world. Even their walking was much slower – Ephraim and I would walk what we thought was slow, to turn and see everyone far behind. There is poverty, but mainly everyone is middle class, and there is a high national pride. The main groups of people were from India or Africa and they spoke English but also another language they called "broken English" that was a mixture of Creole, an African language and they spoke as fast as Ephraim and I walk. A lovely thing to note was that there were few bugs, probably due to the many birds as well as the humidity.

The birds cooed and whistled, very much unlike ours that chirp and caw. There was a bright green wild parrot that cooed a whistle pattern and when I mimicked, it changed the pattern. Every time I whistled back the bird changed it and inched closer. This happened about eight times before it flew away because I turned to see it too quickly. Grandpa caught wild parakeets and I felt so bad for the one that he had now in the cage, desperately trying to get out. I was about to open the cage lid to let it go, but there was always someone close by, keeping an eye on things. Poor little birdie.

In the back yard we picked coconuts, getting Jonas to reach up and pull the tree branch down, teasing him about his height. He liked the machete they used to cut the fruit. The bananas weren't ripe and neither were the mangoes or the sugar cane. We played by a little creek, where uncle Tim said there were little fish from time to time; we didn't see any that day. And we heard lovely church music – it sounded like full gospel – wafting down to my hungry ears. We all shared a coconut and ate the jelly inside and then went into the house for supper.

Grandpa cooked pork and rice and it looked like it should have been gross but it tasted wonderful. Both Jonas and Uncle Tim tried to scare me by tossing a little lizard at me. Not too familiar with my boyish side, both were surprised when I was interested in the lizards and held them in my hand for pictures. The one little guy lost his tail and later research showed that they drop the ends of their tails when birds come after them. The end wiggles and distracts the enemy while the real meal scurries away.

We visited for a while and looked at some more pictures that grandpa had and then we headed back to our uncle's house. The next day we visited another beach – but this one was a community one that was a lot safer and a lot more public. Jonas, Eve, Uncle and I were rearing to go swimming, but Ephraim was reluctant.

"Why not?" I asked incredulously. Swimming in the ocean? Heck, yes!

"Oh I can't see without my glasses," he said; lame. So lame because Jonas was not wearing his glasses, uncle was not wearing his glasses and I rarely wore my own glasses. I don't know why Ephraim refused to go in, but when we saw that he was not budging, we all dumped our things on him – "here, take my sunglasses," "watch my camera," "and my sandals," "and my towel," and on and on until his lap was full. Why not? He was sitting there anyway! Hee, hee!

The four of us splashed and played and once again, all worries and woes of the past and present melted away and I was happy as a lark. Jonas bent his tall frame and let me stand on his leg to throw me into the water…instead of a nice jump; I think I ended up just doing a belly flop. Uncle and I had contests to see who could swim under water at the bottom of the ocean floor the longest (I won against him and Jonas because of better breath support – thanks to singing!).

Eve and I found shells with our feet and Jonas found a really big one that he gave to me, but I could no take it with me because it still had a creature alive in it. We laughed and giggled and splished and splashed

in the warm sun. I looked to shore at Ephraim by himself and we all
went over to try to coax him in.

"Well, I gotta watch all this stuff," he said sheepishly.

"We're close by," uncle said, pointing.

"No, it's okay."

"Not even for a little bit?" I wheedled. No go. We all went back to the
water and Ephraim took pictures from on shore. There was a live band
practicing for a weekend concert right on the dock near by, so we got
to hear the steel band. They sounded good, but I couldn't see enough to
get the rhythm of how they played the drums. But the socca beat and
chutney songs added to our light banter and playful swims.

Soon it was time to go and we took pictures of everything. I went to
take a picture of Ephraim and said "well at least go stand in the water
so it looks like you were in." He did and then Jonas found a crab and
put it on my shoulder. I squealed at that because they look creepy – like
water proof spiders. When we got back Ephraim and I decided to stay
for a few nights with Eve and Jonas at her uncle's place.

Her uncle Ben is an absolutely crazy driver – all the Caribbean
people are, but he was the cherry on the cake! So many times we were
thrown into each other, and within inches of an accident. He would
roll down the window and swear at people and he was quite distant to
Ephraim and me although we did try to at least start a conversation
with him. When we asked Eve about it she said he is old fashioned and
thought that we were a couple. She spoke to him and told him we were
twins and he was much kinder after that!

He took us around another city on the island – to see beautiful
buildings and we took pictures and talked with one another; just the
four of us. We stopped outside of this big old church and when I wanted
to go in, everyone said "no, we should go now," or "I don't think that's
allowed."

"Fine," I said, disappointedly dragging my feet to follow them.

"I think we should take a look," Jonas said, walking up beside me
with a grin.

"Okay," I said and into the church we went. It was Christmas time
so they had many sets and many sections with different saints to pray

to. It was peculiar, but a very lovely church. We took pictures and goofed off a little bit and then Jonas and I joined everyone waiting and we went back to their house.

It was a big blue and white house with big blue iron gates that said "MAMA'S PLACE." Afterwards we went to a local store and then mixed a few drinks and sat on the veranda talking. We watched a horror movie where Jonas kept trying to scare everyone and I constantly made jokes. Only parts of the show were creepy because apparently it was a true story. After that, we all went out and had some drinks and were chatting on the veranda. Ephraim and Eve got along well and they began to talk about church.

Jonas and I were quiet, but then I joined in and he cracked jokes like there was no tomorrow. It was kind of funny, but at the same time it sucked because he was a little bit out of his comfort zone. Eve shared prayer requests and the three of us took turns praying while Jonas tinkered around inside (we prayed for him, too).

At the end of it, Ephraim and I stayed up while the two of them went to bed and I confessed that I didn't pray aloud very often.

"Well you're pretty good at it," he said. I thought it would be a little bit odd sharing a bed with Ephraim, but he was really considerate by sleeping right against the wall to give me more room (I'm sure I kicked him once or twice) – he had my back on the whole trip and I am so glad! We spent the next day just hanging out and relaxing and observing the local action from high up. At this place we were close to mountains where there were orangutans and cougars. It was quite the sight to see palm trees illuminated by moonlight and accented by little stars. We heard on the radio that a fifteen year old boy was chopped up and left to die in a dumpster but someone had found him upon depositing their trash and he was currently in the hospital fighting for his life.

Terrible things like that happen every day there, even after the New Years Day, the murder rate was twice as many as days, even as the days added up. Our uncle told us about how they were hoping for a change in government. He was so passionate about it and about wanting to help people or somehow letting people be heard that Ephraim asked why he didn't work for the government to help.

"There's not much I can do," he explained, "the government won't listen," and he explained that all they could do was wait and hope for better change in the re-election coming in the New Year. On a lighter side, we did hear our uncle Vinny on the radio a couple times. Well our time there was drawing to a close and uncle and aunty took us shopping and Steve and Isabel visited us and encouraged me to play and sing a song on guitar. I played and sang a little bit here and there and there was so much encouragement! Every night before the family went to bed they prayed and so each night someone else would turn to pray.

I did pray every now and then, but it is awkward for me so I made it a bit goofy or I bailed when it was my turn. I appreciate them because they put up with it and quite understood things. Ephraim grew up with the Christian lifestyle and influences; I did not. Yes, there are some areas of life that I absolutely *have* to attribute to God, but I am a young Christian in the fact that things are now becoming my choice.

On our last night there, Steve, Ephraim and I went to pick up Isabel from work after we went shopping for the day, and they ended up taking us on a night out. We went over to Isabel's family's place and they fed us a delicious supper and gave us clean clothes to wear. Here in America, if we lend things, we expect them back. There, when they lend it out, they *give* it out. Isabel's mother showed us how to make roti and let us each take a try at it. I winged it, flying by the seat of my pants, and Ephraim spent a **lot** of time on his (but it did turn out a better than mine, although I did not admit it then), and it was all very good; especially the sweet rice. They appreciated when I played the guitar for them; I did not sing at their encouragement because I don't think I am very good at it, so I just played guitar quietly.

I noticed that most Caribbean people look very angry, but they are so generous! They have a grumpy way about them, because of fear, but when one speaks with them, they are likely to notice the boisterous kindness and generosity within. They are cautious, but not afraid to give without expecting back. We watched a new movie in their galaxy cinema, very much like the ones in Canada and the States. And then we went for a long cruise in the car around the city, and then Steve took us back to our uncle's place around midnight. When we arrived, uncle was not impressed and I did notice that Steve had not come into the yard like he usually did – he said a quick goodbye and took off.

"Hey," I greeted our uncle cheerily…until I noticed he was cross.

When he found out that Steve had taken us out, he was furious "I'm gonna fix him up real good," he said. We knew he just meant talk to him, so we weren't worried. "I tried calling and calling and he wouldn't pick up his phone to tell me where you were," uncle continued, "I was worried sick, you know." Oops. Why didn't Steve tell him?

"Well, never mind about that, you have to get ready for tomorrow," he said and he was right. We had a long night ahead, so we chatted and packed and combined our gifts; at the stores, aunty would just buy me little things – nice elastics for my hair, a fuzzy little puppy…they had such a soft spot for me!

Well Ephraim and I could not believe that this adventure was drawing to a close, and even though we were up quite late packing, aunty and uncle both stayed up with us to make sure we had everything. Aunty had dried and frozen some sorrel and gave it to us, along with instructions on how to make it. Ephraim wrote it down, so I knew I could just get it from him later. I was sad to be packing so quickly.

Jonas and Eve were taking a flight on the same day to another Caribbean island to stay with Eve's mother and father, so we met up with them at the airport at six in the morning. We are so lucky that we all had each other! We cleared customs and were off. Ephraim had to repack his gigantic suitcase in the middle of the customs line because it was too heavy and we were almost late because of it. Aunty had packed us some homemade pizza (not like American pizza, but pretty good), and I ate mine while Ephraim repacked his suitcase – and yes, I teased him and he ignored me the whole time.

Uncle laughed and we could see that he was sad to see us depart, just like we were sad to be going. It was a **great** trip, but our home land was calling and we were anxious to return. We had fun visiting and it is astounding at how different our lives would be had our uncle or grandpa taken us in. Ephraim and I were both glad to be from Canada, but we were also sad to leave our family that we came to adore.

chapter 6: _____

The flights were long, and I got held up and questioned at the border, but seeing my honesty, they let me right through – it was just a check. A fellow checking the passports gave me a compliment "that picture doesn't do you justice – you are way better looking in life," to which I laughed at because it was so sweet, the way he said it. Besides, who doesn't look better than the passport pictures?

Well our flight from New York to Utah went fine, but we missed our flight from Sal Lake City to Winnipeg…by one minute! The plane was pulling away as we came to the window, but we received a complimentary stay in a hotel with a complimentary meal. It was a nice room and we were both grumpy because we were so close, and getting quite eager to just be back home. I had made plans to meet up with Mrs. Krieger and stay the night at her place when getting back so that Noella and Drew could pick me up on their way back from Winnipeg. I had to email that we lost the flight and an estimation of what time we would get it. Hopefully things would work out alright.

I had run clear out of money and did not want to put any more on the credit card, so I saved my free meal for in the morning to take on the plane – which they allowed (surprisingly), but it was sealed. When the plane flew into Canada, Ephraim and I lost our irritability and grew quite excited. Looking out the window we saw three different provinces at once, all white and brown, dusted with snow and highway lines. As the plane flew over Winnipeg, I stared out the window, tracing the roads with my eyes.

"First thing I'm going to do is take a walk at midnight," he said.

"Yeah, me too," I agreed, peering excitedly out the window, "by myself."

"No, first thing I'm going to do is have a hot shower," he continued.

"Ooo sounds nice," I agreed, "I might kiss the ground first," I kidded. Our plane dropped and we drove into the lot. Excitement and a greater appreciation bubbled inside of me. I expected to have to wait for Noella and Drew while Ephraim's uncle picked him up, but it ended up the other way around.

When we came through with our luggage, I looked around, feeling a little bit lost. We walked a little bit and then I saw Noella pacing near by. She saw us before we saw her and immediately came over. I actually hugged her really hard and little microscopic tears welled up in my eyes because I was so glad to see my mommy. Yes, that is what I call Noella. She hugged Ephraim as well and we chatted and Drew brought the truck around and we all waited with Ephraim while his Uncle came.

It was snowing lightly and the air was a bit chilly, but neither of us felt it; the roads were icy with packed dirty snow, but we noticed it not. We did not acknowledge the light dandruff floating down, but we focused on each other and the gratitude of being back in our safer country. The only song circling my brain and coming out of my mouth was the national anthem. I know. I'm a geek.

Ephraim and I goofed off, obviously more close now than we were at the start of the trip and Noella smiled and laughed at my dramatic over joy. Drew hugged me too and called me his "little girl." Soon Ephraim's uncle arrived and off they went. I might have been slightly sad to see him go but I think it is in our genetics to care but pretend we don't – and I knew that I'd see him again. When we were in the truck, Noella gave me a gift that Mrs. Krieger had sent. It was a lovely photo album with twenty bucks to develop the pictures! I was sad to have missed her.

The whole eight hours back to San Frisco, I babbled excitedly and they were glad to see me safe and sound. The surprises and adventures were far from over, though, as soon I was in San Frisco. My lovely roommates had rearranged the furniture in the living room (in a much better way), which I had been nagging Gladys about since forever and due to Alana's persistence, Gladys set up her little drum set in the basement! The upstairs felt a lot homier with the couches along the walls in an L shape, with a big mat on the floor and the TV now lined up against the wall. They greeted me cheerily and asked questions and we piled on Gladys' bed and I showed them my pictures when they developed. It was very sweet to be welcomed back so warmly.

Because of the flight delay, I had to start work the very next day – which happened to be a blizzard to add to the three thousand feet of snow already here, and my car did not start, so I had to walk. Okay that was one moment I did not enjoy Canada. At work I was welcomed back and was a little bit nervous starting up on the acting, but got into the swing of things right away.

Soon Gladys was going to Ontario to meet an online boyfriend named Frank; apparently they did not like Jake anymore because of some dispute between them and he was needy. Well Gladys' friend Denise was going, and although she and I did not get along too greatly, we had learned to put up with each other. Next thing I knew, I was going to Ontario with them! I had the days scheduled off work, so booking days off was not a problem, and we chatted and I listened to music. At first it was really uncomfortable because Gladys and Denise had their little bond and did not include me in their discussions; I was in the back reading and listening to music. Once we got to Ontario, things were better.

Gladys checked into a hotel that she and Denise would share while I stayed with some very good friends that I met in college. We met Frank for about three minutes and he seemed nice, but Gladys was in a hurry to be off with him.

"So what do you do?" I asked bluntly.

"I drive tour buses," he explained. So he traveled a lot.

"Are you musical?" I asked.

"No," he said shyly. He seemed nice.

"Aw, come on, you don't even sing?" I teased lightly.

"I clap," he joked, and that eased the tension; we laughed. Denise came and she was a little bit awkward around him, trying to be funny and such, but then they were off just like that. I had my friend come and pick me up and I stayed with her and her sister for three days. It was nice to see them (even though they worked); they were both engaged to some good boys, which is what they were after.

After the three days were up, Gladys and Denise picked me up and we decided to go to a mall with roller coasters and a huge amusement park in it. Gladys and Frank were not going on the rides, but Gladys bought my ticket, which was awesome. We looked around and went on a ride that shot us up into the air – really high, *really* fast. As we were buckling in and the worker checked everyone, Denise asked me if I had done this before.

"No, I haven't," I answered, adrenaline pumping through my veins, "have you?" "A little bit, not quite like this," she said, "but I have done this one before."

We sat quietly talking like that until – BAM! – We were shot suddenly very high up – there were windows and when I looked out I could see the city sprawled out beneath us. I screamed my lungs out the whole way up. The machine shot us back down only part of the way and then it had to bounce us back down to get a gentle landing.

Gladys was snapping pictures. Looking between the two roller coasters, Denise and I decided to go on the yellow one as it appeared much safer. Well appearances can be deceiving; this roller coaster was scarier than the other one! It did not have too great of bumps and dips, but there were magnetic circles in pairs, some patches of four, other patches of six. When the cart hit one of these patches, it spun around on the track and the edges sometimes hung off the track.

We went on this roller coaster first because I had told Denise that it was my first time – well she freaked out more than I did; but we were both screaming. Because I sat on the outside, I was at times dropping backwards and down – off the track! After that, I wanted to kiss the dirty ground. The next roller coaster was red and it had three large loops. I could almost feel my stomach plummet as we walked over and got locked into the cart. As it slowly drove up, I thought "well this isn't so bad," but then it dropped suddenly and picked up speed so quickly. The drop was so steep that I could see nothing as we went down – no tracks – nothing, not even the edge of the cart we were in.

The little eight year olds on the ride barely shouted, but I shrieked at the top of my lungs. I think I screamed a lung right out, I was so loud. The cart shot us up the loops and I did *not* like the feeling of being driven upside down, but it was cool when the cart raced on a side curve; it made me feel like surfing. After that, I could not understand why people enjoy things like that – I was terrified!

After the ride, Denise and I went to view some pictures that they posted of the rides and sure enough, there was one of me posted that looked like I was dying. We laughed at it and then went to the sea world part of the mall.

We saw a seal show that we had snuck into while Gladys and Frank were strolling about smiling and holding hands. Where we were standing, kids could see and waved at us. The seals came out and did their show and it was tonnes of fun! After the show we went into the sea world which was a tunnel going under ground and it was full of lighted aquariums. In one open aquarium there were sting rays, and I asked if I could feel one.

The worker smiled at my enthusiasm and said "yes, as long as you are careful and go slow." I gently put my hand in the water and held it open, waiting for the rays to swim over it so I could feel their wings. At first they skirted my hand, but patience in feeding wild birds with Jocelyn when I was a kid proved beneficial and in no time they were friendly. They glided over my hand and I felt both sides of their wings – the top and the bottom. The tops of their wings felt like a hard kind of slippery rubber and the under part of it felt almost soft and very smooth. It was neat. Denise took pictures, but I never got a copy, sadly. They are very gentle creatures, actually.

Next we ventured over to an open little pool with a few tiny fountains trickling in. there were real starfish in there, so I asked in I could pick one up. "Well I don't think you should pick one up, because the starfish are very fragile," the worker explained that if you place them wrong they could drown, so starfish are very careful about how they sit "but if you are careful, you can move this one to another corner if you want." I think they only agreed because they saw me work with the sting rays. I followed their advice. The first starfish I went to move was stuck; he didn't want to go anywhere, so I found a big pink one "like Patrick off of Sponge Bob!" I exclaimed happily.

I gently lifted it and moved it to a corner. It was surprisingly hard and a bit heavy, although it looked soft and almost squishy. Denise dipped her hands in here and there to feel the animals, but she was not quite as eager as I was to test the limits. We did feel this creature that looked like a plant – I forget what it is called – and it felt like Velcro to our skin; it kind of stuck. The worker explained that when it is hungry it releases a certain kind of poison which kills tiny fish, allowing it to become a meal; very neat. She said that the poison was not strong enough to hurt a person, but with enough time the effect could wipe out a person's finger prints. The Velcro effect was it releasing the poison.

Then we wandered into the tanks a bit further and stared at the turtles – yes, like the ones from *Finding Nemo*, on the "EAC" – and we saw sharks and exotic fishes. It was fun. We also saw a crocodile and some wacky looking snakes and frogs and lizards. When we had spent ourselves, Gladys and Frank found us and we wandered around the mall until I suddenly parted from the group and found myself drifting over to a music corner where people were holding an open little concert.

Leaning on the balcony rail and peering down from above, I was thinking *I could do that*. I wanted to be the one singing into the mic and addressing the audience. Gladys and Denise found me after Frank left and joined me for a quick second – mostly watching my wistful expressions – and then we went to go back to San Frisco.

"We should have a chat," I said, bouncing on the seat, still energetic from the day.

"Okay, you start," Gladys said.

"Noooo," I whined, pulling out the shy card and grinning. I didn't think either of them would open up, but they did. Gladys said that she and Travis used to sleep together and she discussed some of their relationship and Denise really told a lot about her family. I shared a bit about how Joan left me in a parking lot when I was fourteen and even a little bit about my promiscuity in high school. Needless to say, the trip back was speedy and before we knew it we were back.

Right away I was off to work in between hosting friends who wanted to see pictures and my nicely browned skin. ☺ There were people over all the time, wanting to hear stories and such, and I shared with them some of the things I had brought back. It was all a blurry whir that caught up with me in February when I got quite sick. Refusing to go to the doctor, I had to book time off of work as I couldn't speak and direly needed rest. I got a severe chest infection and was coughing a deep whooping cough for hours at times or so hard that I gagged. I got migraines and fever and was restless in my sleep, so I got some night time Benylin and that helped me sleep more soundly.

At night I would wake to cough and cough and one night I coughed up a bit of blood. In my nose in the morning a painfully huge piece of mucous would slide down my throat before I could stop it. When those got a bit smaller I coughed one out and it was big enough to fill a table spoon; and that was one of the smaller ones. The mucous was hard and black and brown from dried blood as well as green and yellow from infection. This carried on for a good week until one night I woke to coughing and coughed up a chunky solid ball of blood about the size of a large marble.

I knew there was more to be done to get better, so I gargled with salt water and snorted some part ways up my nose and blew it back out. It worked miracles to loosen the mucous and get it out! By the time I was to go to work again I was well on the way to full recovery. It was a little scary, but it's better to use natural remedies rather than take drugs because of chemicals and reactions, etc. it is just a preference; but lesson learned; sea salt water works miracles. My roommates steered clear as they did not want what I had and rightfully so.

Life got a little bit busy for us and I regretted telling Gladys about my promiscuity because she was always coming to me about her struggles with her boyfriend Frank. He lived many hours away, but they talked on the phone and she said that he "had issues." They were always talking and according to Gladys they were discussing their faith. When I asked if she would ever marry him she said a hasty "no," and then retracted to "not yet," and then moved to "but I want to." She was obviously torn.

She ended up going to visit him for a weekend by herself, packing new underwear and her nice clothes; I knew what she had planned and indeed when she got back from that trip, she could not look me in the eye. I made no judgments because it was her choice. Then she and Frank would argue and break up and then make up and then break up, etc. it was very elementary.

I desired to have no part in that aspect of her life, but when she came to me for advice, I thought she was asking to know, but now I wonder. "How do you face things that you've done that you regret?" she asked one day when we were on a walk.

I did not quite understand, so I answered honestly, "I face it and deal with it and take it to God." We kept walking and I pointed out the house where I grew up and the school close by. I pointed to a house down the street from the school and said "I think a lady that used to baby sit us when we were little used to live here. We used to come here all the time; I remember she had curly brown hair."

We paused to look at the dark brown house with petunias flourishing all over the yard and deck. Well, someone liked flowers! Then Gladys turned to me and said "when you walk here, you seem happy, like it doesn't bother you."

I shrugged and said "well I guess it doesn't. Nothing bad really happened here – I liked school because I had lots of friends and stuff…" we continued on our way and Gladys yakked on and on about how even though her friends did not like Frank, she still wanted him. I thought it was hard to like someone when you have only heard negative things about them.

I struggled a lot because Gladys is over twenty years older than me and asking about advice on her relationship with her man. It got to the point where it was all she talked about and all I was thinking about. When I brought it up to Noella, she was apprehensive about it; she did not think it was right for someone of that age to come to someone of my age about their sexual struggles.

I told Gladys that her constantly talking to me about sex was also making me struggle. I also told her that I used to look up to her when she said she had abstained for twelve years, but that I could not look up to her anymore. She said that hurt and it caused her to question her faith; we were drifting apart because I did not want to be a part of that section of her life and for her it is a huge part in her head and heart.

Alana got a nice new fancy car because her parents came over and took the one she was driving (they would give it back when she moved back home). Just as she pulled in with her new car, I was getting out of my car. I had a nice red Chrysler New Yorker, just like my blue one that got hit when I was visiting grandpa a year ago. Same year, same make, but less miles and a different color.

"Nice car...red like mine," I said to Alana, circling the car and peeking in the windows. She grinned; she liked her choice. I went into the house as I was just off work and she was on her way to her job. I had no sooner closed the front door and removed my boots when there was a knock at the door. Alana stood there with a young black fellow I had never seen before.

"He came to me because he hit your car," she said with sympathy in her eyes, "I saw it happen just after you went in." you have got to be kidding! I looked at the boy and thought it was nice that he didn't drive away.

"Okay let's go take a look," I said to him. Alana left for work and I walked with this boy out to see the damage. Sure enough, it was hit in the rear driver corner; I knew it would be written off.

"Okay, they are going to write it off," I said, stooping to look at his nice car. Not too much damage on his car – the front light and a few chips, "not too bad," I said, "they shouldn't write off your car." He looked worried.

"Is this your car?" I asked.

"I borrowed it from my parents," he explained.

"Yikes," I said, "well thank you for stopping in to tell me. I'll take your plate number and phone number." He wrote it down for me and I told him that I was not upset with him, that I would report the accident to SGI. I reported it and then got a call from the boy's father, offering to fix it himself.

"Well it is going to be written off," I explained patiently.

"Well, I could fix it myself," he said; his accent was hard to understand and he was very insistent. I just firmly told him that I had reported it to SGI and they would handle things, because I doubted he could fix the floor of the trunk, the back light, the bumper, the back frame and paint it all himself.

Once I went into the house and things sank in, I picked a pillow up and beat it on my bed, shouting "aaaaarrrrggg! I am very angry!" of course, I thought I was by myself otherwise I would have held much better composure.

I was very surprised to hear Gladys say "well no wonder!" Ooops. Somewhat embarrassed, I went out into the kitchen where she was. "I saw what happened to your car," she said, "Tanya called and told me you might be upset because she saw it happen. She warned me that you would be upset," and then she laughed to try to make things....funny? I don't know why she laughed.

I expressed a little bit of frustration since this was the second car in a year – both times I was not driving. Both times it would be written off.

"Well, you never know," Gladys said, "power of the spoken word." Well, power of experience! I knew it would be written off because this had happened before, and I calmly reminded her of it. Well there was nothing to be done about it, so I just dealt with the issue and they took their time getting things ready, so I ended up still driving the car to work for the rest of the winter, which was awesome.

Eventually Alana expressed some concern for Gladys to me about how much time she spent on her computer – we joked that she had a relationship with her computer, and it was true. When Gladys and Frank broke up it was the end of the world and she was moody and snappy and quite rude. Alana just left when she sensed things and I usually ended up taking the brunt of things.

Soon there was a lot of tension between us and lack of communication. When I would come in from work, Alana would come over and say "hey."

Then I would say "hey, how was work?"

And she would say "oh, it was alright." And that was it. I always tried to ask questions to get some sort of something, but the wall was up and eventually I quit trying. Something happened between Gladys and Alana that they were hardly around at the same time because Alana avoided her. If I asked her if she saw Alana, Gladys would say things like "nope," or "I think she's going to leave soon," or "have you?" but it was the tone of her voice that made those statements unpleasant.

When I told Alana to clean up after herself in the living room she got up and left. Gladys came in shortly after and I was frustrated because I was the only one who did the cleaning – ever. Or so it felt. I was always picking up after her, changing the garbage, sweeping the floors and doing the dishes. Sometimes I would run the dishwasher and then leave the clean dishes in there to see how long it would be before someone unloaded it. It would take weeks and by then I would be so sick of the mess that I would do it myself. I even did the shoveling without being asked and unstuck Gladys' car so she could go to work the next day. But enough was enough.

Gladys said to not say anything to Alana because she thought she was going to leave and Gladys wanted her money before she left. I shook my head because I am not like that. Money does not run my life; if I am frustrated I will show it.

Well lucky for me work was going good. When we had tours off, a few of us would get together and play with the instruments that were props, so now I can play the trumpet and trombone! Maybe not well yet, but I can play!

"We are so talented!" I would joke.

"We should have a band," Joe kidded. We all acted with each other and sometimes I would be acting as the tour guide and think *this is my job,* or **I get paid for this!** *It is pretty cool to have a job that you love.* I even got a little weird and prayed for the people who came through my tours…I would find myself just caring for these folks, not knowing a thing about them. It was nice that a lot of us who worked there hung out, too, having game nights or supper nights and Chloe's house or Justin's place.

Chloe had worked at the local spa that I had worked at and we had talked about music. When she disappeared from there I was not surprised, as there is quite the turn over of new workers. I was very surprised to find her acting at my other job!

"Maybe God meant for us to be friends," she said. At the time that weirded me out, but now we are a little bit chummy. Also good ole Dylan called me up and we started another song in the studio. I picked an unfinished song and Dylan kicked my butt to make me write more words. "But I've said what I wanted to," I would protest. I am a person of few words, especially when I sing – I just get up there, greet the peeps and then sing away.

"Well say more, you need more words….expand…" he would push in a funny way so that I laughed a lot but knew he was serious. It worked. He picked out a beat and I sang to it.

"It sounds…too happy," he critiqued.

"Well the beat sounds happy," I said. And then he worked with me to get a good beat – I just told him what I wanted ("get a clap in there" or "yes, but a bit faster") and he was good for working within my ideas. I showed him kind of how to play the piano part and he made it better and played it in time. I was learning so much about music!

Well after the final recording session, I pulled in front of Gladys' house and saw Alana drop a box of her things in the back. Seeing me and expecting some tension, she got into the driver's seat and started the truck, but not before I got there.

"What's going on?" I asked not angrily, leaning against the door.

"Nothing," Alana said, wanting to drive away. I was concerned because she was obviously upset; poor girl.

"Hey, talk to me, talk to me," I said gently and opened the door of the running truck. She obliged, and I gestured to the truck and said "what's going on?"

"Oh, nothing, it's just I owe a lot of money and can't afford rent and stuff," Alana said quickly, the wall still up.

I got really concerned – I liked having her there! Sure we had little tiffs, but surely the tensions between her and Gladys could be worked out? "Did you talk to Gladys about it?" I asked, thinking they could work something out.

"Yeah, I don't think it would work. I owe like hundreds of dollars to lots of people and my parents said the only way they would help me out is if I moved back in with them." Alana's voice rose at the end, with expressive exasperation. Yikes. I knew she did not want to go back as she had shared certain things about her mother and brother and I knew that situation was not favorable.

"Well, do you want some help moving?" I asked. I did this to show that I was not angry with her. How could I be, when she was standing there, looking so sad? She was so stressed for someone of her age!

"Sure, I just gotta take this truck to unload and then my mom is going to be here soon to help," she consented. As she drove away with the truck, I shook my head and went into the house. When she came back I asked what she would like to do and while we loaded up some boxes – she had been moving for a few days because her room was getting quite empty and she had a **ton** of stuff.

I was also making supper while helping Alana pack up, and was quite startled when there was a fierce knocking at the door. I went over and opened to a stern woman who rapidly and rudely asked "is my daughter here? Where's my daughter?"

For a second I failed to put two and two together and was about to say "who is your daughter?" just as rudely, but then Alana came out and said it was her mom. The poor girl's face was one big apology. Her mom basically stayed outside and barked orders and comments that neither of us listened to.

"Well, you ready to do a bit of work?" I asked, propping up the screen door and handing her things to take to the truck. She talked loudly to me and to herself as she walked the things over. It was a good system and in no time Alana's room was clean. We joked about telling Gladys that Alana was engaged because of her nosiness to Alana's boyfriend woes. Gladys had tried setting Alana up with some of her twenty year old friends and we laughed at it because those boys were drunkards who thought about sex. It was weird that Gladys at forty five was hanging out with young boys like that, but whatever. She had tried setting me up with them too, but I shut them down hard.

"Did you tell Gladys that you're moving out?" I asked Alana as we checked her room one final time.

"Not yet, but I will tonight," she interjected at my facial expression. "I just don't want to face her right now."

"Okay well, if you want to you can text me and then I will come by before you tell her," I told her, hoping that would be encouraging.

"Okay," she agreed and then left with her crazy mother. I closed the door of Alana's room and tidied up the living room. When I went out that night, I received no text. It was the end of March and I told Alana (on msn) that she should really tell Gladys before April; she made promises that she would, but when the first day of the month drew closer, Gladys still had no idea. I thought I should wait until some one was with me because Gladys' moods were swinging more constantly.

My heart was sinking lower in to my chest and the dull ache was becoming familiar, but I tried to be positive and less opinionated. Maybe Gladys was going through really early menopause? I explored my options, but every place that I checked out fell through or was taken before I could even look. I was ready to jump on every opportunity that came my way. I even looked at getting my own place, which was exciting.

I found a place just outside of San Frisco and went to see it, bringing Gladys because she is a real estate agent, just for a look, and it was good and she actually agreed to work with me for free when I could pay the down payment. I spoke to the owners of the place – it was a nice five bedroom trailer – and they agreed to hold it for me for a few months. Gladys actually seemed quite support of this endeavor.

I knew I would not have to wait long because my tax return was coming soon and it would be close to the amount that I needed. Well, sadly enough, the owners sold the trailer and did not tell me; their right, I know, if someone has the money then they can buy. First come, first served, but I began to feel like I was never going to get out of Gladys' house!

Ephraim visited near the end of March and we made a nice supper at my house and went for coffee and had a good old time! We talked about the cooking we did since the Caribbean and contact we had with family, covered how Ephraim was doing in school and how I was doing at work. I told him about my car and he saw the damage and laughed saying "how do these things keep happening to you?" I was still a tiny bit frustrated about the whole car situation because Ephraim was overly eager to tell grandpa and he laughed at my misfortune, but we still had ourselves a good visit.

"Do you know any good pranks?" I asked when we were back at the house, remembering that fool's day was coming up soon. I had to maintain my reputation as a good prankster! I love a good laugh, so I was scheming for something light and fun.

"No," he said, and I was slightly disappointed, but I knew I would think of something. Just after supper, after the dishes were done and we cleaned up, Ephraim started turning the water on and then off, but the way he did it made me want to laugh.

"What are you doing?" I asked with a little grin.

"Hey I'm going to run the water and I'd like you to go into the bathroom and tell me if you can hear it, ok?" he asked. I went in with the door open and he asked "can you hear when I'm running it?"

"Yup," I said cooperatively.

He came over and said, "Okay, now you turn it on and I'll see if I can hear." seeing my puzzled face, he explained that he did something and wanted to see if it worked. Okay. "Turn it on fast," he advised.

I went into the kitchen and did as he asked. When I turned on the water full blast, a spray shot out and soaked my arm and part of my shirt. I let out a yelp of surprise and then laughed. "That's a good one!" I said, turning to Ephraim when he came into the kitchen with a grin. He had put a black elastic band around the spray nozzle so I did not notice. Too funny!

"I wasn't sure if you'd be mad," he said with a goofy grin.

"No, I'm not; that's a good one," I echoed, still laughing, "look at you, pulling out the funny card!" I slapped his shoulder playfully. I tried it on Gladys when she came in but she knew something was up and turned the water on slowly because I forgot to tell her to do it quickly.

Ephraim and I went out and then came back and Gladys was still up and about. "Have you seen Alana?" she asked, "she's been gone forever, must be that boyfriend."

Ephraim and I looked at each other; I had filled him in on the earlier happenings. "Well, actually, she moved out," I said, the smile dropping from my face and concern mingled with caution clouding my eyes.

"Yeah right, is this some sort of early April fools' joke?" she scoffed. I wish…I did not answer and so she questioned some more. "So if I open her bedroom door, her room will be empty?"

My face said it all, but she needed to know "yes," I confirmed. Her mockery dropped when she saw that I wasn't kidding; she went over and opened Alana's door. Empty. I saw her whole demeanor drop and then she asked when she left.

"A few days ago," I answered honestly. I told her what happened and then said "I told her I would tell you if she didn't before April."

"Did she ask you not to tell me?"

"Yes," I admitted. Gladys was not a happy camper. Because Ephraim was there, Gladys did not say too much on the matter but we were both sympathetic, so we thought it best to give her a little bit of time. We went for coffee with some friends and then caught a movie in the theatre.

When I got back Gladys was in bed, and I was glad – I knew I would be hearing a lot about Alana soon enough. When I saw her next, she told me that Alana did not pay rent for March or a damage deposit, so she screwed Gladys over of eight hundred dollars. "That makes twelve hundred dollars that I have been screwed over," she exclaimed. It was her time for frustration, so I just listened. She went on to say that she saw Alana at work and that Alana did not talk to her or look at her; just walked away.

"Well, she is going through a lot," I suggested, knowing more of her story.

"She's a coward," Gladys vented, "she can't come and face me." *Well, not all people enjoy confrontation,* I felt like saying. She went on and on about how she needed the money, so I paid two months rent on the first of April to help her out. On the very early morning of the first, I stuffed the toes of Gladys' shoes with paper and pinned her blanket to the doorway of the bathroom. Okay it sounds weird; let me explain.

The one side of the blanket is black and every single night Gladys gets up to use the washroom. She usually has a little night light glowing so she can see, but when I pinned the blanket up, it looked like she forgot to turn the light on, so she walked straight into what looked like a dark bathroom.

Then I put the black elastic around the spray nozzle in the kitchen sink because she said she gargles with saltwater every morning and night. I also put some sticky soap on the doors and light switches, and saran-wrapped the toilet bowl…and I switched the things in the mirror cabinet, filling Gladys' side with rolls of toilet paper. Feeling quite satisfied with my little pranks, I snuggled into my nice warm bed and drifted into a happy, cozy little sleep.

In the morning, I heard Gladys up and about and giggled to myself, picturing her walking into the dark blanket. I heard her outside of my bedroom door and contemplated opening the door, but chose to fall back to sleep. Later on, when I tried to open the door, it only opened part ways because there was a string attached.

Okay, I thought, *not too bad.* I got some scissors and cut it. As I went about the day, I noticed that Gladys reciprocated some of the pranks back to me. Lame…she put the stuffing I placed in her shoes into my boots and oiled the handles of my car, which froze in the night. I don't think she noticed the soap on the light switches or door knobs.

When I saw her at the end of the day, she said she quite enjoyed the blanket joke and caught the toilet bowl one. In the morning she swore because of the spray of water. I had walked into the grocery store where she worked for groceries and thought again. Going over to the clothing department I asked for Gladys.

"One minute," the young girl said, calling her on the store phone, "She said she's busy," the girl said, hanging up.

I leaned on the counter with a mischievous grin and said "how are you at acting?"

"I dunno," the girl said with a shy but friendly smile.

"Can you call her back and say there is an angry customer trying to return an empty hanger?" another worker heard and came over laughing. The girl went ahead and pulled it off. When Gladys came, we just laughed and had a quick visit and then I went on with my day. "I was like, what the heck?" she exclaimed, making a "Grr" noise at me.

Well with April fool's day out of the way there was nothing to do but enjoy work. It was hard to sing outside of work because of all the speaking, but one thing is for sure – I learned how to breathe properly and stay supported.

I changed my costume at work and that ended up changing my character to a much more comical one. It is so funny, the things I get away with because I use a funny voice! I also trained a lot of new workers getting ready for the summer – the busiest season for us – and it was a blast. I tried to make it really fun for them because if you enjoy what you are learning, you tend to remember it better.

I also called my grandpa Stardens to go car shopping with me. I had to drop my car off at SGI and needed a ride to look around and then across town to my house. I was glad to drop the red car off because there were engine problems with it – it was having great difficulties accelerating, and switching gears even though it was an automatic. I did manage to drive it down to its last few drops of gas before turning it in, so that was nice.

"Okay," he agreed, "why don't we look for cars first?" he asked.

"Sure, okay," I consented "as long as I get the car in before four."

Well, I tell you what! I had a surprise coming. We drove around some lots and my eyes kept falling on this one light blue car – I just liked it!

"What about that one?" I asked.

"Why don't you get something smaller? Maybe less people will hit it," grandpa joked. I smiled and then noted that if I was going to buy a car, I might as well like it.

"Plus the newer cars are not as good quality, and I need one big enough to fit my keyboard on the back seat," I continued. We tried out a few lots and everyone tried to spin some kind of deal, then we went back to the first lot and my eyes were drawn to the light blue car again.

"Go test drive it," grandpa suggested. I did and it opened up real nice on the highway. I came back smiling. Of course, the sales man had some story about how it was only ever owned by an old lady – they all say that – but I did note the low kilometers. We sat at the table to negotiate and I was a bit surprised when grandpa joined, but thought he knew more about cars and would offer good input.

"How much is it?" I asked the sales guy.

"Eight thousand," he answered.

I was preparing to negotiate when grandpa started itching and scratching. He was looking for something. "How much did you say it was?" he asked, clicking a pen.

"Eight thousand," the guy repeated. Grandpa dropped the check for eight thousand in the guy's hand!! My eyes fell out of my head – I could not *believe* it!! I still can't, and it is a whole year later! Grandpa bought me a car. He just laughed at my face and said "it's like your sixteenth birthday, only a few years late."

Of course I felt terrible because I had no intention of anything other than bumming a ride when I asked him to come along. "I know, you just wanted someone to drive you around," he nodded with his grandpa grin.

"Well, thank you," I echoed for the billionth time. He laughed and said he had wanted to do something like that for a long time. It was so sweet! I remember feeling envious when some of my friends had their parents buy them cars...mine was much nicer! And now it has sentimental value!

"Take care of it," grandpa advised, "don't go hitting things with it," he teased.

"Oh I'll take care of it!" I promised. And I do – very good care.

We took my red car down to SGI and I cashed a check for three thousand from it and gave grandpa two thousand. He did not want to take anything – I wanted to give him every penny, but he thought ahead and said "you gotta put gas in it and you gotta license it, so you keep the money." We were at the bank for me to deposit the check, so I transferred two grand and he said "okay if it makes you happy." And it did.

I drove right to where Gladys worked because it was close by and near the end of her shift. I parked, ran in and got a few groceries. Seeing her with a few groceries in the lot, I was surprised to see that I had parked one car space away from her car. The car beside mine was gone, so my new car now rested beside her old white Buick.

I strutted right up to her and she said "where's your car?"

"I dropped it off at SGI," I was eager to inform.

"How did you get here?" she asked.

"I got a ride," I said, excitement bubbling inside as I helped her load her groceries into the back seat.

"Do you want a ride with me then?" she asked.

"Uh, no, that's okay, I might walk," I said, thinking she might catch on by now. It was opposite ends of town and still pretty chilly out. No way was I walking.

"Okay, see you there then," she said.

"Okay," I picked up my groceries and was about to go when she offered the space in her car because it would be easier to walk without them.

I turned back, a huge grin spreading across my face. Gladys knew there was something up, but she had no idea why I was so happy. "No thanks," I sang out, floating away, "I think I'll put them in my car."

Gladys looked at me as I walked over to my new vehicle. Thinking that I was pulling some weird joke, she was surprised when I unlocked the door and stuck the groceries inside.

"What, really?" she exclaimed, happy for me. I nodded big. "Did you get that today? How much was it?"

"My grandpa bought it for me," and I described the story for her.

"That's amazing!"

"I know!"

"I'm impressed! You actually like big cars," she continued.

I looked at her like *uh, yeah* and said "yup, I do."

"I thought you just liked them because you got deals on them or something, but here you are with your own car – and it's your choice. I'm impressed."

"Okay, I'm going to drive now," I said eagerly beaming.

I took her and Travis who was around for a ride in it. Of course he made fun of the car, but all in good humor. I knew he was jealous, (just kidding!). Actually, Travis and Gladys teamed up to do something quite nice for me. Knowing my love of animals and my tender little spot for my cat, Gladys agreed to let Travis' cat, Troy, stay for a couple weeks while he and his wife took off to BC. I was happy as a lark.

Of course, Gladys lumped all the responsibilities (changing the litter, feeding, water, cleaning the extra litter up, making sure he didn't get out) on me, but I didn't care too much. She got annoying with it, but I was able to brush it aside and shut her up for a while. She did her part in covering the furniture with blankets and removing the living room rug for the duration of his stay.

The floor was light hard wood underneath, and the room was so much brighter and more inviting without the dark carpet that I told her that I liked it. Well, Troy moved in while I was at work, but I knew his presence in the house because of the cat carrier, full litter box, food and water dished and toys arranged in Alana's old room. I searched the house and was told that he was shy, so I flicked on a show and made supper. Lo and behold, Troy ventured out in his own time and in no time was purring and rubbing while I petted him. He was a nice kitty!

Gladys and Travis and his wife soon came in and I showed them that I was petting him and they took him to show him where everything was and then left.

"He's cute!" I said, pleased as fruit punch.

"Watch out, he likes to scratch people," Gladys said "he's mean."

"Well he won't be mean to me," I said "if he bites me I'll bit him back."

"Don't let him in your room," Gladys advised, "he'll pee on your bed." Gee, for someone who used to be a vet, or wanted to be one, she sure didn't like animals! She said she was allergic, but the whole time the cat was there, I think she sneezed twice. He ended up staying with us for a lovely month and it was because of this kind gesture that I stayed with Gladys over the summer.

Troy, or as I called him, Mr. Tumnus, was my buddy in no time. At first he would just hide under my bed, nesting on the tote bag and backpack stashed under there. I did not smell anything strange, so I figured as long as he was being nice, he could go. It was only a couple days before he would come with me to bed and leave as I fell asleep. I left my door open so that he could come and go as he pleased.

He was a fuzzy black and white cat with round yellowish green eyes and nice white little paws. His pink nose and white whiskers were adorable and he was a nice healthy weight – still young, so a little bit small for a boy cat, but he was fixed. He had a little quiet meow that I would imitate to him and a nice rumbly purr and he was a delight to have around. When Gladys wasn't in the house, he would skit about, jogging here and there happily, and I played with him, bouncing some strings about.

He wondered at my fish, but did not cause any damage and he would nestle on the top of the couch near me when I wrote or read or watched TV or painted. He didn't even mind my singing or guitar or piano noises; he was my buddy. Gladys was surprised that he was such a lovable cat; apparently he wasn't like that for even Travis and his wife. Things were good for me for a small while, with my little friend there, but Gladys was up and down and all around because of her issues and struggles with Frank.

I had just started attending regular church in about early March, because I knew it was something God wanted me to do – I don't know why or how I knew, I just knew. I figured it is probably better for me to listen rather than to be driven to the point where I **have** to listen. I am not saying that God blessed me with the car because I was going to church, but I am saying that it was a blessing to be able to share that story as a praise item for the church to hear.

This church is special. It is called Prairie Winds and I think it is the only church that is a church (that I have been to). Oh, there are many churches that are churches, but they are only buildings that people go to in order to fulfill themselves. This church is one that is reaching out to the community and I started going with friends who went there, but when they moved, I had to go alone.

It was rather tough once my local college friends left because I did not know many people except for Chloe and Derek, whom I work with. The pastor's name is Russell and he is brothers with Pastor Harry, who is still friends with Joan, so my guard shot up when he recognized me and informed me of this. He backed off a little bit, seeing the tension enter my face and other than that I thought the church was weird when I went.

I will admit that I was not optimistic when I first started going, but after the friends who brought me there and encouraged attendance moved away and the church relocated and got a few things in order, I have grown to appreciate this church as I learn of their mission statement of reaching out to present a "bridge of hope." Sounds cheesy, I know, but they are unlike the stiff churches I have been to.

This church helps one another within and outside of itself. They have a 24hr prayer line at Prairie Winds Church and many things like pantry room for specific needs. One room had food bags and they say "if you bring the bag back, we'll refill it," another room has clothes, and another had things like soap and toothbrushes, etc. and there is another room for things like cutlery, pots and pans, furniture, washers/dryers… all donated and all given away for free. I think it is remarkable. Every Sunday they have a meal afterward and have prayers and things for the students within as well as community suppers on Thursdays where people can have a warm meal and pick out things that they need. The meals are great too – not just processed or cheap stuff, but actual pork or beef or homemade chili or potatoes and actual ham or sausage or salads…it is good for hungry stomachs. It definitely motivates me to go to church because it is almost right after I get off work – I have enough time to dash home, change and then go out. At first it was difficult on an empty stomach, but knowing that there is supper after helps a great deal.

There are many people that go there, but someone always remembers and greets me, Pastor Russell usually asks how I'm doing…when I speak in church – I don't know the lingo – so the folks usually laugh and don't mind it. They say I am real and they like that. This is the first church where I feel like no one looks down – of course there is room for improvement, but this is the first church that I see really working at it.

Well this year opened up with a bang, and although there were a few hard times in store, the blessings were definitely still raining down. I learned a lot about forgiveness and the effects of free will. God had me in the classroom in so many different areas of life and yes, growing means being stretched and stretching sometimes hurts.

chapter 7:

As I was growing, it seemed like Gladys was dwindling in her faith and stature in my eyes. She holds a lot of knowledge, but little experience. When I asked her questions about faith or anything like that, she had all the right answers. Soon her moods began to swing really low sometimes and she would snap at me for no reason, or say comments that made me feel like dirt. She never apologized for it unless I approached her about it first then she would go on and on about how sorry she was.

At first I was able to let these things go quite quickly, but the more they happened, the worse they got. A fellow that went to elementary school with me, by the name of Joe came by and looked me up and we hung out. He plays guitar so we did some music together and we used to hang out a lot with a few other friends.

This time it was a little bit different though, because I sensed and felt a different kind of attraction. He drinks a lot, so I shared but did not get wasted, and the reason I shared is because it is not wrong for me to have a drink so long as I am not drunk. Soon we were holding hands and he was cooking for me and we had some romantic times. Neither of us talked about being together or anything, but we just were. Gladys was surprised when he came by but also allowed us some privacy.

The snow was gone outside by now and it was warming up. We went on the roof with the booze and ate cherry frozen yogurt and shared a blanket and cuddled and snuggled while the stars and moon observed, and it was very sweet. We were waiting for Gladys' shift at work to end because we were going to scare her by calling out to her while we were on the roof, but she took forever, so we went to my room for a while. We were wrestling by the time Gladys came back and neither of us had heard her, so it was a surprise to see her when I was hanging upside down off the bed (Joe was pushing me off). She laughed and said my face was hilarious when I saw her.

"It's good to see you happy with someone," she said, and I felt that she meant it.

We were moving real fast and in the moments I enjoyed it, but when he was gone, I kicked myself and always thought *what am I doing?* I knew that it was wrong to be with a fellow you weren't even dating, but it just happened and it was very sweet and very mutual. We had a lot of fun but he ended up moving far away, and although I was really sad to see him go, I was kind of glad because I needed to sort things out.

It threw me for a loop and I realized that Gladys' talking with me about sex all the time, **all the time** had made me want it. And I usually get what I want. That shook me because I usually catch onto things like that, but this one snuck up and bit me in the butt! When Gladys came to me again about Frank and her feelings for him, I had to tell her to stop coming to me. I explained that her wanting things like that so badly and constantly talking to me about it had made me want it and I had fallen right back into my high school days without knowing it.

I did not want to back to those days for a reason. I'm lucky that Joe and I were not hurt by this, but situations like that can get real messed up. I realized a few things, then, one of them being that I am still easily impressionable. I cried out to God, because I felt that I had really been stupid. Joe is great, but we may never have gone anywhere, being as he is anti-Christian, which means a full relationship would have cost one of us our beliefs. I was just surprised at how easily I "fell away," and how much I liked it. In a matter of seconds I had dropped my pals, the church and focused on one person.

Gladys kind of hit a low, then, and she became really super moody. I pulled away from her and she noticed because I played no games about it. She invited me to a conference (she goes to millions of them each year to increase her faith) and it ended up being Josie from way back in Carrington! I went and she tugged at the heart strings and Gladys was crying and I thought it was good. We did a line of prayer after, committing ourselves to Jesus, and I joined in. I had texted Drew and he came because he Josie, and although this event was open to anyone, it was mostly women there.

After our line and praying, there was a black woman who was crying with many people praying around her. Something compelled me to hold her hand, so I did. It was so weird because I am not an affectionate person at all! Gladys wanted to leave right away, so Drew and I stayed for a quick visit with Josie and she said she heard my new song called *No Say* and that it sounded angry.

"Oh, yes, the electric guitar," I half joked.

"No, it was *you* that looked angry," she said with a friendly smirk "you sound good, just be careful. Keep those creative juices flowing."

"I will," I said. I had noticed that in the song I sounded angry and Dylan had said "well of course, you're using this as an outlet." Maybe I was angry? I didn't feel angry. Drew bought a book for Noella and Josie signed it and wrote a big flourishing message of affection for her. We visited for a bit and then it was off to bed for me.

A few days later, while I was making some food, Gladys offered up some of her food for me to cook. I was pleased, but I knew that she offered it up only because it was going bad and she did not want to cook herself. So I cut and peeled and cleaned and cooked and she came home and ate. Soon she was saying what kinds of foods she liked and how to cook it. I was distressed doing that because I felt like none of this was my choice – I had become the little Karee that I was for Joan. Somehow Joan seems better because she is also afflicted by the wounds that she inflicts, but Gladys just seemed... proud of the wounds she inflicted on both me and Frank and other people.

"I offered the food so you could have something to eat!" Gladys protested. Maybe so, but we both knew that was not the only reason. I acknowledged that and told her that I did not even like cooking. "But you always look like you're having so much fun when you do it," she said. Well I don't. I know that I am a good cook – hours of standing there watching Joan and then doing dishes have proved beneficial – and I like to share this gift with people, but as soon as I feel that I am used or it isn't my choice, it sends me running the other way. Gladys made me feel this way.

A few days later I noticed that she was really down, so I went to a local bakery to buy some treats for my lunches and bought a few extra for her. Putting her name on the box and leaving it for her on the counter, she thanked me later when I asked if she got it.

"How did you know?" she asked.

"Because you were that obvious," I stated.

"You are such a good friend," she said, but I disliked when she said things like that because it just didn't sit right. She informed me that she invited Frank to stay over for a week or so.

"When is he coming?" I asked immediately.

"Next week," she said, studying me carefully because my guard had shot up.

"Then I won't be here," I said firmly. No games.

"Why not?" she asked indignantly, I said something about how the church talked about staying safe and not putting yourself in situations, implying that was what she was doing. That was not the real reason. Dear reader, I will tell **you** the real reason. Gladys said that on the weekend she went to visit Frank at his place, they were fooling around in the bed after sleeping together (she made sure to tell me that they were naked) and then he pinned her arms above her head and said "what if I took you right now?"

She had answered "then we would be done." Manipulation. She made him want her more by doing that, and she had allowed that situation to happen in the first place. He refrained, but then Gladys went and told that story to her pastor, counselor, friends…and roommate. What she also told her roommate is that all these people thought he was a rapist because of what he said and they did not like him. Now she was inviting him over? She was not taking the whole time off of work, otherwise I might have stayed.

Alarms went off in my head and I had to listen. "I need you here to keep me accountable," she protested. Her trying to keep me there was putting me in a dangerous situation. If he was a potential rapist, how could she invite him here and expect me to stay? I am young, people say I'm pretty; people – men – are attracted to me; that is one bad thing I did not want to chance.

"Nothing bad is going to happen," Gladys protested.

"Well the point is to avoid something bad happening," I said, feeling déjà vu – I had said these same words to Chrissie in Portland. "I don't want to wait and see if it happens, because then something bad will have happened." Did she honestly think I would be okay with sticking around the house with him on my days off? She got angry with me because I was not sticking around and that told me to leave all the more.

I felt a little lost, then, because Gladys would not tell me when he was coming so I could make plans to get away. I went to the church for prayer. They listened and offered places and prayed. My friends, Helen, Chloe, Derek, even Noella and Drew all supported me in avoiding the situation. One day I walked in from work and was making supper when Gladys told me that Frank was going to be there that night.

I felt so lost and like a sad little child all of a sudden. Helen offered up her room while she stayed at Chloe's. Helen was living in the dorm room of an old school that had…eight students. When I was there, she informed me that I was not allowed to cook or use anything downstairs, unless she was there because that's the way it was.

When I was downstairs, waiting for Helen to come down because we were going to cook (it was a rule that the landlord made), I played piano until a girl I know (and have hung out with) named Lacy entered the area and said "okay, Karee, no."

I looked up at her brightly and said "hey Lacy, Layne said I could as long as it was before nine." Layne was the landlord, and she had complimented my playing only minutes ago! It was shortly after six.

"Whatever, Jill is sleeping in her room and you have to realize that people have to get up early. You're probably not even supposed to be down here anyway," she said coldly. A few minutes passed and Layne came down and confirmed that I could play the piano until nine at night. I looked triumphantly because Jill walked in and unlocked her dorm room door; she had been out all day. Way to go, Lacy.

Well Lacy was not finished. She had a chat with Layne and soon enough, she had her way. Music was not welcome and I was not allowed downstairs.

"But how am I supposed to cook?" I asked, while a little surge of panic welled up inside of me. And this was supposed to be a Christian place?

"I know you're going through a hard time right now, that's not my problem, no one upstairs is allowed to come down except for Helen," she said. Alrighty, then! I went upstairs and repeated everything to Helen who did not like it. I was greatly annoyed because Lacy used my own troubles to make me feel worse.

"Yeah, these people are not good at living in community with each other," she said. Her eyes got big, like they do when she gets upset and she said "I just don't understand why they would do that." We shook our heads and ate sandwiches for the next couple days. It was nice of Helen to open up her place like that. She stayed with Chloe in the night and I slept on her bed in the dorm.

I was really struggling because I could not do music and it was calling to me in everything. It was like the more time went by the stronger it called in the wind, it was sad. I felt alone and worried and sad. I could not believe that Gladys, who opened her doors and told me it was safe had caused me to run. Helen said earlier that I should have only paid half the rent because I left for two weeks on Gladys' account. I agreed but did not think that much could be done about it.

The next day a young lady by the name of Melody accidentally locked her keys into her dorm room. Unable to break in, they opened up a spare room for her and I went to help, happy to see a friendly face. We ended up sharing the room and chatting well into the night. Work was hard during these times because there is nothing like having to act like you're happy when you are not, but it made me feel better to laugh. I even felt weird because Helen had left me in this cold place while she stayed with friends, which she did all the time. Well someone had an issue with me and the landlord left a note on Helen's door telling her that the room was meant for her and I would have to leave or she would be charged more. Great; I had no where to go, just like that.

Once again Helen was put off by it, so she suggested Chloe's place, but I didn't want to because I did not know her well at the time. No other options forced me to suck up my pride and I found myself knocking at her door.

"I have no where to go," I said tearfully when she opened the door. I just felt so unwanted and *sad*!

"Well you can stay here if you want," she offered. Helen was sleeping in Chloe's roommate's bed because they were good friends the girl was out of town, so before Helen came over, I explained everything to Chloe.

"It sounds like Gladys has a lot of knowledge but she isn't very wise," Chloe observed. I nodded in consent and Chloe tried to be encouraging. I bottled things because I did not want to be too vulnerable and Chloe already saw me cry. I prayed to God and thanked him for at least getting me somewhere safe.

After a week went by, I texted Gladys and discovered that Frank was still there; I stayed for almost two weeks at Chloe's place, but I bought groceries and left them with her to help her out. She had a lot of her plate, as a volunteer at Benny's Place (a youth center for teens), she got a call at one in the morning and I answered to a troubled teen.

"Is Chloe there?" she asked loudly.

"Uh, she's sleeping right now," I said tentatively.

"I need to speak to Chloe, lemme speak to Chloe!" and she went on and on, freaking out loudly – I was holding the phone away from my face.

"What's your name?" I asked gently.

"Asia," she said and continued freaking out.

"Okay, Asia I'll get Chloe, but you have to calm down," I said and kept talking quietly until she did quiet down somewhat. Chloe heard and patiently took the phone, calming this girl down. Soon Asia came over and was talking to Chloe in her room in a loud voice. I am a light sleeper, but there were also neighbors in the building probably trying to sleep. I got up and knocked quietly on the door.

"Come in," Chloe said quietly.

"Hi, uh, Asia, I'm just trying to get some sleep it's four in the morning and I work at nine, would it be okay to keep your voice down a bit?" I asked, looking right at her. The same proud smile was the one I used to wear. She had a scar going down one of her cheeks and a haughty look that truly hurting teens wear. She went on and on about her boyfriend and drugs and…it was a late night with a long day at work the next day. Chloe is probably the very most patient person I know.

After work that day, I decided to write Gladys a letter expressing how I felt because it seemed like I could not talk to her. I prayed about it and went to scripture because she claims to be a hardcore Christian. I looked up scriptures that caution the use of words – that advise against slander and gossip because Gladys is also a youth leader. I did not want to point fingers, I wanted her to see where I was coming from – and that I went to scripture first. Then I wrote about the whole Frank situation, and, dear reader, what I told you earlier on is what I wrote in the letter. I couldn't sleep that night, so at three in the morning, after reading it to both Helen and Chloe, I drove. I dropped the letter in between both back doors and then I drove off into the night and wanted to cry out to someone – anyone who would listen and **care.**

Chloe was still up with Asia who was still being loud about not having weed, so I knew the door would be open when I got back. I did feel better leaving the letter there, because then it was sure that Gladys would get it and at least start to read it. The night air was clean and sharp and the clouds were illuminated by the city lights underneath. I could not sleep because of the anxiety, which is an uncommon occurrence for me, so I sang softly in the car and drove in the clear night until my eyes drooped.

The next day I got a text from Gladys saying to come back home because Frank was gone, apparently Travis was there, too, but had left already. I dreaded going back, but went anyway. When I went in, she was smiley and said hello. I nodded and went into my room to unpack. I'm sure the hurt was on my face and in my eyes.

"Can we talk?" Gladys asked politely.

"Sure." I followed her into the living room, not knowing what to expect. All the folks that I talked to about this issue (which was not many) agreed that I should get out of there, but for some reason I felt that I couldn't. I just felt that I had to stay and I don't know why, because all it did was hurt me.

"When you wrote that letter, it broke my heart," Gladys started, "I had no idea that was why you left." Really? How do you forget abut telling someone something like that? What was supposed to go through my head? She had the right words, but her tone and her eyes did not match the words; they were not heartfelt. I did not voice this aloud; I just knew it in my heart. I stayed silent and thanked her for apologizing. Something happened, then. I pulled away from her and she seemed to think that she could walk all over me and both parts showed in our actions.

I stopped talking to her and she continued to freak out randomly at me – even saying some mean things and then going into a room to slam the door so that she would not have to hear me defend myself (and know that I was right). Of course, the door slam was the most aggravating because it left me with her rotten words. I could tell that she felt bad after, but she had too much pride to say sorry.

Okay. I do not understand people like that – sure, we all have pride and it is an issue most human beings face – but here was Gladys hurting someone over and over and too proud to say sorry. Proud of what? She was sticking a needle into my heart and pulling it out only to stick it back in to cause fresh pain. At first I could see that she felt bad, but she *never* apologized without me approaching her about the issue first.

I decided to just keep her at bay for a while, so I was still friendly but not so trusting. The summer was better for the both of us and I even sang again in a local competition. I thought it was just a one time singing thing, but it was a karaoke competition, so I did not practice. I did not know that people practiced karaoke. Well I should have practiced! It was fun, though, and I was the only performer who took the mic off the stand and went to the edge of the stage to sing.

Hearing my voice come out of the speakers, nice and full, was cool. I was on key for the most part, but the first song was a gong-show. Anything that could have gone wrong did. They played the wrong song, the cd wouldn't work, I was too loud, so they turned the volume down and cut me out, then they had to restart the song…on and on…then the mic cut out because I was too loud again, so I had to go to the other mic – all while singing. I can't help it if I sing loud – actually I could, I could learn to sing more quietly, but they liked my voice and said I had the potential for super whatever, whatever.

They said if I could find someone to mentor me, that I could go far… and that I should practice to really nail the songs. It was cool. I did not even think I would go to the next level because the show was that bad, but I did. And I did not practice the next song either because…well I don't know why. My friend, Rachel was there and she did very well. Her mother even sang a song! It was great fun. There were also what is called "side-walk days" where the streets are closed along the main street and stores will sell their merchandise outside and have all kinds of deals.

New bands were jamming and animals were there to pet and so we went and pet some raccoons and kittens and they were cute! Rachel had a rabbit and kitten at her place, and dogs with her parents, so she was very fond of animals. In between singing and work, the month of June sped by fairly quickly. Rachel and I went to a bar with Emma who came down for a visit and then Rachel and I went again in July.

We were singing at a karaoke night and I sang *Little Gasoline* by Terri Clark and people actually stopped talking to see who was singing and clapped at the end, which they didn't do for everyone, so that was nice. Then I sang *Basket Case* by Greenday, I had fun. The DJ asked to sing with me, so we sang the song that neither of us knew too well, and at the end I grinned smartly because I held the note for the longest. We held onto it to see who would give out first and he did with "I don't know this song." I used to listen to it in high school, years ago by now, so I was off key as well. Rachel sang a couple songs as well, but did not do so well on the first one because she had switched it or something. We were just having fun, though.

When I signed up for a song, a man named Luke came up to me and chatted. At first I was nice enough, but then he started putting his hands on my waist, and I would move and he would lift his hands in the air. As soon as I relaxed, they would go onto my waist again. Everywhere

I went, guys shouted comments at me or invited me outside or offered me drinks. This has happened since I was fifteen. I used to take those drinks and go outside. I know better. I think it is quite annoying, but Rachel was like "every guy here has his eye on you," as if she thought it was flattering. It isn't; it's annoying.

When I go to the bar, which is not too often these days, I prepare. I play it safe and dress in layers, because I know how guys like to use their hands. Well this night was a bit chilly and rainy, so I wore jeans and a jacket that I kept on all night. Rachel wore clothes that did not fit right. I don't know what she was going through, but everything about her demeanor changed and she wore pants way to huge to stay up, so she would hold it up, walking down the street! I have been to her house, so I know that she has clothes that fit, and I would constantly tell her to fix her clothes.

She actually reminded me a little bit of Gladys because she was going online and shacking up with random guys in Portland that she met online. She would tell everyone what she was doing and post it on face book so that friends and family would say "don't go!" and then she would go and come back with unclear stories of things that happened. It was so weird! I tried to help her by getting her to focus on positive things, but she just let herself sink low. It is like she wants to stay there!

At the bar, she went to sign up for another song, and I guarded our table. We only had a few drinks, yet, so I was not drunk. While she was signing up, four guys came and sat with me. I talked to them but very casually, careful to not make any suggestions in what I said or did. The one guy's name was Anthony and he bought Rachel and me a drink and kept his eyes on me.

"Take your jacket off," one of the guys said.

"Uhh….no," I said lightly but firmly.

"Hey isn't this no-shirt Friday?" another asked. Ha, ha, funny. Not.

"No, it's three shirts-and-a-jacket Friday," I rebuttled sarcastically. They were a little put off because I wouldn't put out. Anthony talked to me and asked for my number. I gave him some random combination of numbers and grinned as he typed in a false name – I said my name was

Ashley – and then the random numbers. It was funny. I looked over at Rachel to see how she was doing and gasped in horror.

She had wedged herself in between to guys and sat with her shirt and bra up to her chin. They drunkards were laughing and touching her boobs. What the **heck**?! They turned and laughed at my reaction, making some comment about me doing that too; pigs.

"Rachel what are you doing? Put your clothes down, now!" I commanded.

She did and I turned to Anthony. "Get your friends out of here," I ordered.

"What? I didn't do anything," he protested, not moving.

"I know, but you know what your friends are like and you need to get them out of here right now." I looked around and assessed the situation to get out if I needed to. No help and four drunken guys. The one on the end was practically sleeping; the two in the middle were trying to get Rachel to lift up her shirt again, but a lot of their weight was muscle; they were pretty big guys. Anthony was the most sober, but he was a big guy and he was blocking my way out.

"They are just having fun," he tried again; right.

"At my friend's expense so we are going now. Get out." He actually listened. Good, because I would have lost a fight with him, but was prepared to try. He and his friends got up and left. Anthony had ordered a new beer and it wasn't cracked open yet. I downed the rest of mine and took his, leaving the cap on the table.

"Lets go, we're getting out of here," I said to Rachel. Boy, I was *livid*! Outside, I started walking fast. It was cold and rain was coming down in stinging little pelts, but I was hot and quite angry so I did not heed the weather. Rachel stumbled along, but I knew she wasn't drunk because I had about twice as much as her and I was tipsy, but not drunk. Not even close. I walked fast and when Rachel fell behind, I said "pick it up, I'm not waiting for you." And all of a sudden Rachel was there, walking just as fast beside me.

"What the hell were you thinking?!" I asked angrily, "I did not need to see that."

"I don't know," Rachel answered like always.

"No, don't give me that – you know. Why did you do that?" I asked again.

"I wasn't thinking," Rachel threw out. Well that was for sure. We walked all the way across town and she said sorry, but there are many things that she has done and it was getting worse with time. She bought me a tea because she felt bad and we walked until I no longer felt the tip of the booze. Then I drove home angry.

Then next day I told Gladys about it because I needed to tell someone. Sally was having issues as well – she had been avoiding me, so I asked to talk. She got angry when I said that I had enough people going crazy in my life, thinking that I meant her. I had actually meant Rachel and Gladys, but Sally didn't know much of what was going on because she was too busy being angry at my brother for calling her a Debbie downer about a year ago. And she got mad at me for laughing. That's what friends do: tease each other or forgive each other.

She got mad at Helen because when she came back from a trip somewhere in Illinois, Helen was quite different. I agreed with Sally, but I gave Helen some space and now we are good friends. Sally got angry with a few other friends that I didn't know and complained about it to me many times. Sally got angry with Rachel for things she was doing. I think Sally needs a change – she lives at home and is my age and has many dreams and talents, but allows her anxiety to hold her back.

Sally ended up leaving the house angry, kicking things around saying "whatever Karee, I'm not a psycho, and by the way you have a horrible singing voice." She smiled with grim satisfaction and said "I've wanted to tell you that for a long time," and then she left slamming the door. Well, before me Sally had been getting angry with many of her friends, dropping them like flies; it was a pattern and it was my turn. I tell you, if you look for flaws in a person, they will jump out at you. I am not a perfect person, what did she expect? I appreciate criticism if it is constructive and Sally did say some things that were good – and she did come to me about it after I told her to. We had many good times and I am sad to see the door to that friendship closed so easily.

I grinned at her words and said "well you could have told me that sooner." Helen called to see how I was doing and I was in quite low spirits so I told her what happened at the bar and with Sally. I asked for prayer at the church because I did not know where else to go. I prayed for both girls and Gladys and read my bible.

I did count my many blessings; besides Gladys' moods, I liked where I lived. The neighborhood was great – stores were within walking distance, the neighbor was nice. I had a job that I liked and my boss was really considerate and laid back most of the time and the workers are great! Things calmed down at the homestead for a while, but only for a little while.

I was processing things in my mind – between music and Gladys and every one else, I felt like if I didn't have some down time, I was gonna go mad. Work was busy, but I had a little bit of time and space to think a little bit. I had to encourage myself and remind me that God *did* intend for life to be **good**. We do have a devil for an enemy, folks, and he will always enjoy every bit of sadistic misery that anyone could ever imagine.

Sadistic is not even close to the things that Rachel has done. At work her mother, Gail, called and left a series of worried messages on my phone. During a break, I called and she asked that I meet her after work as soon as possible. Her voice was strained with worry and overtiredness. Right away I thought *okay, what did Rachel do?*

Work was great because the script is second nature and the other workers could tell I had a lot on my plate because as soon as my character dropped, my composure remained downcast. I did not mean it, but I found my head hanging low, my shoulders drooping, my smile dropping, and my eyes clouding over. I was not happy.

Giving these tours to many large groups of people every day, I even took in a negative thought that none of these people cared. They thought I was amazing – lots of people said so, so many people take my picture and I am always making them laugh. It was all pretend during these times; just a happy façade. But at the same time it felt good to loose myself in a character that was so unfazed and silly, although it made Karee's life a little bit harder to face.

At the end of my shift, my heart thudded into my mouth and every swallow was a heavy one. My chest sank with the weight of oppression and my head wanted to stay lowered, ducked, as if I were a child in trouble. I changed out of my work clothes and actually told Gladys what was going on for a change, to see if she could help.

"I think that you need to realize that you can't help Rachel," she said nicely, "you can't always be the hero."

"Yeah, you're probably right, probably," I said, dragging my heels and dawdling as I went out the door. She had good advice, and in this case was definitely right; not probably. I drove over to Gail and Lance's house and tried to prepare myself for whatever was coming. *You'll be okay,* **you'll be okay,** *you'll be okay,* and I repeated this mantra over, not feeling very well at the moment.

Gail welcomed me into the house; I had been friends with Rachel for a period of time, so I had experienced this change over her first hand. She offered tea, which I took her up, as I was sensing a long chat ahead. I won't go into details, dear reader, because some things were said in confidence. Gail shared about the changes in Rachel and she tried to keep things light.

"Rachel called me up on the weekend crying and throwing a fit because she said she blew it with you," Gail started seriously.

I grew solemn and quiet, not knowing what to say. I knew that Rachel and I were pals, but I didn't know that I meant that much to her. "she said she did something horrible and that you would probably never speak to her again," Gail continued, "can you tell me what it was?" sensing my hesitance, she said "I'm just so worried, when she called, I have no idea what is going on now."

"Well, we were at the bar to sing karaoke, it was her idea, and we were having fun. We hardly had any drinks; I had twice as much but was not drunk. Some guys came and sat at our table while she was signing up for a song and one kept talking to me and when I looked over, she had her shirt and bra lifted right up for them to see and stuff..." I trailed off, looking down, not really wanting to recall this recent memory.

Her mom got real worried and apologized for her. "Rachel used to have lots of friends you know," she said to me, "but she alienated them by doing things like this. If you want to stop seeing her, I understand." I understood too. I understood that her mother had no idea what to make of the situation. Then her mother told me in great details some of the most horrid things ever.

She said that Rachel used to have a boyfriend who lived close by and when they tried to break up, she would sit and just zone out, staring at his house for hours at a time. They think he tried to hurt her; I think they are right. Then Gail told me that she was sexually abusing her little kitten and bunny. Rachel was so distraught at what she was doing that she called a help line, and they got her location and called the police. Bestiality is against the law, and rightfully so.

When her mom told me that, my jaw literally dropped in horror. I could not fathom that – still can't. "If she can do that to an animal, she could do that to a child," her dad, Lance, said. That scared me because it is true. Among other things there were accusations Rachel has made about other people very close to her. I had heard many accusations from her myself and wondered at the validity because the stories and people were so inconsistent. Rachel always started the story with "I think so-and-so did this..."

Well I know from experience that when people do things to you, you do not question it. Even if you deliberately block it from your mind, it is still there, inside, taunting you, and the only way to stop it is to face it, otherwise it could drive you mad. Something happened to Rachel, I think when she was young, but who knows. Now I was horrified with her because of these infidelities. Well, that is all I can mention of the conversation that took place.

I know that Rachel's family is not perfect – her dad has quite the temper, but something more happened to her. I don't know what it is, but I was suspecting schizophrenia. Rachel even admitted to hearing voices and seeing people or forms watching her. She has tried to seek help by checking herself into the mental ward of the local hospital. Sally and I visited her once when she was there, and I had snuck in some homemade pumpkin pie for her. It was a creepy visit.

I had to get out of there, so I made a speedy exit and acknowledged their confidence in me. Later, when Emma was visiting from Portland, I asked if she had heard from Rachel because Rachel chatted with her online a few times and was open with her.

"Yes," Emma said, "I don't know how she is doing, though." I asked if she admitted to anything having to do with animals and then Emma knew that I knew, so she said "yes, she told me, but asked me to not tell you." I see. For a while I tried to pretend that I didn't know and still hung out with Rachel, but it was just way too hard. What if she tried something with me? What if she tried to blame me for something?

Eventually I told her when she was over for a visit and I know that Rachel feels like she can trust no one now, but it's like she enjoys doing things like this to tell everyone and see their reactions. My reaction did seem to hurt, though, but how could it not? She was going down a path of dark that I just could not follow.

I really struggled with this situation, because I felt that the last thing she needed was another person pulling away, but Gladys was right. I am not a hero. Not in this case – I have been before, but this was entirely up to Rachel. When I got back, Gladys saw that it was eating my insides and killing me. I had lost my appetite and thank God for the next day off work because I could not even think. I was so disgusted and angry with Rachel and I cannot understand what drives a person to do that – but I don't *want* to understand.

I told Rachel that I knew and if I ever caught or heard anything like that again then I would call the cops, because her parents had told me that they had let her off with a warning. Seeing as it was a mental case. "Go ahead," she said smartly, "my cat has a new home and my parents have my bunny." That disturbed me because there were no attempts of not doing it again, there was no apology.

I again was driven to the church for prayer, but it felt like it wasn't helping. Who knows? There is probably much more than the eyes see. God probably spared me from more than I realize. After work a few weeks later, I got a text from Rachel saying *I have something creepy to tell you. It's going to creep you out.* So I texted back **then don't tell me,** and she texted *but I have to,* I almost texted **no, you want to,** but refrained and she texted *I'm gay.* That was it for me. Too much.

I just knew that if I stayed friends with her through this confession that I would be put through more traumas. **I need a little break for a while,** I texted. *Does that mean you won't be my friend anymore?* She texted back. When I didn't answer, she sent a few texts saying things like *are we still friends?* I just sent one more saying **I need some time for a while,** and I let her go for real then. I do not mind being the push or the nudge that a person may need to boost their efforts, but when other people suck the life out of me something is drastically wrong.

I had to let Rachel go because no one could help her. She has plenty support around her with her mom, sister, she had me and was going to see counselors and doctors. Well they did tell her that she had aspergers, which is a start. So, as you can see, a lot was piled onto my plate at once. It was hard to wrap my head around things. In a fight over email (before Rachel got so incredibly odd), Sally had said "Karee told you things that happened in her life and now you are creating those situations for yourself."

I hate to say it, but she was right. Dead right. I also started her on drinking by offering Rachel her first drink and having good foresight, Sally had cautioned "be careful not to open a door with that, you know how Rachel is." Well it was Emma and me before I went to the Caribbean, and we had mixed a touch of rum with egg nog for Rachel to try. I could not help but hear these words looming in my mind after the matter.

I shook my head at myself. How could I not see? Rachel asked questions about my past to learn how to better create it for her self. Why would she even want those things to happen to her? Why would anybody want those things to happen at all? Was it all for attention? Then I thought *who am I to judge? I don't really know what is going on.* No one but Rachel knows what is truly going on with her – and I don't think she even knows most of the time! It is a terrible situation, but she has to be the one to face these things and then to help herself. Life got a bit tough for a while, so I used music as an outlet, singing with my guitar or piano, writing songs…it wasn't too long until things got a little worse.

chapter 8:

Well as the saying goes, where there is good, there is bad. It is such a fact of life, but all bad things can be overcome. For me, belief in Jesus Christ as my personal savior does the trick. Also, even though it sucks, because it shows other people's trials, learning about other people really helps to open eyes and put perspective. Chloe shared details about her own family life and I realized I have not had to deal with things like that, and her life is very tough. She is probably one of the strongest and most patient people I know, and she depends of God for her strength.

I needed God's strength a lot lately, even on a day to day basis. I read the files I had received from social services way back when. I had ordered them to use for my first book to validate the things I put in there, but I had already put the summary that Jasmine had read, so there was no need to read these. I had a bit of time, so I pulled them out and began to read – from front to back, page after page.

As I read, it almost hurt more than the things I went through because Ephraim and I were not mistakes. We were planned. Joan took fertility pills **so that** she would get pregnant, and she knew that she would probably have twins because of those pills. We are not twins genetically, but only a result of some stupid pills, which might explain our differences. I wondered which one of us would have been born if there were no pills involved – would it have been only Ephraim? I have this strange feeling that it would have been. Did I take the bullets for him? I often feel like I did. Would I have been spoiled and rotten if it were just me born? I'm glad I'm not spoiled, seeing as most spoiled people are usually quite unhappy.

Oh, that fact of it all just angered me something fierce! Why did Joan want more kids? Why did she treat us that way when we were so planned? I also learned that Jocelyn and Jonas were in foster care when Jocelyn was only one year old because Joan "could not handle the kids." I do not think that Jocelyn knows that to this day, and I am not about to tell her because she is just becoming happy, finally, because her friends and art helped to pull her out of her deep, dark shell.

I also learned from these files that Daniel had tried to commit suicide after Jonas was taken away. He overdosed on Comet and Lysol. Even typing that, my heart breaks for him, especially after seeing that lovely picture of Daniel and baby Jonas at our uncle's house. Daniel cared; he really did, but how could he just stand by and let Joan ruin things? I guess he really does love her – so much that his whole family life is torn up and now no one carries on his generation. When Ephraim and I went into care, Daniel would get up and leave angrily during meetings with the workers and lawyers – well this tells why – because the same thing that was happening with us had already happened with Jonas, so his emotions were repeated as well.

My heart grew colder toward Joan because for *years* she made me feel **horrible** for causing her great physical pain – at birth. She whined about a c-section, that her teeth were shattered and her bones were crushed and we were eating her intestines when we came out and she almost died and blah, blah, blah. She used to say to me "I have scars all over my belly because of you." Well I now have doctor and nurses notes (signed) saying a "normal and safe delivery." Why would she say things like that to a small child? She also said that we were about two and a half months premature, but we were only about three or four weeks early, which explains our combined weight of eleven pounds that is normal for early twins.

When I was five I weighed 12.2 kg and my bones were at the maturity of a young three year old – and deteriorating quickly. It is a miracle that with all the abuse and falls and hikes and all, that I have never broken a single bone. God's hand is and was around this little child. I cannot help but give Him the glory, as kooky as it sounds; it stands undeniably true in the eye of this beholder.

I had osteoporosis when I was a teeny bopper and the doctors kept me in the hospital for months to treat it in my right leg. That explains the scar I had pondered over for years; and the faint memory of me walking around in a hospital crib with an IV attached. I had asked where the scar came from, but Joan had always answered that she didn't know. How could she not, when she was right there? The notes said that when Joan came, she was unresponsive to her little child. I would tug at her red sweater, trying to get attention, but she would shoo me away or ignore me rudely; she was only there because the people involved made it mandatory.

I read about how Joan confessed to a worker named Lexi that a lady had put a curse on her when she was twelve on the beach; something I had heard and asked about before – something she had flat out denied to me. I also read that one of the ladies who used to baby sit Ephraim and me was worried because we were left alone for long periods of time. Her name was blanked out for safety reasons, so I am not sure which one lady it was; Sarah or Esther. When I left for good (at fourteen), they wrote **"Karee steals, she lies, she's evil and Joan hates her!"** imagine seeing that written about you. I suspected it all along, but there it was, confirmed before my eyes in black and white; the reason why I was abandoned by my mother. The plain truths instead of what she said. It's one thing to read these things, but there were also recorded phone calls as well. If I had wanted them I'm sure I have rights to hear them as well, but the writing is enough for me.

A few years ago Ephraim and I had went to meet with the Stardens to try to talk to them and Joan still feels that contempt for me. Ephraim hates how she talks in different tones to me and refuses to shake my hand or really even look at me. She has always accused me of lying even when she knows I did not and to this day she still piles the blame on me for everything gone wrong. At the time that we met them I mentioned that I had files from social services and she thought it was a lie so she said she had files from a lawyer. I hadn't read these files yet otherwise I could have told her that I had records of that lawyer too.

The lawyer was to help her with her case when she got pastors and church members to sign saying that she was basically a good lady to help her case with the kids and it all helped with the house to get the funding to expand it. She has told so many lies and she hates me or fears me for whatever reasons…she believes these lies without conscience even today.

Well, too bad the lies I told were lies that *she **forced** me to tell*. And too bad I was considered a thief even when I wasn't – I was blamed for every single thing that went wrong – from a bad day to poor health to stealing things that I had no idea what they were to being infatuated with my dad. I think I remind Joan of either herself or someone threatening. Eventually I was probably just a big mark on her conscience and that is probably why she would always say "get out of my eyesight," after crushing my spirit or striking my body.

The social workers had me tested for ADD or ADHD and discovered that I was not positive for either; just a child with imagination. When I was around other people, my creativity would come out, but around the family, I was dead – a shell that was breathing and deteriorating. They also described the three of us, Ephraim, Jonas and me, at different parts of our lives as sad, battered children, especially me. It broke my heart. There were notes that Jocelyn was also tested for ADHD and for behavioral issues and that Jonas had emotional outbursts, (probably very similar to the tantrums Ephraim used to throw), and Jonas was tested for a few similar things as well including behavioral studies. It was later noted that Jocelyn was treated like a princess and that not much was known about Susie other than that she was treated royally, which I remember because apparently she was the "miracle baby." Joan used to say that the doctors told her she could not have any more kids after the birth of us twins because we were so terrible at birth and blah, blah, blah, but I saw no record of any of that.

These files contained quotes and dates for recorded phone calls between various parties of the foster care system – calls of Joan asking for me back but not Ephraim because she thought he was a bad or demonic influence on me. Boy she sure missed the boat on that one because Ephraim is the best twin in the world! For years again she used our separation to beat me into the ground, saying that Ephraim couldn't stand me; he wanted to stay away from me; he wanted to come back but he couldn't because I had forced my way in. Well, what about when she pried his little arms off of her and threw his few belongings out onto the front lawn when Ephraim begged to come back? How dare she? Maybe I would not feel this way if there was a bit of space between each event, but the people, the files…everything just piled up on me at once and it was overwhelming. Ephraim knows how blessed he is to have gotten out when he did.

Moving on to the foster places; I learned that Fran really did care for me as did the Swazies. I also learned that the social workers thought I "played games" a lot and what actions led them to think that. I had heard the term, but never understood its meaning. In my mind I was not playing anything, but now I understand their perspective, but they had made a few mistakes in their perceptions of me. Well it's all okay because they are only human and we all make mistakes. I turned out pretty fair despite these things.

There are records of things that I would say to them that didn't make sense to them – like talking of relations with a boy…but I was so evasive or spoke in riddles so they dismissed it as a game. From my point of view it was probably a cry for help without me wanting it to be a cry.

I also learned that the serious thing I was blamed for at the Swazies was acquitted due to "*lack of evidence*," as in the "witnesses" were not credible. Good, because I was innocent! Also Kim's behavior and actions regarding the whole issue led the cops and social worker to doubt the accusation's validity and giving me a clean slate. That was a huge relief to me because I always wondered if it would haunt me in the future – I was blamed for things that did not even cross my mind! Kim knew my innocence and while she did not out rightly profess it, her words were enough for me to know that she knew it. Well, it is laid in the grave and I thank God for that!

It was interesting to see how the social workers started off rather cold or distant – as I was just another case – and then gradually opened up and then grew to like me. They still kept the files and notes official, but they were not so quick to discredit me and were there to defend quite rapidly in time. The turn around in all this was around the time I found Jonas and decided to stay in Carrington instead of moving twenty-four hours away with some friends. I remember how Josie had walked with me and said "what about me? You're my best friend…" and although she tried to put it off as if it was her acting skills (later), I knew she meant it all. When I mentioned this to Noella she said that's because it had become my choice at that point to stay there with them. And she is right.

The social workers noted my musicality showing in earlier years and encouraged it, saying that they thought I was quite talented (very flattering) and they recommended that Noella encourage me in the arts. I thought Noella did very well at doing so. They recommended that she check out performance or music camps and I wonder why she didn't. But she did encourage writing and drawing, and then later, my singing.

Also, when I had eating problems, it was Bertha who was concerned and recommended that Noella take me to the doctor. Noella also wrote notes to the workers, asking to speak to someone who had more experience. It was kind of cool because Noella really wanted to help this young kid save her own life. I know that reading these files kind of seems like going back for more abuse, but it really did some good; questions were answered and I knew things and where I stood. It was good closure. I had answers and honest truths – legal documents to back me up if ever need be, but it was a tough read. I prefer a hurtful truth than a nice sounding lie.

Well I needed a break from the hullabaloo, so I visited Noella at the summer camp she was wrangling at. Watching the dust fly up behind me as I drove was liberating and I wondered what little adventure lay ahead. It was so sweet to watch Noella put on her cowboy hat and boots and saunter out in the field with the kids and horses, as if her age wasn't catching up to her. Don't tell her I said this, but she is so precious! When I first went out there, I was a little bit out of my comfort zone because I had been immersed into a world of performance and arts verses outdoors and horses. It was not long before I let my hair down, so to speak. Simon came and visited with me, saying "you're quiet."

I answered with "well, I'm out of place." He left it go because he knew I would warm up in a few minutes. I think Noella may have been a little uncertain, as was I.

I relaxed and knew some of the camp kids, and laughed and visited and ate with them and Noella. It wasn't long before I sat on a horse again – my first time in a number of years! We were doubling up on the horse and I have ridden many horses bare back, but **never** with another person. We were pretty crazy!

Noella line the horse up to a fence and hopped on. Then she lined the horse up to the fence, but it was too far away for me to hop on, so she brought him over to some buckets set up for the kids to step up, and the horse moved away. I think he was enjoying himself. "Hold on a second," Noella said, and tried to cup her hand to give me a boost. It failed because I did not know what I was doing. If it were just me and the horse, I could have hopped on, but when there is a person up there already, things get tight.

We laughed and then she lined him up against the fence already. He was pretty far away, probably getting exasperated by now, but I hopped on. "There!" I cried out triumphantly, "oh, just a sec," I was slipping off. Noella started the horse going, and she looked so stable in her position on the horse, so I placed my hands on her shoulders and tried to pull myself the rest of the way back on the horse while he was walking.

As if in slow motion, Noella kind of leaned forward and…fell of the horse! And me too! I had never *ever* fallen off a horse before! I am quite loud, and my job helps me to be so, what with projection and all, so of course I hooted and hollered when we were falling and everyone looked and laughed. Noella and I just laughed are butts off – good thing they were on the ground! It was a riot. Yes, it did kind of hurt, but not nearly as bad as I thought it would. I just thought *this is it?* It is not nearly as scary as people make it out to be. We just got back on and then the horse ambled his way to our destination. It was fun to just goof off and laugh at a silly mistake – all riders fall off, my time was coming sooner or later, and it just happened to be on a good day.

I had brought the files from social services and spoke to Noella about it before hand. Later in the evening there was a camp fire, and we were going to burn the files while the fire died. But while the campers were at the happy little fire, we snuck into the shack and took out the canoes. Man, I learned that I have no balance! Walking in a canoe on water is hard! We took them out and it was neat because the sky was as divided as my soul at that point. On the western side was a storm a fair distance away – we could barely hear the thunder – but we could see the bright flickers of lightning that seemed quite close. On the eastern side it was clear; stars were out and the moon sang away with the crickets. Talk about cool.

The water was still and the night seemed to sleep in a blanket of silence, daring the storm to come before morning. It was so peaceful, hearing the campers sing some songs (including Rudolph the red-nosed reindeer) and laughing as the tiniest hint of a breeze toyed with a strand of my hair, stroked my cheek and then left to play with the leaves. As we floated, everyone visited and I just listened and soaked in the distance from my woes. The dark night is not so scary out here…it is daring and inviting at the same time, mostly calming and serene. The horses snorted and we mixed each other up with our paddling patterns, laughing and shushing each other.

It is always fun to visit these camps – such a getaway! When our ears told us that most of the campers were off to bed, we paddled up shore and snuck around the fire and saved it before it died completely. Soon we had a nice fire toasting our wet feet as we teased each other and laughed.

"Go get it now," Noella said to me with a big noisy yawn, "before the fire dies out." I went to my car and got the bag, coming back to the fire pit with it. It felt so nice to run in the clear, cool air.

"What is that?" everyone asked. I looked at Noella. There were only six of us – two of the boys were sons of Noella and Drew's friends from church, and one is a rancher friend of Noella's (named Simon) and the other was…a nosy camp worker? The two younger boys got tired and (they are the sweetest boys *ever*) so they bid us goodnight and wandered off to bed.

"Never mind what it is," Noella said in her *I'm pretending to be defensive* voice. I snickered. We started taking papers out and burning them. The nosy fellow tried reading them, but the writing was small and hard to read in the dim firelight.

"Karee, are you burning your report card?" Simon teased. I laughed out loud.

"Yes," I said sarcastically "it wasn't straight A's like I wanted."

"What is it?" the nosy guy persisted.

"They are…illegal papers from the government," I revealed in a voice that said I was obviously lying. Noella came for another stack to burn. As I looked into the flames, I could not help but grin as the papers burned and wilted, turning to dust; my past.

"…Is it really?"

"Of course it is," Noella interjected, carrying on the joke, "we are running from the law…" and she went on, making up some funny story. I remember laughing even though my thoughts had wandered. We looked at each other and shared a knowing smile. Simon stretched out on the bleachers and continued observing. I knew he was guessing, but he was kind and keeping quiet. He never made mention of the papers again, that I saw of him anyway. We finished and seeing the last paper shriveled before my eyes, and watching Noella keep one more piece of burning paper from escaping in the night wind, I felt like I could actually smile for real. What a wonderful feeling! I grinned and smirked and smiled away. Noella did, too, a little more subtly because she was wiped out. I really appreciate how careful she was to make sure everything burnt completely.

"It feels like I can actually smile," I explained with a huge sigh of… release.

"I know," Noella said, beaming. We were all tired, then, so we went to bed. That was it now; there were no more questions, no more self beatings…it was finished. Like Jesus Christ said on the cross: "it is finished." What a great moment that was! Well we all got into bed and the storm answered the night's taunts to come disturb the peace, but even then, it hardly disturbed. Snuggled under the blankets, watching the lightning and listening to Noella sleep, mingle with the thunder, accented by the soothing rain; I soon fell into a peaceful slumber. Lying in the little trailer with Noella snoring away beside me, I could not help but thank God before I slept.

Even though the returned to San Frisco meant facing the hard things that had come to pass; I knew I could do it. I needed this break to renew my resolve to keep going forward, and that it what it did. In the midst of the troubles, I felt blessed. When it was time to go, I headed back with a lighter heart than what I came with, and I walked away knowing that there are people who care.

Needless to say, I was not quite so cheery about the drive back, but remained happy about the little adventures. I had received some texts from the Addams out in Carrington saying that Juliet was in town and wanted to catch up. I met up with her and her husband, Steve. They had to do some shopping, so I tagged along with them, still stinky and sweaty from the camp trip. Juliet had watched for me from the restaurant where they ate, so when she spotted me, she opened the door and waved.

When I ran over, she said "do I get a hug now?"

"Oh, I'm pretty stinky," I said, my voice very peppy, "I was out riding."

"I don't care," she said, "Come here," and she playfully tried to hug me. I gave her a half-hug and teased Steve. We had a visit and I shared about my job and things going on and then we journeyed over to the mall and right away Juliet bought me things. It was weird because I just looked at a shirt and set it aside and then she bought it, but they really help me to learn to accept things. We looked at wacky clothes and visited a local fudge store and walked around.

At one point during the day, while Steve was out paying a parking ticket, it started to rain a heavy, beautiful fall. The sky was dark on one half, but even though it was raining over me, it was still sunny. I loved it! The big drops were warm and refreshing, so while people on the sidewalks scurried into buildings or vehicles, I laughed and soaked in the rain. It was beautiful! The way it fell at a curve without a wind is unique and I enjoyed the sight of birds flying in the clear sky above. It was a nourishing rain for the earth, as well as my soul.

"You're gonna get wet!" Juliet called out, sitting in her van with the door open, waiting for me to join her.

"I don't care," I laughed, "it's so nice!" I spread my arms out and leaned my face toward the sun; the rain was inviting. My eyes sought a rainbow and did not find any hints of one, but then I thought *maybe we are at the end of a rainbow* because even though it was raining heavy, one half of the sky was clear and sunny. The thought made me smile. I always wondered what it would be like at the end of a rainbow.

All in all, it was a good day. We had a nice visit and Juliet apologized for not keeping good contact. "You feel like one of my own kids to me," she said while we looked at shirts on a sale rack. They had sequins in big brightly colored pictures on the front, and the same bright pictures on the back without the sequins. I thought they were neat – not too common.

"You should get one," I teased Juliet.

"Yeah right," she scoffed lightly as we flipped through them. She ended up buying me two of them and then she relented and got herself one too. "Then I will think of you every time I wear it," she said. I smiled, because I kind of thought it was funny that she bought one. Well I hope she did wear it sometime; these shirts were wacky!

"Awww....look at you, getting all soft," I teased later on, "don't worry about it, I'm not great at keeping contact either." Well soon enough, it was time for them to go and she kept sending texts back saying things like *I had a good time,* **we should do this again,** *you're welcome any time...*it was nice to know that people really cared. They are very sweet.

When I got back, Gladys was there and I filled her in on my little adventures. She liked the shirts and said maybe if I wore them when I sang it would help my stage presence. What she meant is that when I act for work, I own the character and the stage, but when I sing, I'm fine when I sing, but in between songs, I pull out the shy card. She thought that maybe the costume at work helped me stay in character (which it does), so maybe these shirts could kind of be like a costume. "Because even when you sing, you are not just a singer, but you are supposed to entertain," she explained, "so people are coming to hear, but also to see you." Dang, she was right! I told her so and took her advice to heart. I think she is onto something there.

The rest of the summer was peaceful, lots of sunny, warm days – I went outside as much as possible – long walks with my ipod that

Ephraim gave me, runs, walks in the park, feeding the little duckies, reading outside, painting outside…anything when it was beautiful. I chatted with my uncle on Skype and showed him the place up north in the fall when the leaves began to change colors, and I showed him my nice blue car.

Gladys went on a trip for a week and when I asked "where?" she said to Ontario.

"Oh, ya," I said, sensing something else, "any particular reason?"

"I got friends there," she said evasively. She did? As far as I knew the only one there was good ole Frank, and she had great speeches about how she was never going to put herself or him in any kind of position because her sole purpose in life was to bring people closer to God and she wasn't living if she wasn't doing that….

"Who?" I asked, giving her the benefit of doubt.

"Oh, friends," and I left it at that – she did not have to tell me anything if she didn't want to. Her friend Denise came over and there were awkward silences, so I flicked on the TV and ignored them. I knew there was something about that they did not want me to know, so I let it be. It didn't even bother me, really. Gladys took a long shower and Denise had to use the washroom.

"Knock on the door and ask," I suggested. Gladys always proclaimed great friendship between the two of them, so I did not think she would mind.

Denise knocked on the door and said "can I come in; I have to use the washroom." It seemed like no big deal, right? They shared the washroom before…

"I'm almost done!" she sang out. About a whole hour and a half later she floated out and Denise finally used the washroom.

"That was rather rude," I chided gently while her friend was in the bathroom.

"What, did you expect me to come out here naked to let her use the washroom?" Gladys retorted sharply, staring from behind her glasses.

"No, but I did expect you to show some courtesy. If you are such good friends it shouldn't have been a problem for you to pull the curtain and let her use it, or to change in your room," I pointed out quietly.

"Really?" she burst out. I looked at her like she was being stupid and she said "really?" again. When I nodded slowly with dramatic emphasis, she said "fuck you," and watched my face with glee. It did not crumble as she wanted it to.

"And you too," I said. Her comment did not offend me at all; it would offend her more because she is the one who wears the Christian title all the time. It's just that she *said* she shares everything and blah, blah, blah and I was weird when I said that I don't share bathrooms with friends because for me it's strange to do so.

"Are you joking?" she asked.

"Are you?" I retorted.

"Whatever, Karee, whatever," and she flounced off to her room, joined by Denise a few minutes later. Well she left and I did music and played hockey in the house and left my dishes on the counter and sang as loudly and as long as I could...it was great! I even had a little party with some friends and watched movies with others.

When Gladys got back, the house was spic and span. "How was your visit?" I asked pleasantly, but keenly observing her face.

"Wonderful," she sighed, going into her room and avoiding my goofy gaze.

"How were your friends?" I asked in the same pleasant tone.

"I don't have any friends there, I went to see Frank," she confessed. I wasn't even fazed. "When you came in that day, I was texting Denise that you were here and to not tell you," Gladys explained, "because you said you used to think highly of me and now you don't." I am not sure if she meant that to hurt me, but it just caused distrust. Why did she tell me that? I'll never know. It didn't hurt, though, because I did not consider Gladys a friend – she had made many proclamations about what a great friend I was to her, but I have never been able to reciprocate it because I did not feel the same way. Well she just proved that her words were lies because if I was such a great friend there would be no need for this dishonesty.

She talked a lot about her trip and how he had this great heart and was a kind person even though he has all these issues. Everyone has issues. "Well why don't you tell people about that?" I asked, meaning his good heart. She said people wouldn't believe her…well, I wonder why; she had given him quite the bad name around here.

"Because people already have this negative idea about him," she said.

"Because of things that you told them," I voiced out loud. She knew I was right. Here she was, coming to me about how he was so good and nice and stuff, but she had already slandered his name before getting to know him so well. It kind of sucked for Frank. Gladys and Frank chatted for hours and hours, days after day, and then the high school drama settled in. Gladys could be seen crying and wanting to be alone because they broke up, and then on cloud nine because they made up… she would snap at me one minute and love me the next.

We had a little squabble over food because I make tasty meals and save up to get the food to do so. Also, when I am super busy, like I was at that point, I cook a lot of food to count out the meals for the day. I had made a nice chicken dish and told Gladys I was counting out the meals, as I am not wealthy. When I got back after a long day at work, one of those pieces was missing.

"Can you please not eat my chicken?" I asked blandly, as more of a statement.

"Really," Gladys burst out, "the one piece of chicken? You ate my food, so now I'll eat yours." She did, but she eats a **lot** more than me. Now let's get something straight here; when I moved in with Gladys, she offered me food until I could afford it. That was what she said "you can eat my food if you need to, I don't want you to starve." Also she had said "anything in my house is yours, this is your home too," well, now it seemed she was retracting that. Whatever food she wanted saved, she had only to tell me and I would refrain. She bought boxes of cheap burgers for two bucks on sale and with employee discount, very different from twenty dollar chicken. Chicken breasts are expensive – we all know that. Plus, she had been eating my food just as much the entire time, if not more than I ate hers – plus I cooked and cleaned for her! What more did she want?

I eat a **lot** more healthy than she does because she doesn't cook, but she ate my bananas, perogies, pasta, juice…and I ate some of her bread or canned soup. We were okay with it, but I had long since stopped eating her food and she damned well knew it. So she offered food to help me out and then held it over my head in order to manipulate me. I did not bother fighting because talking to her was like talking to a brick wall – only the brick wall is a bit friendlier. I soon thought that anything she said was a lie, because she did not have the actions to back it up. It got to the point where I just pulled away and made sure that she minded her own business while I minded mine.

I thought it would be best, but Gladys was on a roll now and if my pulling away from her was hurtful, she wanted to do the same to me and would not stop until she brought me down. One day I swept the kitchen floor and received a phone call from a friend needing help, so I abandoned all, left and it ended up being a late night. That was my last day off before a busy week of early mornings at the spa or late nights at the spa followed by early morning acting. It was tough and I quickly forgot about the little dirt pile swept up under the broom propped against the wall by the door.

To her credit Gladys had spoken to me quite a while ago, about leaving the little dirt pile on the floor beside Alana's old room because she now kept her hair dryer in there to not wake me up in the mornings; which I had thanked her for. Well I forgot entirely about the dust – it was not a priority at all and it did not affect Gladys as much as she said; in fact, she could have bent over and swept it up herself, but she chose not to.

Well she slammed doors and blew dry her hair on high right outside my bedroom door at seven in the morning, knowing it would wake me up. Feeling that I could not talk to her about this, as I had before, I simply took the dryer and hairbrush lying on the desk in the spare room and put it in the top drawer. If she wanted to play this way, then I would play. One thing about Gladys is she can dish it but she cannot take it; at all.

Then next morning I was up early, getting ready for work, when Gladys ambled out of her room. The tension between us only mounted, even if we did not talk to each other or if we did become civil, you could still cut it with a knife. *Dang,* I thought. I wanted to be out of the house before she got up. Oh, well, I just kept on my merry little way – I had a feeling it was going to be a good day at work and then I was off for a visit with Chloe at her house to watch a movie.

"Where's my dryer?" Gladys asked.

"Check where you usually leave it," I said stiffly, pointing to the spare room.

She stood in the doorway and looked in the room; not much searching done, here. "It's not here," she observed. "Have you seen it?"

"I don't use that stuff," I said tiredly glancing at the clock. It was like she sucked out all my energy and happiness, fifteen minutes until work – five minutes to go.

"So you don't know where it is?" she asked again, to see if I would lie.

"Check in the desk where you leave it," I repeated with exaggerated patience. For a woman of so much knowledge she wasn't smart. I didn't even close the top drawer all the way so she would see it open. She went in and found it. "Why did you do that?" she asked. As if she didn't know, really. I smelled trouble looming in the distance.

"Because you were blow drying your hair in the mornings to wake me up," I said bluntly, losing patience with her stupid games.

"Because *you* left the dirt pile over here again!" she retaliated, "it takes *two seconds* to sweep it up." Well then why didn't she sweep it up?

"You know sometimes things happen and people forget things like that," I defended. She was not on the top of my list of importance! She is not my whole world.

"Whatever Karee," she said to stir me up. It did not work. I kept my cool and just went quiet, watching her carefully. "You're not going to say sorry?" she asked. I shook my head; why should I? She did not say thank you for sweeping her floor, which I did **all the time**. "When I sweep the floor, I always sweep it up," she lied. I caught her.

"Bullshit," I said quietly, "I have never seen you sweep the floor since I've been here and I am here a lot more than you are."

"Yeah, you don't see it because I sweep the dirt up," she flailed.

"Then there should be no way that I pick up that much dirt every time I sweep," I pointed out calmly. She knew I was right and it angered her. She was a ticking bomb.

"Why do you have to be such an immature bitch?" she yelled. Her eyes looked crazy. I started to gather my things to go to work, but she would not let me leave the house. I thought about punching her, but that would just open another door for her to cause misery. "Why can't you act like an adult?" she shouted, "instead of a stupid, immature bitch? Stop punishing me for other people's sins; I am not Joan, I am not those foster parents," she cried out, "why can't you just act like a mature adult?"

I looked at her with mild amusement and said "like you are right now?" Well, I tell you that drove her straight up the wall! She went crazy! I had to text by boss quickly, telling her that I was running late because Gladys would not let me leave. She shouted insults and names and her face got red and her eyes went wild. I stayed calm and the more calm I was, the angrier and crazier she got. I only told myself to catch it if she tried to strike me; to not fight back. Gladys knew I am stronger than her, so I doubted that she would try, but at this point I thought she was ready to try anything.

"Why won't you talk to me?!" she bawled loudly in her tantrum.

"Because talking to you doesn't go anywhere," I shouted back to see if it would matter. It didn't. Why ask questions and demand answers if you aren't prepared to listen?

"If you won't talk to me then you can just leave," she said, "I don't need you to take care of me," she added, "take care of yourself, Karee." *Well then stop asking me to*, I thought. She didn't even take care of herself. She always said she wanted to change her life style, to get more fit, and I was ready to help her on that, but she has closed her ears to everything. It is *her choice* to eat out every single day – sometimes twice a day – and **her choice** to not be active; she proved that she could do it if she wanted by getting her real estate certificate. She worked her butt of for it and aced the tests; she liked to be as difficult as she was, or she does not realize that change comes with effort.

"Is this my notice?" I asked calmly looking right at her.

"Yes," she said tentatively, quieting down; the eye of the storm.

"Okay. I'll be out by end of this week."

"That's it?" she steamed, that anger rising up again. I shrugged and said nothing. She needed the money and I needed the place, so she retracted when I told her it was up to her. "But you can pay me a damage deposit," she stated matter-of-factly.

"No," I said firmly, "you said that when I moved in, I would not have to, that was our agreement, as long as I gave you a thirty day notice."

"Then I'll raise the rent until you pay it off," she said. Not fair. I could not afford that and I knew at this point that if she had the extra money then *she* would turn around and scam me. Why was she so short of money anyway? She got about nineteen bucks an hour at her store job and was delivery for another job plus whatever real estate things… where was her money going, that she needed to wring my neck for more coins? Now I was angry; she got the reaction she worked for.

"**Do** not tell me how to spend my money," I advised sharply. She went on and on about how I had to do that to ensure that I wouldn't screw her over like Alana did. Well by this point I would not be in the wrong if I did!

"What about '*you're such a great friend, Karee, I trust you,*' how true are those words?" I asked. Wow, the second part of the storm *is* the worst part!

Gladys entered the spare room to get her dryer "how true are they from you?" she rebuttled. Lack of originality; I had never said those words to her.

"You know what, all those good things you said are just *hollow words,*" I shouted over her constant mockery, "nothing but **hollow lies.**" And that was all I had to say.

"La, la, la, I can't hear you, what? Oh, what did you say? Oh I can't hear you," Gladys mocked, but I knew she heard me loud and clearly. Talk about acting like adults? I left angry and slammed the door in the middle of her mockery. Work was not as difficult as I thought it would be; I steamed for about an hour and then lots of really good groups came in and we had some really funny moments. Many people will bring cameras and snap pictures of me; sometimes I feel like they are paparazzi, especially when they sneak the cameras in and then flash it in my face. Usually I ask if they want to be in the pictures with me and that gets them a bit more excited. Well this one lady said "no," and had a team of three people with her telling her if it was a good picture or not.

"Oh, ya, that's a good one, use that one," a team member said. I was confused. The lady saved it on her phone and then pulled out a pad of paper and a pen. "I work for the paper," she explained, "I would like to do a story on you, is that okay?" she asked. I consented because I didn't know any better and she already had the picture. She took notes while I acted and then a few weeks later I was part of her story in the local paper! Front page! My boss was a bit upset about it because I did not ask her first – how was I to? The group was here for the tour already and everything is set on a timer…and the lady already had my picture. Whatever, I still thought it was exciting.

After work, I snuck back to grab some things and was super cautious, looking around my shoulder, checking corners, I ran in, grabbed some things and then bolted off to Chloe's. I told her what happened and she did not think it was good; she actually recommended that I speak with a lady at the church by the name of Sandra. Chloe came with me because I thought it was really awkward and she had chatted with this lady. Chloe came with and actually did most of the talking ☺ and then they prayed, but I did not feel better. I even shared about it in church and told Helen.

"I would be mad if you did that," Helen explained, "but I wouldn't freak out that way. That's just crazy."

"Well there would be no need for me to do that because we communicate," I pointed out. I am a good communicator; if a person has a problem I appreciate them coming forth an addressing me with it. Of course, I am also absent minded, too, so I forget things, but I am not mean and I am not ignorant. I stayed away for a few days, crashing at Chloe's and when I got back, Gladys was there.

I felt something then; that I hadn't felt in years. That old knot of dread that used to fill my stomach when I walked up to the house when I was living with Joan…it came back. Gladys had become a baby Joan in my eyes. I went to my room right away without saying anything. Her nephew wanted me to play, but I was not in a great mood and did not want to be a built in babysitter, so after telling him nicely that I was going to eat first, I told Gladys "not today, I'm not in the mood."

"Well then you had better stay in your room then," she retorted snottily.

"I will," I said, but that statement bothered me because when I told Gladys how Joan used to keep me shut in my room, she had said "I will never send you to you room." The first time Gladys approached me about the dirt pile was in letter format and she had thought I was "punishing" her for other people's sins. I am not Joan, she had written. I had written back to her that the dirt pile was retaliation to her blow drying the hair in the morning, and we had resolved the issue – she blew her hair in the spare room, except for the one day, and I swept the dirt piles up.

Now it seems she went back on her word yet again. I did not let it show, I did not tell her anything about it and I did not let it simmer, but it was in the pot on the back burner. I picked up my laptop and turned it on, reclining on my bed. I did not want to leave because there are all kinds of people everywhere and running would be way too easy; I wanted to figure something out because I believed that Gladys was a good person.

How to live with difficult people, I typed. A lot of handy things came in, like staying calm in fights, empathy, not getting too close, but then something came up that made think for a while. Control freaks. Two types; one is they have to be in control of the situation at all times, the other is they have to be in control of you and the situation at all times; type A and type B.

I think anyone can be a type A – I sure am – but not that I have to be in control, but that you don't mess with me; let me live my life and let me be me and then you will be fine. Gladys, I realized, is a type B. She had to be in control of the situation around her and the people involved – that is why she was so manipulative. Hm…I wanted to learn more because I really thought we could figure something out; I am kind of foolish that way – I give people benefit of doubt sometimes when I ought to know better.

As I read more, I learned more about myself, such as learned behaviors. For me it is the retreat and high guard; I realized that I am always on guard – when I walk into a room I assess the situation before me before even thinking; that is a learned behavior to the point of second nature. Likewise Gladys has used her words to get people to think what she wants them to think – whether it is to want her or to give her satisfaction…in my case it was to bully and hurt me, and I am not sure I am the first to experience this.

I went on a psychology site to look up how to deal with manipulative people and there were some interesting things on there! I feel like Gladys' manipulations are intentional; she knows better just like Joan does, but there are people who manipulate without knowing it. I realized that is what the "game playing" is. Social workers had written that about me a lot in high school, and I never understood until now. Game playing can be anything from little mind games to downright vocal/mental abuse.

The site also had what types of manipulators there are some tendencies of theirs. I came to the conclusion that Gladys is a master manipulator because of the way she camouflaged herself with the different groups she hung out with. Because she hung out with eighteen year olds, sixteen year olds and people of my age, early twenties, she was stuck at that age, which means something happened to her that she is unable to move past. The fact that she sleeps with a huge stuffed toy displays certain strangeness for someone of her age to be doing so. She has very few friends her age and often tries to appear cool to younger people. It works, because Alana and I both thought she was very cool for a while. When she manipulates, she leaves you thinking that it is your choice to need her or to stay or that you don't have a choice at all – I have felt like that a lot. When people manipulate, they are twisting the situation and if they are masters at it, you often don't know it is happening, like it was with Gladys.

I won't go into details about it now, but the site also had some tips on cautioning yourself if you thought someone was unstable. They described a few things to look for in "unsafe people." I saw almost every single thing in Gladys. Manipulation/bullying, lack of consistency in relationships (her and Frank made the rollercoaster look like smooth sailing), sudden shifts of character, and consistent play of characters. Both I had seen first hand; control. Always wanting to know where I was, or to meet people in my life; always wanting me to do things with her, always telling me what to do, saying things like "you owe me your life now, slave," because I put a pot of soup in the fridge and she changed it to a plastic container. Making me feel like I *had* to cook for her and help her out all the time; the getting angry when I didn't, but turning things around to point at me. The fights over simple things that most people overlook, the way she toyed with Frank...things about Gladys just fell into place and I learned that she is not a safe lady.

I know what you are thinking, *that may be a little too much Karee*, but I just knew that this was right. It was as if my eyes were truly opening and I was able to fit pieces of what I had experienced and seen first hand right into place. Gladys just **had** to be in control – that probably came from her childhood – the manipulation is a learned behavior, and she most likely mastered it at an early age, and because of her age now, she is unteachable to try to break the habit. I felt that she was not safe, that anything I did caused her to justify the way she treated me like shit. So I figured out her game, but now to find the motive...

The site advised finding the game and not giving in, but also not reacting to the manipulations. I think I failed, but she worked with me until I was downright angry and then she bailed, which left me angrier... which is what she wanted. The site said that people like this do that because they have been hurt. After learning all this, I felt more prepared to go forth and try to work things out – but I needed to be cautious.

Gladys had told me of her family life – both parents are deceased, and she is not close with her brothers. She had raised her younger brother since she was eleven and said that her parents used to yell hurtful things to her all the time. That's where the promiscuity had come in; by the age of fourteen, she needed to feel loved. I could relate. She recounted how one time her brother had beaten her until she passed out and she said ever since then she has held a spirit of murder.

"I used to fantasize about killing him or having him dead," she explained, "but then I gave my life to God and it went away." Well now I was having doubts about that. I have dealt with a lot of mean and crazy people in my young life, but if you could have seen the look in Gladys' eyes, you would have told me that her murderous spirit was still there. Joan often looked at me with distaste or anger, but somewhere down the line she did care once. The files from social services showed me that when we were seven and going into care, Joan and Daniel really did try to seek assistance. The anger and distaste in Joan's eyes were also directed at herself. The crazy look in Gladys' eyes reminded me of Bo in Portland when he was angry and on drugs. As far as I knew, Gladys was sober; she did not like alcohol in the house, a boundary I tested frequently.

I did not discuss with her any of these new findings because I knew that it would not do any good – and things like this are hard to hear, especially from someone you hate. I don't know if Gladys did hate me, but it sure felt like it at times and her actions sure declared it. Later on I ambled out of my room and joined her and her two year old nephew in the living room, putting some music on to dance with him. He had been coming outside the bedroom door asking for me, so I thought I'd play.

We danced and then watched a movie, and the little bugger was glued to my side. He is a little cutie, although I'd never admit it to Gladys. We went outside and played hockey and then Gladys asked if I would watch him while she went. I consented.

"Could you do me a favor?" I asked just before she left.

"Yes," she answered quickly because she still felt bad.

"Could you pick me up a scoop or two of almonds?" I ate them for calcium.

"Yes," she said immediately.

"Thank you," I said. She came back with them and said not to pay her back. She felt horrible and so I stayed pleasant until her nephew went home. When she got back, the guard was higher and she brought her laptop out into the living room. I brought up the fight we had a few days earlier, as this was the only time we had spoken since then.

"I'm sorry," Gladys said while she typed. I studied her carefully. She looked at me and said "when you said that about hollow lies I could hear the hurt in your voice, and everything I said could be said right back to me."

I paused carefully and asked "so why did you do it?"

"I don't know," she said; a cop-out. She professed all these terrible guilt and regrets and seeing the pain on my face crushed her, etc, but I could not believe her because this had become quite a constant thing.

She even said that she did not want me to leave and had looked in my room to see if I had started packing like Alana had.

I shook my head slightly and looked directly at her saying, "why do you treat me like this? You say I'm good friend, but I *never* treat my friends like that." I treat my friends like gold because that's what they are to me. Precious.

"Well I think it should be obvious," Gladys said, staring at the computer screen, "I don't consider you a friend, I consider you family." A bomb shell just fell on my head. She was not honest because she could not look at me. Earlier on, when I had first moved in just before Alana did, Gladys praised me one day, saying "you are such a good roommate and a very dedicated tenant…and a good friend." At that time she had looked right at me very openly and her tone and eyes said she meant it. Now, she was glued to her computer and she just threw it out there; her tone sounded flat and insincere. You do not lie about family to someone who does not have one. I felt that her saying this was unnecessary and mentally allowed her to justify how she treated me. "I know that everyone thinks Denise and I are so close, but ever since she turned her back on me that one time, she has not been in my heart, and she never will be. I know that you would die holding my hand before letting go." Sweet words but they felt ominous. I had a feeling she *wanted* me to hold on until I died, so I metaphorically dropped her hand at that point.

When I stayed silent, she glanced over and I peered into her eyes. No sincerity. Shoot; that is not what I had hoped for. I have decent discernment in reading people, I could tell when foster parents were lying, at my job I can tell when people give me false names and I can tell when friends are hurt and not wanting to show it. I am not blind.

Gladys followed up with a gift; a poster of guitar chords. I loved it, but I had to be careful because abusive people often do this. They abuse and then gift to bribe, then it sucks the victim in further and then becomes a pattern. I thanked her kindly and hung it in my room, but I did not let that action go into my heart, and I am so glad. Later on we were having a chat and I asked if she was okay.

"Yup," she said, her eyes scanning the screen as she typed away.

"Are you sure?" I asked out of concern.

She sighed heftily and said "I dunno."

"Well when your nephew was here and you said 'good job' to him, I couldn't hear any feeling, and I know that he usually gives you great joy," I said gently.

She looked at me and her eyes filled with tears – sincere or not, I still don't know – and said "I don't know why, but the last few times I've seen him and felt nothing. I feel nothing at all. And I don't know why I treat you like that, you are the only one I do that to, and I don't know why," she wiped away a tear and sniffled, looking at me.

I wanted to show the compassion I felt for her, but had to be careful. I did not know whether to believe her, but I do know that it is her choice to feel this way.

"The only time I have heard you say something you meant was when you were angry the other day," I said quietly. I did not say this to make her feel worse, but in hopes that she would see it and change somehow, or at least begin to…or at least **want** to. She just cried and whimpered about how she didn't know why and stuff.

After that I did pull away. I remained very general in conversations with her and very curt because I did not want to allow room for games to be played. She still talked to me, though, trying to pick my brain and still talking about Frank. He came to Portland for a dinner with her because they had to talk through some "issues," and he had told Gladys that she needed more stability. I used to ask her about how things were going with him, but she threw my own evasiveness back at me (to get me to want to know more), and I just let it go and let her come to me about it.

I sat clipping my toe nails on my bed and Gladys stood in the doorway talking about Frank. She shook her head knowingly and said "he has no idea, he just has no idea," as if he was out lunch!

"Maybe he thinks the same about you," I said as nicely as possible.

"Whatever, I can't talk about this with you," she said and flounced away. Huh. Okay. I went back to my nails and she came back and tried to explain that he was mixed up "you know how everyone is afraid of being alone," she said.

The question mark on my face said it all. "Okay, well most people have fears that they don't say, and for lots of people it is being alone or dying…what's your fear?" she asked; danger bay. Red flags went up, so I was general.

"I don't know, most of my fears have come true anyway, you know, trusting people with things and having them turn against you," I said honestly, just barely skirting her question. She took it in. That night I had a dream of her holding a knife in her hand, trying to stab me. I fought the knife away by grabbing her wrist and twisting the knife out, throwing it far away. Then Gladys came at me with a wheel chain saw, holding the handles – one on each side, and I couldn't fight so she cut open my chest with it.

When I mentioned this to Sandra and Chloe at church, they said "I think you need to get out of there," but for some reason I felt that I couldn't just get up and walk away; I had to stay to work this out. I thought it was God keeping me there for some reason – what a lie! Well Gladys did not come at me with a chain saw, and when I mentioned picturing her in mind with the knife, she said that was how she pictured me when I said "maybe he thinks that way about you," when she had recounted her dinner with Frank.

I realized that part of Gladys' game is camouflage and the other part is reciprocation. She will take what you do and turn it around to give back to you – I gave her tonnes of gifts for her birthday and asked her favorite kind of cake and then made that (which she hardly ate any, and I had to throw it out), and so for my birthday she did the same. Christmas was indeed great with Alana there, but I know that she played a huge roll in all the surprises – it was a three way street. I wonder if we had done nothing at all, if Gladys would have still made the effort.

Well life was busy and Gladys was succeeding at bringing me down. Lucky for me, I prayed and mentioned it to Uncle Tim in the Caribbean and he and Aunty prayed for me as well. I did not forget my many blessing in the past year, but counted them and was surprised to find yet more little blessings and surprises waiting for me. God is good at what He does…he has quite the sense of humor!

chapter 9:

With music in my brain all day, I dreamed about it – about playing guitar and singing in front of large crowds. I dreamed that I was in the Carrington high school, to sing on the stage there with lights, and in a practice, I saw Joan sitting with some young kid I didn't know. She tried to talk to me and I ignored her (which is what I would do today), and then I left the gym, trying to find some medicine to get better before singing. As I ran through the school halls, a teacher helped me find some medicine in her classroom and then I ventured to the kitchen (they used to make roast beef on a bun for our games – volley ball or hockey) for some food to enjoy. There was lots of chicken, but it wasn't quite ready to eat yet.

"That's okay," I said cheerily to a lady who apologized about the meat not ready, while breaking off a piece of unleavened bread. I asked if they needed help in the kitchen, but everything was under control. Afterwards, in the evening, I ignored Joan in the audience and sang my heart out under the bright blue and purple and white lights. Back in reality, I looked up what the dream meant in a dream interpretation book that Gladys kept on the shelf in the living room.

That book is based solely around scripture, so I kind of liked to use it, just to see what certain things meant. The bread meant spiritual food; the running in the hallways meant a journey; the singing and performing meant leadership or prophesying. It was cool but I'm not sure what the medicine meant, though. It was a dream about a journey to music. I decided to look up music events in San Frisco, and came across a little church that had music nights every Thursday night. Great!

My first night I just went to watch and it was a laid back atmosphere with a lot of people many years older than me. I did not mind, as these are the folks to give good input. Since it was my first visit, I did not have to pay the five dollar cover fee, and was greeted very warmly. The next week I brought my pal, the guitar, and we went onstage for a duo. I did not practice, as I was short of time (that's always my excuse).

When I first started singing, I heard someone say "oh, wow," and realized that people were actually listening. That kind of freaked me out, and I screwed up within a few short minutes. It sucked because I was so nervous and flustered, all alone up there with the guitar, and it seriously bothers my ear if I'm not on key, so when I first fell off it spurred more errors and I ended up walking off, shaking my head. The audience was kind about it, trying to get me to go up again, but I had had enough for the night.

The next week I practiced and then went up and sang. I was a bit earlier, so there were fewer people, and I dunno why, but I was on a roll. I sang six songs and could have kept going, but then the place filled up and people were itching to play. Each set is about fifteen to twenty minutes, so when I had sang three songs, I looked over at Edna (because she was next) and she said "keep playing." So I sang another song. At the end of that one, a man who used to be friends with Joe, the father of a friend named Dorothy whose family I used to live with, came and set up a bass, saying "keep playing," so I did. He was really nice, just like Joe was, and I hadn't seen him in years; I don't even know if he remembers who I am, but he is quiet; kind but quiet.

After the sixth song, my throat was getting dry, so I wandered to the back for some water and was sipping away, wondering where to sit when a woman breezed through the door and approached me.

"Hi, I'm Esther," she said, setting her guitar down and then extending her hand. Something in my head recognized her hair and her voice. I reacted before I thought.

"Esther who?" I asked quickly, doubting and surprising myself.

"Johnson," she answered with an easy smile. No way! My mind pieced together who this woman was before my brain had time to process it, but the dots were connecting! It couldn't be, could it?

I paused and then asked "do you know Joan?"

"Yes," she answered. Her voice sounded really laid back and low, "I used to baby sit for her a while ago," she continued, "why, do you know her?"

"I'm her daughter," I said, studying this woman under a new light. Is she the one who reported Joan and saved my life?!

"Really, which one?" she asked with a laugh. She had a good laugh.

"Karee," I answered, all of a sudden very shy.

"Are you one of the twins?" she asked. I nodded. She remembered. We chatted a bit and I told her that I acted for my job and she mentioned that she and her husband Wayne had come on my tour recently and enjoyed it immensely. They had not recognized me in the costume, and I had not recognized them.

"Did you remember me?" she asked sweetly.

"Well I remember your hair," I said with a grin, "and the tone of your voice."

She laughed a big laugh at that. Her voice kind of reminded me of the character Jesse off of *The Parent Trap*. "So are you musical?" she asked.

"Yeah, I just sang like six songs," I gestured to the stage.

"Now I want to hear you," she said with a smile. I smiled but didn't say anything. I ended up going with Esther on her set and singing *Knocking on Heaven's Door*. She liked the way I played it and people said that I have a nice voice. After the set, we sat for a little visit and Esther gave me her number and said to call "or I can be the first to call, whatever," she concluded with a kind and knowing little smile.

I did not know what to make of the situation, so I let myself mull it over for a few days. I told Helen and Chloe and they both agreed that she was in my life for healing. I tried calling the number but got the wrong place; I had dialed it wrong. I did not know until I looked at the paper she wrote on a few days later. One evening she called and we set up a meeting at her house (which was pretty close by) to "do some music."

I considered bailing out, but if I say I'll do something, I usually will, so I sucked up my pride and went. As I walked up to her house, I recalled walking there with Gladys a while ago and saying "I think a lady that used to baby sit us lived here," and pointing at the same house. Well as it turns out, she did live there and it was the right house! I also remember that it was almost hard to walk up the steps. I cannot describe how it felt; I wanted to go, but at the same time I held back and it was exciting, but at the same time I felt uncertain. I sucked in a lot of air and went up the stairs timidly.

I don't think I was nervous, but my heart was pounding. I reached out and rang the door bell; my hands were not shaking, so I was not scared. Boy, I was out of my element – it was kind of exciting, though. Esther opened the door and said "she came!" and greeted me cheerily. She was excited…which was good. I set the guitar down and she ushered me into the living room, saying "have a seat, do you want anything to drink?" I declined and she sat on the couch across from me with an excited grin. We spoke very generally at first, how our days were, and what kind of music we liked. I could tell she wanted to say something, but was debating, so I waited it out.

"So what do you do?" I asked, meaning work.

"Oh…anything that comes my way," she said with one of her bubbly laughs. I looked at her inquisitively and she went on "I do odd jobs, but my kids have families and they come over a lot, so I take care of them." I understood; a full house can be quite a handful at times. Her husband was at work with his window installation company.

She took a breath, hesitated, took a breath again and I waited. She was looking at me in a way that I did not understand – I knew she was excited, but there was something else there; like she *cared*. She took a breath and said "I wish I would have taken you in," and shook her head as tears filled her eyes, "it made me so angry to hear when you and your brother went into foster care," her voice was choking with emotion.

I did not know how to handle that. I didn't say anything – I'm sure my face looked shocked, but my guard also went up, so I sat still and waited. Seeing my face and the overwhelmed look in my eyes, Esther dried her tears and said "I probably shouldn't have said that," with a goofy little laugh.

"It's okay," I said with a gentle little shrug. I had heard people say things like that all the time – but it was always *shoulda, woulda, coulda… but didn't.* With Esther it felt different, though, because she really did care; she had carried this guilt for a great many years and she had no idea about my return for seven more years. It takes a lot to come out and be vulnerable like that. I did not respond to what she said because what do I say to that? "**I wish you would have**"? That would have made her feel worse, and she had obviously carried this guilt for twenty years. I just kept it and pondered it in my heart. So this was a resolution for her too, to meet me.

Her daughter, Alice came in and Esther introduced us. For some reason, we clicked instantly and then Esther asked if I would like to stay for supper. I hesitated and then said "sure," and visited with Alice. "Are you musical?" I asked her.

"Not really," she said. She picked up a guitar and I showed her a few chords. Then we went downstairs to visit her drum set. I played on them and then she did and I kind of coached her. Her drum teacher taught her how to read and hand positions for holding the sticks, but she had not played much in lessons; I had learned hands-on, so I can play. We had fun goofing off and doing music and I played guitar and sang while she played drums and then Esther came down and played guitar and sang while I played the drums. It was fun. Esther came downstairs with a camera and when I flipped the finger (a rudely natural instinct in front of the camera), she said "no flipping the bird!" which Alice and I laughed about later. Apparently Alice does not play music for other people so it was quite the achievement that she did it for me. Good, because music is fun.

Alice has a really good heart and quite the quirky sense of humor so in no time we chatted up a storm and found some things in common. Esther invited a few people over for supper, including her mom, Ruby, who is hilarious, and her brother, Mack (who is weird – he is the weird uncle of the family) and his son Shaun who is our age. Alice invited her good friend Samantha who lived down the street and then Wayne came home.

While I was helping to set the table, I paused and stared, seeing something in my mind's eye. "What are you thinking?" Esther asked.

My eyes narrowed as if zooming in on the image floating in my head. For years I have wondered at a memory of Ephraim standing in a door way – the door was brown and it opened into a bedroom. I remembered a long dinner table – much like the one I stood at now, but not quite as long – and having difficulty climbing onto the chair, because that's how small we were. I had asked grandpa Stardens about it many times, hoping he would remember something, but he has a good memory and that is not how his house on the farm looked.

"What about a piano?" I would ask.

"Nope, we didn't have a piano," he would answer every time. I was so bewildered by this memory, and right now I was standing in its midst in reality.

"Do you remember something?" Esther asked again, studying my face.

"Yeah," I said, "I remember standing here, and there was a piano here, and did that used to be a bedroom?" I asked, pointing at the door that was now white. "Did that door used to be brown, and that room used to be a bedroom? And the piano was a brown upright?" I asked, also pointing to where it used to stand in the living room.

Wayne nodded and said "yes it did; you have a very good memory."

"I remember sitting here and then Ephraim sat at the piano and I sat beside him later. I don't think the table was this long, though." Esther stood observing with this look in her eyes…I do not know what the look meant. I wonder what she was thinking. She was smiling a bit and her face seemed warm, but there was a look and I still don't know what it means when she gets it. Her eyes go almost…distant; perhaps she was walking down memory lane? I do not feel that it is a bad thing, but it definitely made me wonder. We had a *wonderful* chicken dinner and Esther had felt bad because the chicken was slightly burnt – but it was a healthy meal that I didn't have to cook. I liked it.

I visited with Alice and Samantha and Shaun, and observed everyone else. Esther was also taking the scene in and Mack was teasing his mother while the dog mooched for scraps. Some of his jokes were funny, but sometimes he just went too far. Later on, when we relaxed in the living room, he tried to have a battle of wits with me and lost. Then he and Shaun had to go do something, and he started searching for his car keys.

"Okay Karee," he said "where did you put them?"

At first I thought he was joking, so I said "who knows?" but then he wouldn't let it rest and everyone was searching, including me.

"Where did you hide them?" he asked again. I did not know how they would take it, but I insisted that I did not have the keys. I knew they were watching my reaction and my face, and was not sure if they believed me. I racked my brain trying to recall seeing the keys he described. Everyone was nice about it, but I did not want to admit to anything I didn't do. I searched the big recliner chair that he was in earlier and when he went to double check the chair, he found his keys.

"Oh, found them," he announced to the world, holding the keys up high, "Karee stuck them in the chair!"

"No, I didn't," I insisted with a slight smirk, trying to keep it light. I just didn't know if they would believe him or not.

When Alice and I were recounting the story at Samantha's house later that night, she laughed and said "you looked so guilty!"

"I know!" I laughed, "I didn't know if you guys would believe him."

"Oh no," Alice said, "Did I ever tell you how much he creeps me out?" when I shook my head, she said "I usually avoid him. He tells all kinds of stories so no one really believes anything he says. He probably had the keys the whole time." I felt better, then, and relaxed a bit more. Now I laugh at it because I was so shy and uncertain!

Shaun came over to Samantha's and the four of us joked and ate junk food while watching a "pro-life" movie. I learned that Samantha was off to Russia for two years with a youth with a mission type of group. "So you're a Christian?" I asked. She nodded and told me her story. As I listened, I saw the heart that she has for young teens and young adults, and I thought it was very neat to see someone so young with that kind of heart. We had a good time and soon it was late, and I had to work the next morning, so off I went. My head spun quickly because I could feel myself growing quite attached already – and I did not like that!

Alice and I hung out almost every day that she was in San Frisco; she about to go off to school some eight hours away for an English education degree. We had reading parties and avoided her creepy uncle and hung out with her cousin Shaun. We went to a barbecue to meet up with some of her friends and I met so many people – I think that was the first dry party I had ever been to, and it was alright. I only just barely knew Alice and Shaun, but they knew most of the people really well, and Samantha was there.

When Alice left for school, I promised to go to the pasta night to support Samantha's trip. Somehow the topic of Christmas came up between Alice and me, and I told her that the year before, I had been by myself, but that this year my roommates had done something for me. "Well, you won't be by yourself this year," she said in her goofy way, "you should come to my house, it'll be fun."

"Oh, I dunno," I hesitated, "Christmas is kind of hard for me." I get really bitter.

"We'll make it fun;" she offered again, "my family has people over all the time."

"Oh, I'll probably forget," I said dismissively. Or so I had thought.

"Well, I'll remind you!" Alice said in a way that made me laugh. "You should come for thanksgiving, too." I was just as hesitant about that too, because family celebrations are not my cup of tea! I can be rather cynical. Thanksgiving I was more open to, so I was apt to exchange it for Christmas. "Just come to both!" Alice said; what a generous little heart! She is hilarious; she makes me laugh so hard sometimes!

We exchanged our information and have stayed in contact since she had left for school. I got to know her grandma a bit because I had been to her house a few times, hanging out with Shaun who is two years younger than me. He lives with his grandma and his father is….not much of a father, so I thought Shaun could use a few pals. I invited him to my church and then attended the house church his aunty, Esther, pastored. Sitting in the house for church, I remember looking out the window while they sang worship songs (that I didn't know) and thinking *God is really pleased right now.*

Somehow the fact that it was a house church with a meal afterward and seeing them sing with heart and listening to them talk about God, this felt like it was more biblical. It was an interesting experience and I went a few times since, but I usually work Sundays. I was still trying to go to Prairie Winds in the evenings, but with all going on between Sally, Rachel and Gladys, my faith was slowly dwindling.

I invited Chloe to Samantha's pasta night and she came. As soon as we walked in and as I was teasing Shaun and Samantha, giving them a hard time at the ticket booth at the door, I saw none other than Pastor Harry himself.

"Hello," he greeted when I looked at him.

"Hello," I said politely. The memories of when I ran away came flooding back.

"How are you?" he asked out of courtesy.

"Fine, how are you?" I countered automatically.

"Good, good," he nodded with a strange little smile. It was weird – and so awkward talking to him!

"Are you…here for some pasta?" I asked, pointing at the ticket table.

"That's good," he said…okay. Maybe he thought I said that I was here for some pasta. Whatever, this was still strange and uncomfortable, so I nudged Chloe and we went inside. I explained that he is friends with Joan and she understood right away. We were wandering to the back room where the guests were eating and just about as we were to enter the big room, a nice old gentleman reached out to me.

"Excuse me," he said politely, "are you Joan's daughter?" I stopped in surprise. You have **got** to be kidding!

"Is your name Karee?" the woman standing beside him interjected. I studied them quickly; clean-cut, kindly appearances, about the same age as Noella and Drew.

"Yes it is," I admitted reluctantly.

"Oh, we used to baby sit you when you were just a baby – you and your twin brother!" the woman exclaimed pleasantly. For real? Chloe was quietly observing things and I was feeling the shock. They went on about how cute we were and that they had some pictures and they knew Joan and Daniel. I was kind to them, as they were excited.

"You've got a good memory!" I commented with a nice smile. They let us go, as more guests came and they were the greeters.

"Do you know them?" Chloe asked in her quiet way.

"I don't remember them," I answered with bewilderment.

"They seemed nice," she said ever so positively.

"They did," I agreed, "let's go get some grub!" We picked a place to sit and joined the line to serve ourselves some pasta. As we were going to do so, the couple reached out and said "hey, do you remember Pastor Harry?" I looked over at him. Of course I did.

"Yeah, we met just outside the door," the pastor interjected with renewed enthusiasm. "I've seen you around, but I never said hello because I wasn't quite sure if it was exactly you," he said. What a choice of words! The wit that I use for my acting job kicked in as I replied with "well, it's a good thing you checked because there is another person about eighty seven point nine three percent me running around." The couple laughed, the man really enjoyed the joke – good, and Chloe laughed a bit and pastor Harry smiled abashedly. We went on our way to the pasta buffet.

As we were in line dishing up, the older couple told Pastor Harry that they used to baby sit Ephraim and me before he came to pastor the church. "Yes, her mother was in town the other day," I overheard Pastor Harry say, "I just saw her, she had stopped by." All of a sudden, I froze. The back of my neck tingled and my appetite plummeted through the floor. I stopped and just stared at the pasta, my mind whirling a thousand miles at once.

"What?" Chloe asked, noticing the reaction, "what's wrong?"

"Shit," I said quietly, forcing myself to dish up a healthy serving, "he's still friends with Joan. I worked so hard to get her out of my life!" Chloe went quiet until we sat down at our table, I almost felt like the hard work to get better had failed. She was never going to be fully out of my life, was she? Chloe did not know what to say, so she changed the topic and I went with it. The food was great and within minutes our table was full – and I knew most of the people from the barbecue that Alice and I went to a while back. We laughed a lot and I felt my despair melt away and my appetite returned.

There was a lot of goofing off and seeing how much one could eat and laughing and meeting and greeting. Samantha was all over the place – bouncing from table to table, helping serve, thanking people for their support, etc.; it was fun. The night was busy as we ate and joked and I met some of Samantha's friends from the barbecue – Rita and Shaun and a few others.

Even though it was a good time, my mind was a little preoccupied. I could not help but wonder what was going on, because it seemed like people from my past were bouncing into the present – my kindergarten teacher saw me and recognized me in a grocery store, the lady who lived down the street from Joan (I used to run errands to her house all the time) came on my tour at work, my grade six teacher and grade two teacher saw me at local stores…what was going on?! It was overwhelming!

During the summer time at work because the schedule is a lot more hectic at work because of tourists, the lunch hour gets a little bit longer and as long as it is nice out I am sure to be found outside. I had wandered into a random store because I wanted to see a store I had never been in before. The girl working at the counter was polite and asked a few questions here and there. We got talking and I discovered that she had indeed sang a song called "Run to the Cross" at church when I was about nine or ten years old! I even remembered her name and she said she had been off to do music since then. It was neat and I am sure she felt exactly how I felt with all these other people remembering me.

Another time I was out shopping with Noella and we saw Dorothy. I did not like the looks of her, and did not want her back in my life in any way, so we looked around the store and then left without buying anything. Even old friends from elementary were popping up! I just stayed positive and did not dwell on things. I kept going to the music nights and at first it was hard because I could not focus and that is hard to do with lack of practice. I got so upset when I was off key that I just walked off, even if it was one note off. I know it is not a big deal, but I think I make high demands.

One music night Esther and I were talking and sipping tea when she suddenly said that she knew life was hard and that it wasn't fair…but that it would get better someday. I wanted to believe her. "Did you know that Joan was treating me like that?" I asked openly. That question had never rung around before; I had just asked it spur of the moment.

Esther paused, looked away and said a slow "yes."

"Did you try to stop it?" I asked, suddenly feeling very small and childlike.

"No," she answered honestly. Her face fell when she answered and I could see that it bothered her so, but I still could not fathom it. I sat back and looked away, sadness creeping into my soul and wanting to pour out of my eyes.

"But I had my own issues," Esther explained, "I had just gotten married and that was traumatic for me," she laughed, "Wayne probably wouldn't like me saying that."

"Why was it traumatic?" I asked, looking over at her steadily.

She looked away, but I could still see her eyes. They were nice blue with long black eye lashes. "Well because of my dad. My dad was great, but when mom remarried, there was a lot of fighting and I just couldn't handle it." She looked at me and continued with "I wanted to find someone like my dad, and I did." She was happy. "I had a lot on my plate as it was, but then I had twins and a young baby too, right off the bat after I married I was pregnant with my twins." All five of her kids are very close in age, so I can only imagine how crazy it must have been. My heart did soften a little bit – not because of her story, but because of her honesty and the trouble it caused her to turn away.

"I could tell that Joan needed help," she said, her voice getting tense with emotion, "things will get better," she insisted. *When?* I wanted to ask her how she knew that everything was going to be okay, but I knew that Wayne had stuck beside her – they are very close; a rarity today. That is something I am searching for in a man…and it is also something I am thinking I will never find these days.

Well this was going on along mixed in with Gladys' freak out shows and Rachel's creepiness, and work was busy and there were tour buses packed with people coming in, as well as I had just read the files from social services, so I was overwhelmed and angry. The hurt just burns – as it does now (but not so severely) – and then I understood why they call it heartache; because your heart actually hurts. I listened to a radio show that said heartache is a real pain – they did an experiment on it and when a person going through something painful like a divorce was tested, they showed similar symptoms to having heart burn or a heart attack. Well who are *"they"* anyway?

I feel like I was driven to God at that point, because most people didn't understand and did not know how to help me figure this out. When I told Gladys about Rachel (before she freaked out so hugely), she had said "you have to realize that you are not a hero; you can't save everyone." And she was right, but it seemed like people were always coming to me, asking me to help them.

"What about if I need help," I had had cried out in despair, "Why must I be driven to this point, that I have to ask for it?"

"Because you don't let anyone help you," she said. Wrong. All a person has to do is care and *show it*. Not just like me when I bring them treats when they are sad, not just appreciate me when I do things for them – I just want someone to care and I am thinking that it is getting harder and harder to find. Her answer was a cop-out...or so I thought.

When I spoke to Noella, she was empathetic and listened with a good ear, but she always said "you're strong, you'll get through it, you'll be fine," but it felt as if it were in passing. *I'm not invincible,* I felt like saying; **don't just assume that I'll be okay.** Drew was sympathetic and encouraging. He actually told me how he stood up in church and confessed about his swearing because he sings on the worship team and realized it was wrong to praise God with the same lips that he profaned from.

"I'm so proud of you!" I said. I was – he had changed so much in the past few years, and for him to do this *of his own accord* was amazing! I needed some help to get me through these tough situations, so I dragged my feet right back to the church. I lifted Gladys up for prayer and just said that she was causing me a lot of grief.

"You are being tested, sister," the pastor Russell said with a knowing little smile. Oh, I knew it. Part of the service was going into little groups and talking about things – so "God is…" and we could fill the blanks, or talking about prayer needs or about church. When I got to the church group, I shared that I had not had good experiences in churches; that

147

I had been hurt and looked down upon by Christian people and that Gladys was a Christian as well. I was starting to dislike the word, and disassociated myself with it.

They said that she probably did not have the Lord in her heart as she was saying that God brought the sin in her life to teach her. "I think that God allowed me to sleep with Frank so that I could see that this *giant* I made out of sex is just sleeping," she had said. Sure it might sound good – but she is lying about God. God does not need to allow promiscuity to show someone that. It seemed like Gladys was proud of her promiscuity, whereas I am ashamed of mine. She told herself that to justify the actions to herself, hoping that I would agree. My church suggested that I should get out of her house immediately. At the end of the service, a young man (who spoke and led worship sometimes) offered to pray for me.

"Is there anything specific?" he asked.

"Healing," I answered. He could see the pain on my face.

"Are there any names you can give?" he asked when I was evasive again.

"Joan, Daniel, Susie, Jocelyn, Gladys, and a pastor that could have helped but didn't," I said angrily biting my lip and looking at the floor. When I looked at this man, he looked in my eyes and started to weep! He prayed God's protection and I left abruptly, unable to do this anymore. Thankfully when I got back, Gladys was out. I went into my room and cried out to God. **Why?** I demanded **you could have stopped this from happening! Why didn't you?!** I was so angry and hurt and disappointed because I had really thought I had moved on – and in many ways I have.

I moved on in the fact that I did not need Joan in my life; in the fact that I no longer blamed myself; in the fact that I was not angry with Joan and the people I listed, but at their actions toward me because I was INNOCENT!! I had not done anything to them to warrant that kind of treatment. I could feel my heart becoming hard and it showed in the next song I recorded in the studio.

It is called *Leave Me Alone* and is directed to various people in my life – Joan, foster parents, false friends, boyfriends, classmates, Gladys… well, it's posted on the infamous youtube, anyway. When I finished recording it, I played it for Gladys. These times were **so** hard because I was dealing with a lot of things that I had never faced before all at once. I did not know how to handle someone who chose to stay in dark places, or someone who was to afraid to try to live, or someone who lied so much. I did not know how to handle the many people coming up to *me* and recognizing me from twenty years ago, wanting to, but choosing to not help. They are people who turned a blind eye. I did not know how to face the truths I learned from the files.

Through it all – the angry words at God, the wrestling at night, the dreams and the angst, I suddenly and abruptly realized that God was the **only one** who worked to stop the bad things from happening. My grandpa praying in the Caribbean – a 24 hr flight away, my prayers when I was young…He was the only one who worked to stop it all. The downfall is that He gave people free will, so if people choose to do terrible things to other people then God has to live with it too, but He can protect and deliver and present hope. I told Chloe, I told Helen, I told Noella and Drew and Ephraim…what a great revelation!

I turned from anger to gratitude when it came to God. All of a sudden, through my grandpa's prayers, I could see the hand of God in my life. Grandpa's prayers mingled with my tears are the reason why I am okay (for the most part) today. They are the reason why I have kept a job that I love for a couple years, I am on my own and doing alright, slowly paying off student loans, I have a nice car and people who care. Talk about being put in your place! God slapped my head around and I liked it because it renewed my fire.

Gladys was searching for another roommate and soon Drew's niece Gina checked the place out. I had hung out with her a few times before and she was pretty cool! She was the first of the Fairmonts to not judge me – it took a long time, but the other Fairmont's have finally accepted me now, for the most part; and I accept them now too. When Gina came, we were friendly right away. She left saying she had to think about it.

"She's not going to take the place," Gladys said knowingly.

"I think she will," I said staying positive, "power of the spoken word." A few days later, Gina agreed to move in at the end of the month. I looked at Gladys when she told me, beamed and said "hate to say it but I told you so," I sang out the last words.

Gladys got up from the kitchen chair and said "you were right about the power of the spoken word, so I broke the curse of what I said in Jesus' name. It's gonna be weird to have someone else living in the house!"

"I think it'll be good," *actually I think it'll be great*, it'll pry Gladys' negative attention away from me…or so I had thought. Gina had moved in while I was at work and her family was there to greet me. I knocked at her bedroom door and visited with her for a bit to show her that she was welcome. I almost wanted to give Gladys my notice on the spot, now that Gina was in because then Gladys wouldn't be short of money, but I refrained because Drew informed me that Gina had moved in because I was there.

When thanksgiving lumbered around, Alice was true to her word and texted me up. Next thing I knew, I found myself sitting at their big family table for dinner at Ruby's house. I had expressed some concern about it to Shaun when we were talking one day, and he said I should try it. I *wanted* to be a part of this family for some strange reason, and I did not like it! I was so concerned that I spoke to Jade about it. Jade lives twenty minutes away and is one of few people whose opinions I really value.

I used to like her son, who is a year older than me, but then I learned a little bit about him and certain things just didn't sit right with me. An example would be going to church because I am there. I do not want to be the reason for a person to attend church – if a person questions their faith and I invite them, or they go because they know I'm there and they don't know anyone else, fine. But when you go to the church because I am there and that is it, it kind of scares me because the bible says "I will cast down your idols before you," and if I become an idol then I will be cast down. Well, this is what I thought at the time, so I let it scare me off. Looking at it now, I see how it is an overreaction; so what if he is coming to church because of me? But I had too much on my plate and was really hurting and quite thrown off by it, so a boy was not something I was looking for.

Well anyway, Jade and I met for coffee and I expressed the woes of going to the Johnson's house for thanksgiving dinner. I confided about my bitterness and that I did not know how to feel about certain things that Esther had said.

"It seems like God is trying to show you that there were people who cared, like they wanted to help but couldn't, that's probably how He felt," she related, "I think you should just take a chance and go." *Okay, I thought, I could take a chance; I'm good at taking chances.* Not much to lose at this point anyway.

"You have a lot of hurt," Jade observed, "and you need to let it go or it can haunt you for the rest of your life." I went quiet then, because her pain was so raw and this was true advice… "Like it does to me," she continued her voice a bit higher now because she was crying. She looked me directly in the eyes so I could see her pain and know that it was real. I told her about possibly meeting with Sandra from church because three people had given me her name on different accounts and those people don't even know each other. Jade said she might follow suit to help sort some of her own troubles out.

I was glad to have gone for coffee with Jade because it made me respect her even more. I look up to her because she comes from a dark background and is doing good things about it, by helping people that are in similar situations get out. I admire that. I prayed and hummed and hawed over thanksgiving, and then just went.

It was so good to see Alice and she had been after me to meet her sister Megan because she is a musician as well, so I finally met her. One thing about that family is they are soooo accepting. I felt no dissonances or tensions when I was there. Wayne sat by me and his son, Larry, and Alice sat on my other side, and at times I was quiet, but the oldest sons, Lyle and Larry remembered me from when I was young.

"Do you remember Karee?" Esther had asked, standing behind my chair and putting her hands on my shoulders. "Ephraim's twin," she continued cheerfully.

I watched her son's face twist with concentration. All of a sudden his eyes got big and he said "no way!" a few times. I am quite used to that reaction by now, so I just watched with mild amusement. "Yeah, you're Ephraim's twin, right?" he asked.

I nodded and asked "what's with the reaction?" making a joke out of it.

"It's not at you, it's at *him!*" Larry exclaimed and dramatically shared the story of how when he babysat us, he tried to get us to put on our boots to go outside in the snow. Not wanting to go outside, Ephraim called the cops on him! I loved it! I laughed and said "for once I'm not the bad twin!" Ephraim was quite the child when he was young.

"Yeah, who has the police number memorized," Larry continued. Well we chatted about memories for a while and then everyone dug in; the meal was fantastic! You know a meal is great when a table of about twenty falls absolutely silent. The sounds of forks scraping plates, knives cutting meat, people chewing and sipping drinks was all to be heard for a while. There were homemade perogies, turkey, ham, potatoes, veggies, sweet potatoes, cabbage rolls, jello, ambrosia salad, and for desert many pies – pumpkin, lemon meringue, apple, peach…all homemade. What a meal!

Looking around, I couldn't help but feel a twang of pain. Esther's words floated around… "*I wish I would have taken you in!*" with the echo of me "**did you try to stop it?**" followed by her saying "*no.*" These words toyed with me, circling around and around, daring the tears to come out. Looking around, seeing the family resemblance between all five kids and the loving parents, seeing the nieces and nephews running around, hearing their interactions, I could not help but to feel cheated.

Esther's words hurt a little more because now it felt like I was always seeing what I could have had. I have always longed to be a part of a big family. I could have grown up with one; I could have grown up with music and encouragement and love and faith. I could have grown up in safety; I could have grown up with gold, but because of that one split second decision to turn away, a life was ruined. I am not pinning the blame on Esther for I am not angry with her personally, but I do not *comprehend* how things like that can happen. That split decision to walk away cost me twenty one years.

She could have helped in other ways than taking me in as her own child. It just feels as though my eyes were opened to more abandonment is all.

She said that social services had been vicious at the time, but they had probably saved my life. I have put myself out of my comfort zone and right in danger to help someone, so maybe that's why I don't understand.

I have no choice but to let it go because dwelling on it does not go anywhere, and I had realized that shortly after the thanksgiving meal. I was grateful to be there, as years before I had not really celebrated it, so now I knew that it was about giving thanks. Counting your blessings is hard to do.

I decided that Noella and Drew are my parents and I had given them the starting papers for legal adoption before leaving for the Caribbean with Ephraim almost a year ago, but then I struggled with that too, because I don't even know any of their kids. I am not close with them, and I had to know who I was calling my family. Drew understood and Noella thought I was being judgmental, but I was only going according to my own personal experiences with her kids. The last experience of hanging out with some of her kids was very crude and I was ashamed to have been in public with them. What else did I have to go by? Noella came to understand that her kids do *not* need to change for me to call them family; I just need to know *who they are* before deciding whether or not to call them family – and right now I cannot just call a bunch of strangers my brothers and sisters. For me family is important, so if I am going to call someone family, they will be of great importance to me – it is not something I take lightly. Like the word love; I don't just throw it around.

I need an example of a family to look to – Noella and Drew are divorced and remarried to each other and their kids have their own lives, so I cannot look to them in this one aspect. I have decided to observe the Johnsons because as a family they are strong – the parents are strong in their marriage and loyalties to one another and the kids are strong in their respect and loyalties to their parents. Of course every family has issues, but this one is also strong in their faith. I want that for my family if I ever have one.

After the turkey dinner, we did many things – played games, nibbled on food here and there, said good bye to some leavers, played with the kids, watched movies, read books; it was fun to just have a day to hang out like that. I hung out a lot with Alice's sister, Norah, the eldest one, and ended up laughing a *lot*! We played games and visited and then went for walks. Seeing the familial bickering was a bit awkward because I did not know where to stand in it, so I mostly ignored it, or teased them, saying "now, now…" or "hey now." But that day I realized, *this is what families do* and for a little I longed to be in the Caribbean again because I had that same sensation there, except that I was part of the family there because they **are** my family. I yearned for it to happen again.

Norah also invited me over for Christmas and I quickly declined. Alice would not take no for an answer, insisting that the whole thing had started over Christmas.

"It did?" I asked, thinking she was joking. I had forgotten all about that!

"Yes, and besides," Alice continued as we strolled along, "I already told mom you were coming." What, really? I was surprised. I got along with everyone well enough, but this was thanksgiving. Christmas would be just too hard, but I didn't dwell on it – Christmas was a ways away yet, so time would sort that out. We had supper in between Esther and Ruby's house – the large family group was split between the two places – which were only a few houses down from each other.

Norah and I joked around as we did the dishes and teased Ruby and Esther. In the evening we went for a walk, us four older girls and the clean air wisped on my face. The stars twinkled in the velvet sky and the wind had a chilly bite, but the night was quiet, shading everything to darker hues. The stars played hide and seek among the feathery clouds and the clean, crisp air was refreshing. The street lamps shone down, little spotlights on our paths and we ran, shuffled, walked very goofily and teased each other. When the tips of our noses were cold, we went into Esther's house and all of us "big kids" (who are all adults) gathered to play a game of some sort. It was almost abnormal for me to experience what families do…still is today.

While Norah searched for a game, the rest of us piled into the living room, squishing onto the couches and talked about everything and nothing all at once. I mentioned going in for pharmacy to Lyle and Larry had lots to say about that – good stuff, of course! We ended up talking all night and Larry's wife, Reba, said she could tell that I would be a good music teacher because of my personality. At dinner I did not get very much interactions from her, so her encouragement was surprising. She was really nice and had a lot of friendly words. She said she came from a hard life too and could tell that I did and she is a photographer so we chatted a bit about that. Esther came home and then went to bed and Wayne stayed up for a short while with us, eventually falling asleep on the couch. There's one man who doesn't snore.

Shaun had disappeared during the day, fixing the roof of Ruby's house with some uncles, so when he finally showed up we had a brief greeting about how our days went. "It wasn't as scary as I thought!" I exclaimed happily.

"Good, so are you glad you came?" he inquired.

"Yes," I answered sincerely, "but I gotta go now." It was getting late and my eyes were starting to droop, so I was anxious to get to bed and to lay out the events of the day in my mind. I am glad that I took Jade's advice and went despite by qualms about it.

All in all, God had thrown me for a loop and life was getting hard, as I was faced with many things I never had to deal with before, kind of all thrown in at once. I did (and do) count my many blessings along with God's hand working in my life; it is the one pearl among the rubbish. I am lucky that God chooses to be on my side and this year has taught me the value and extremity of free will and how much it can affect other lives.

chapter 10:

Things at the homestead got better when Gina moved in; Gladys wanted to invite her pals over for a party for Gina's birthday. She tried to include me in it, but I just waved it away. I thought if we were to throw a party for Gina, then *her* friends should be the ones coming over and from the looks of it Gina already had different preferences.

"I have a little present for you," I said to Gina a little later, when Gladys was gone, "I didn't have time to wrap it up." I took a little candle set – one was a flower and two were leaves – and gave them to her.

"Aw, thanks," she said, cupping them in her hands and beaming. She looked so happy about such a small thing! Well I know she likes candles so it went over well. I planned a trip to visit Alice, we had planned it since thanks giving and I chose to invite Ephraim along. He hummed and hawed and then said yes.

"Are you sure?" I prodded. He has a terrible habit of bailing out at the last minute.

"Yes," he insisted.

"Are you *sure*?" I pried again, "because I am booking these days off work."

"Yes," he resolved, "the only way I won't go is if I die!" I laughed and all plans were set in motion. "Do we want to see Joan and Daniel?" he asked.

"No," I said firmly.

"Okay, well how about if we just hang out with Susie and Jocelyn," he suggested. I agreed reluctantly, as long as it was short. We had visited with just the two girls before and it wasn't too bad. I had thought that I was probably the most creative of the immediate family, because I write and draw and design clothes and act and sing and play instruments, but looking at some of her art recently, I see that Jocelyn is the true artist. Jocelyn was really becoming more positive and more confident in both her art and also as a person – I thought it was great to see. She is a great artist actually – she can draw anything, paint anything, color anything, but anime is maybe her favorite. She also writes poetry and designs clothes and had asked me to model some in the future when my hair was long again. I answered Ephraim's question with a "maybe."

Sue also draws often and is now getting into detailed art – she is quite good. She also claims to be musical, but I have yet to hear her play or sing, but I believe she has some musicality of sorts. I think she is the most like Ephraim and Jocelyn is the most like Jonas, leaving me the odd one out (but I'm alright with that). After all, they all have blue eyes – I'm the only one with green.

We had started the day off at a car show but as soon as I realized that they were repeating the cars, I got bored quite rapidly and wandered off on my own. Finding a book store, I popped in and was soon absorbed into the pages of a book by Denise Jackson (I forget the title). She is married to country superstar Alan Jackson and it was her perspective on things as well as their growth in faith; a remarkable book.

Anyway, they found me soon enough and we all went for a walk. It had been a nice summer day out and the leaves shone bright shades of green and rustled while the gentle wind hummed through them. Coming to a stop light, Ephraim and I did what small town folks do – looked and seeing no cars, walked across the street.

"You guys, the light is red," Jocelyn said, holding her boyfriend's hand.

"What are you guys doing?" Susie screeched in alarm as we kept walking. I said "crossing the street" and Ephraim said "are you guys coming?" they didn't and it was the longest light in history! No cars were in sight, so Ephraim and I teased them by making a big show of stretching, yawning and checking our wrists for the time. They did not budge until the light changed – it was hilarious. Well Jocelyn soon ran off with her boyfriend and Susie suggested going to their house; an idea Ephraim and I declined.

Later on, we had ventured to a little bar with Susie and met some of her friends – it was a good time. She still carries guilt about being a "favorite child," but I have no resentments toward her and neither does Ephraim – actually he is more open and receptive to the family than I am, but he has had seven years less abuse from them, too.

Susie was drinking on an empty stomach, so she started talking and getting sentimental. "I'm so glad you're here," she said, "we are still family." I usually pull out the silent card when we see the Stardens; quite different from myself around my brothers or close friends. I stayed quiet for most of this trip and was not about to start talking now, so I looked for Ephraim for he had disappeared during the pool game. He came back from the washroom to where we stood in the doorway when suddenly a fellow kept going back and forth between us. We moved for him each time, minding our own business.

"Yeah, I know, I must be so annoying right?" he said sarcastically.

"Well now you are," I shot back and he went away. Susie laughed and said it was a good one. I attributed it to my job with a grin. They began talking about a "family" business – Ephraim would doctor or give medicine and Susie would counsel the patients and I would…play the music. Ephraim said that if he would hire anyone he would hire me because when I walk into a room people just notice me. I never noticed that before, but it probably comes from being a performer. Ephraim and Susie talked about girls because she had decided to be gay a few years ago, and I was far out of that loop, but they were bonding and it was interesting to listen to anyway. Susie really seems to want to know Ephraim and I think it might be good for her.

As the night drew nigh, Ephraim was ready to tuck in, but I was having a decent time observing things. It seems our little sister would like us to be a family but the poor girl doesn't realize the efforts that would need to be made – on *all* our parts. It is always Ephraim and me driving out to see them or making the arrangements. I had long since grown weary of walking this one way street. Susie had mentioned earlier that she knew that Joan didn't treat me right. I had begun to tell her to not apologize for Joan's mistakes, but when I said Joan, Susie's eyes held a question mark. "I don't know what to call her," I stated honestly.

"Just call her mom," Susie had said. "I know she wasn't and all that, but you should just call her mom." I went silent, but skepticism was on my face. *No way,* I thought, *she does not deserve that from me.* To me the term "mom" is one of love and affection for a motherly type of figure. That person in my life is Noella. Not and never again Joan. Well Susie tried to persuade me to hang out with her for the night, but I declined because if Ephraim left then my quiet demeanor would no longer suffice.

That's right; I let Ephraim do all the talking because he uses more tact. Plus Susie promised that Joan would give me a ride back to the hotel since she used to work there anyway, but I just did not want to see that lady. All in all, that trip was decent – not a favorite time, but not the worst either. I think Susie has a good heart but not enough to reach out when we are about seven hours away; she never sends emails or chats with me, so it is moot.

Well this one trip I had planned to get four nice days away from Gladys, but because Ephraim was coming I lost two days. We agreed to split the costs of going and to take his car for the better mileage. He called on Friday (we were to come back on Sunday), and said he got into an accident and we could not use his car because he had nicked the front bumper. He said it was pretty bad, but dust on the car is pretty bad to him. I agreed to take my car and to pay the whole amount of the trip – it was costing me a lot all of a sudden, but I felt kind of manipulated into it. He dawdled and did not get to San Frisco until five thirty, so I cancelled the trip because it was not worth the expense to drive for sixteen hours (there and back) for one day's visit.

"Well let's still go," he wheedled. Yeah, right! I was ticked off! If I had known this would have happened, I would have left when I wanted to, three days ago! I told him off and he did not apologize because he did not think he was in the wrong; whatever.

"There's nothing I can do to make it better," he had said. Bullshit, he could apologize, but I should not have to ask for that, so I just let him go and hung out with Shaun and Ruby at their house. I had just wanted to get away from Gladys for a while, but even that seemed too much to ask. When I spoke to Alice about it on the phone she said what no one wants to hear in moments like that "maybe it is all happening for a reason, maybe God wants you to stay there for a reason." Cliché, cliché, cliché...

"For what?" I cried out angrily, but maybe something would have happened on the roads or who knows...maybe if I would have seen Joan I would have punched her. That is how I felt after reading those files. I had no choice but to let it go, so I did. This experience also helped me realize that having spats with Ephraim, being frustrated by him is actually quite normal. I never grew up in a normal home setting, so there is much for me to learn, like what is personal and what isn't. Well Gladys was up to her old tricks of favoring Gina, and shafting me. I was trying to deal with that, too, but it was so constant. It really felt like Samson in the bible where Delilah nagged him to death. The story is about a man who had long hair that gave him superb strength and he was instructed by the Lord to not tell anyone where his strength came from.

This lovely lady named Delilah had been with him for a while and was always questioning where his strength came from. Every time he said something like "tie my hands behind my back," he would wake up and her attempts were futile, but he never seemed to catch on that she was trying to destroy him. See, Samson was a judge for the Israelites for about twenty years and was rather harsh to the opposing Philistines, so they wanted to knock him down. They paid Delilah to find the secret to his strength and she was so persistent that in the end Samson told her it was in his hair and he woke up very weak because she had his long hair shaved off.

The Philistines captured him and humiliated him, but when his strength came back (when his hair began to grow again); Samson destroyed thousands of Philistines by pushing against the two posts that supported a great temple. He killed thousands and probably saved Israel from another attack by doing so, although he ended up dying as well. The story is recorded in Judges Chapter sixteen. For a strong guy, Samson seemed kind of dumb when it came to Delilah.

I felt that Gladys was persistent in the way of Delilah – and up to no good. It is peculiar how Samson never caught on to Delilah's tricks, perhaps because he loved her so. Well I did not love Gladys, so perhaps a bit too late, I caught onto her ways. One day I was very chipper and had burst out the back door on a beautiful fall day singing "good morning, good *morning*, it's great to stay up late…" and the lines from that song (from *Singing in the Rain*) and, still in my pajamas, I began to walk outside to check the mail before work. When I had opened the door, I had flourished my arms out and up dramatically, while belting the song loudly.

I did not know that the neighbors were out on their lawn until I saw them looking at me like I was weird. "Good morning to you…" I sang to them, pointing at them. Then I turned around and went inside, blushing – so embarrassing! Good thing I know how to laugh at myself, and it was hilarious, of course the very few people I told about that - all laughed at me, but in good fun. I like when things like that happen – harmless but humiliating at the same time and sometimes goofy things like that just happen!

When I told Gladys that she said "I know, I could hear you singing, it woke me up." It was nearly eleven, so she shouldn't have been sleeping anyway. She asked me to stop singing in the house in the mornings – which I did every single day and loved every single minute of it – because it woke her up. I was disappointed, but considerate, so I stopped the joyful singing.

"Gina doesn't mind if I sing – I asked her," I pointed out sadly. Well soon Gladys had it so that I could not sing at all if she was around – if I sang in my room, she blasted the TV, saying she needed to turn it up that loud to hear it. So when she was around I played keyboard with the headphones in and plucked the guitar without a pick. Let me tell you something, no one can squash the music in me – if God put it in there, it will be more resilient than Gladys – it's more resilient than I am! I have tried to quit so many times, but it bubbles up inside and keeps pushing opportunities at me. It comes out of my ears!

I used to think that because of the events of my life, maybe music is **not** meant to be, but lately I have been thinking that perhaps music is my destiny – *despite* the things that happened. Maybe I **was** meant to do music because of the songs that I write and the instruments I play and the sounds I hear – all without training. I don't know, but these days if I can't express musically somehow, I feel anxious or desperate…

So I sang in the car, driving around for a half hour before work, and it felt *so good!* It was a huge outlet and I found myself thanking God every time I sang, even if it sounded horrible, because I was just *so* glad to do it! I had to stop going to the music nights because of complete lack of practice – Gladys took two weeks holidays twice almost back to back and stayed in the house for the entire two weeks, and I didn't have anywhere else to go for practice.

When Travis came over I was frosty to him, but warmed up when we talked of music – I was told that he was a musician, so he played a song for me that he recorded. It was alright – kind of generic, but simple can be better sometimes.

"Now you play a song," he said. I did and he said it was better than he thought it would be – everyone says that. We switched off a couple more songs and then I played *Leave Me Alone* and told him that I wrote it about Gladys. He said he didn't understand why she wanted to marry a man that she didn't want to be with anyway, meaning Frank, and I agreed. Travis had had long chats with Gladys about him a few weeks back, because Gladys was going to **everyone** (including me) for advice, or so she said.

I had been in the kitchen cooking when Gladys spoke to Travis on Skype, so I could hear every word they said and she knew it and was fine with it. He spoke of his marriage and how with his wife what they actually want to do when they are alone is talk because if you don't have that communication it is easy to drift away. He was being sincere and for the first time I felt myself respecting him, but Gladys was just saying "uhuh" at the odd times and not even listening because she was chatting to more guys online! It seemed incredibly rude since she was the one approaching everyone.

I don't know if she is as close with him as she proclaims because she had this nasty habit of whining to me about how he constantly made her feel like shit for everything. She would tell me that he made her cry in the car or that he called her terrible names, but some of these actions seemed out of character, even for him, and some of these things, I felt, were exaggerated because Gladys is kind of a wimp. Gladys had said that when she had invited Frank over Travis had called her a "condemning bitch," but again, I don't think it was entirely true. She said he would only do certain things when it was just the two of them, and while that may be true of him I thought it also true of her. Did he know she was going around saying things like this to people? Travis can be annoying and if he is honest he can be harsh, but I don't think he is overly cruel.

The fact that Gladys acted one way around him when I was there and another when I wasn't said something about dishonesty. I felt that she was trying to turn me against him, but I just played a mutual card because I didn't know him too well. I know that Gladys and this young man had…relations years before he married, but I know that he is loyal to his wife and rightfully so because she is a sweetheart, but Gladys was holding on to him even though he is in early thirties and she is in her late forties.

Her treatment of Travis when he opened up to her ended all of my encouragement and advice giving for Gladys because if she closed her ears to Travis, her "best friend in the whole world" (because he knew her "like no one else"), then she was *not* going to be receptive to anyone else. I had agreed with what Travis said out loud and Gladys did not like it "stop it," she would say, as if a joke, "you two aren't allowed to agree anymore." I dunno, but when I go to friends for advice – which I did a LOT about Gladys, I take what I can if it is applicable. I listen and consider what they say. I told Travis about how that was bothersome and he admitted that it had to be her choice – well now she was pining after a man who did not want to be with her because of her own actions! Frank had said she needed more stability…and he was right.

Gladys told me a story of how in elementary or high school she crushed on a boy and he called her stupid or something and her feelings were hurt. "I resolved to never hurt someone like that again," she had said; her deceptions are way worse! I would prefer the direct hurtful truth to a false friend. She went out of her way to cause misery and her face lit up when mine fell as she entered the room. Yes, for my job I act, but in life I do not pretend that everything is alright when it is not because life is not a play.

I told her it bothered me that she was so quick to dismiss Denise even though the girl kept on thinking that they were best of friends. "That's mean," I told her honestly.

"I only do that because she needs me," Gladys said as if it were right. I did not understand so she continued, "Denise is like a needy child, she needs me to be there for her. You don't need me like that, so I don't have to pretend with you." Oh, but you do!

"Yes, but if she is as good a friend as you say, then you should be honest with her," I said, talking from experience.

"But I don't want to hurt her," Gladys said. No excuse – she was being deceitful and working the situation so that Denise was becoming dependant on her. Not good.

"Sometimes you have to be honest – even if it might hurt your friend. It will build the relationship," I explained. Wasn't she the one who said "you can't always be a hero"? Well I mentioned this to Travis while we listened to the music and spoke to him about Gladys because I knew he would tell her and that she would listen. I wanted her to know that I was not okay with how she was treating people. Someone who was quick to hold the name Christian and point out the "power of the spoken word," was using her tongue to cut people down. I had figured out her game of camouflage and words for manipulation, but I did not figure out the motive; did she have to feel needed? Wanted? Did she want people to depend on her to feel important? Was it all just for control or fun? I did not get it…but I do know that younger people are more easily swayed and she knows it. That would explain the age group of her "friends," as well as her youth group leader status…as well as her immaturity.

Well she came back and Travis joined her and they went out. I sang like crazy when they were gone. I missed the music nights – a fellow named Neil had actually stopped me from walking off the stage one night. "You have to figure it out up here," he said, pointing at the stage where I stood, "because you can go home and I know you won't have a problem singing these songs. Each time a performer gets on stage, they learn something, but you have to figure it out up *here*." He was so right. That night I had forced myself to finish the songs and everyone was nice enough about the whole thing.

Esther was listening in the audience and said that I needed more airflow, so I worked on my breathing a little bit – but the thing about music (much like a sport) is you have to work on it constantly – like every single day! I'm not used to that – life tends to sweep me away and I fall behind as I have done now, yet again. It was so great to play each week, the nerves slowly moved to excited anticipation as I picked up my guitar and winged it each Friday. One day I would not sound so good, the next day would be great, but after Neil spoke to me, I learned to stay up there and finish each set, and he was right – I had to figure it out up there. So hard, but that is what the classroom is all about – learning.

I praised God for this opportunity because I felt like I was in the classroom – which means if I can put my nose to the grind stone for real, then I will come out much better than before I went in. I sang one night and it was great – I had nailed every note – I sang *I'm With You* by Avril Lavigne and when I was done, I knew I had nailed the song good. So one night would be great – lots of people and on key and fun, and other nights just were not my cup of tea; a part of life in the performance world.

Neil said that when I sang sometimes I would sing a harmony line – which most musicians cannot do without someone playing or singing a melody line. I was singing the right notes, but one third above what they were supposed to be sometimes; which meant I needed to lift the key or sing lower. He said that I have a really good ear – and a great voice – I just need to get them to work together. It was good and honest input – I was on cloud nine, because we were figuring things out!

Esther would invite me to her house to do music and she noticed that sometimes, for example in the phrase "or would you simply laugh at me and say" (from Randy Travis' song *I Told You So,* covered by Carrie Underwood), I would be too low on the word "or" and that would pull me off for the whole phrase. Esther was right, and I noticed that I also do this at the end of phrases, when sometimes I should stay on the same note, I drop off. Just little things like that have filled me with excitement because I am learning to get better! Esther said that maybe I shouldn't sing so high – but I like to because the range is there, but the notes are sometimes sharp and I know how unpleasant it sounds, so all in all, more practice is needed.

It was great because some of the other musicians started to work with me as well, getting me to play guitar and singing with them – it was kind of hard. Edna always sang worship songs and stuff and she asked me to do a set with her. I did the first time and it was fun because there were many musicians up there and even though I didn't know the songs, I was able to follow along somehow.

Then next time she asked me to do a set, I couldn't follow! We would play our guitars and she would suddenly step back and say "now you sing," but I didn't know the song at all! So I would refuse, just playing the guitar, and then she would get up and sing. Sometimes if I did try to sing, I would be quiet and she would say "sing louder!" I would get frustrated sometimes and just stand back, playing the guitar and shaking my head.

Well last I was there, some musicians were having troubles with each other and saying hurtful things into the mic and it ended up being that some of them are not coming at all anymore. "Aw, why can't we all just get along?" I said plaintively.

"Well we can't because if we did then we would have world peace," Neil said, ever the literal one. Well I haven't been to a music night for quite some time as life swept me away on a current dropping me to unknown shores. My heart is longing to go back and soon I will. Well Gladys might keep me from going to the music nights – but it will not be for long! She was still up to her old tricks; Gladys told Gina to close the bathroom door loudly to make sure it shut properly which was unnecessary, and it just kept me up at night and in the mornings; something Gladys knew very well.

Gladys used to keep her bedroom door open and I had told her a little while ago that I used to duck in to peer out the window or to turn on the front light when I had visitors. She was alright with it at the time, as she admitted to going into my room when I was away to use the mirrors. I had no problem with her doing so, and vocalized that for her. One time Noella came over for supper and Gladys had left her bedroom door open when she left for work, so I went in and peeked out the window and shut the heater off so I could hear Noella's big truck pull up. We had a lovely visit as I caught her up on the happenings, and she listened with a good ear and advised me to pray.

When she left Gladys came home and asked why the heater was off. "I forgot to turn it back on again; I had just turned it off so that I could keep an eye out for Noella when she came," I explained honestly, "I'm sorry and it won't happen again."

"Don't ever go in my room," she said, turning away darkly, "ever again."

Okay, her saying that was unnecessary because I had just been honest with her and sincerely apologized. She had just said that to make me feel worse and it worked. She had also slammed the bathroom door to leave me with that remark; a common trait of hers. Noella said that Gladys' romps with Frank were inviting all kinds of troubles into her life, and I think she was right. In the year that I lived with her, Gladys' heart slowly disappeared. I wrote her a note addressing the issue of her always insulting me and using her words to cut me down. I went to scripture again and used verses about how life and death is in the power of the tongue (Proverbs 18:21). The bible says to keep your tongue from saying evil as it is not what you put in your mouth that makes you clean, but what comes out that shows what is inside. Proverbs 15:4 says *gentle words are a tree of life; a deceitful tongue crushes the spirit.*

That is exactly was Gladys was doing; hurting me on purpose. My soul and heart were aching and I told her in the letter as kindly as I knew how. I also wrote that my friends were thinking that she was being verbally or mentally abusive. I had to write the letter because that is the only way I could get the words out without interruption, a scene, or unnecessarily hurtful words. I knew Gladys would read it and she ended up coming to me and saying "I read your letter and I am going to pray before I get back to you." Something in her eyes, tone and body language hinted that that was not the case.

"Sounds fair," I admitted and wondered what she was really up to.

Well, I was about to find out real soon. She waited until my money was in her hand and then kicked me out in November, the hardest time of year to find a place. She works in real estate (worked her butt off to get the certification, but then let it dwindle), so she knew from looking around that November is the hardest time of year to find a place.

"I won't throw you out with nowhere to go," she promised. Yeah, right.

"Places are hard to find," I told her, but at the same time I was relieved because I realized that God had kept me there because it had to be *her choice* to let me go. I thanked and praised Him that day, but I was also filled with despair – where was I going to go? I did not try to protest, because this was the out that God had provided and by golly, I was gonna take it! If it meant jumping with both feet and not knowing where I was gonna land, then it was chance worth taking. Gladys mentioned that Travis told her everything and she figured that I talked to him because I wanted her to know that there were still issues. I admitted that she was right.

"That hurt because you did not come to me," she said. Well, what good did talking to her do when all she did was cut me? I said nothing.

"I want us to be friends," she continued, but I knew that when I walked away, it would be without looking back at her. I was gonna shake the dust off my feet. "And I'm not just saying that," she continued, "I am saying what's truly in my heart." While she said these things she did glance at me but it was like she was waiting for a reaction.

I wore my disagreement openly on my face and said "I don't think we'll ever be friends because there is too much distrust." And her face fell, but I had to say it otherwise she was still open to play her mean little games and once I left I was out of her life.

From what I saw of Gladys, her spirit of murder was still in her heart and she based her faith on her ability to pretend; to manipulate. Her tongue just caused deceit and was only used to lie – even her compliments are a farce. I began to feel around her as I used to feel around Joan. There are few people who can bring me down and Gladys succeeded because she thought it gave her power, but the power to overcome is stronger than the power to suppress. I needed my friends greatly because I was sinking to a new low, so I hung out with them even more to try to lift my own spirits.

One day Shaun and I ventured into a valley near by at night. All of a sudden he perked up and was running off here and there and we leapt on slippery rocks. I was not as quick as he was but it was fun. We went down to the river and walked on trails and Shaun tried to run away, taking the light with him. "I can still see you," I call out, noting the light flickering and then his form in the moonlight. It was chilly and winter was drawing nigh. We ran around for a bit but I was quite drained from everything going on, so we headed back to his house after a short while.

At his house his grandma watched a movie with us and we ate some grub. It was a good time. When I went back to Gladys' she was in bed when Shaun texted me, informing me about his auntie's house being robbed.

"What?" I asked in surprise.

"They took a TV, DVD player, a computer and jewelry," he explained "they would have taken everything but the neighbors came home and spooked them away." He went on to say that a house three doors down got robbed when we were out. We both noted a red van that was running, but with lights off and a man was carrying something like a drawer. I had noticed them because he had shouted something to the man in the van. We had paid no heed at the time, but now details were fuzzy.

Gina heard my part of the conversation and looked inquisitive. "A person I knows house just got robbed and then another house three doors down from more people I know got robbed tonight." I explained, "I'm going to start locking the door," I vowed. Gladys was *obsessed* with locking the door – day in and day out, even if all three of us were inside. "I don't want to tell Gladys," I said "because I don't want her to get all worried."

"Well she won't know if we don't tell her," Gina said with a mischievous grin.

"Okay," I agreed. The next day Gladys was up to a little confrontation and I could tell by the way she sidled in and stared, clearing her throat constantly. I ignored her.

"Hi," she said in her weird way. She was in a mood, I could tell.

"Hi," I said briefly, mixing up some pasta for the next day. She came over and stood right close to me on purpose because she knew it would invade my space. I moved away. She did that a number of times as she bustled about the kitchen and then said she was going out. "Where you going?" I asked, expecting her to throw back my own evasiveness at me.

"To a conference," she answered smugly. She went all the time, but I have no idea what good it does for her.

"What's the point of going?" I asked.

"I know what you mean, so I'm not going to answer if you are going to *insult me all the time*," she said, taking some words from my letter out of context.

"I was actually asking you a question, but okay," I retorted, going into the fridge for some sour cream to add to the now cheesy pasta.

"It is to experience things in a bigger way and to learn more about God," Gladys answered suddenly very helpful. I did not understand because Gladys proclaimed a great love for God, but her life did not show it. She treated people poorly, went out of her way to cause grief and did not take care of herself. I think she has a lot of knowledge about God, but has not had any experience whatsoever in dealing with Him. He changes lives, and I know that if Gladys would let God in even for half a second, her life would change.

Gladys was always whining about wanting to change her life and be happy and become physically fit. "So do it," I would say. I have had to fight for my life and face a great many trials, so things like this seem somewhat trivial. If you want to change your life, just do it. Same thing for Rachel on her dark path; "**why is the mental health department as helpful as a piece of crap?**" she wrote on facebook, "**I should be in jail, they aren't even helping…**" and on she wrote. I checked to see how she was doing, but seeing these statements, I feel glad to have stepped away for a while.

She is the one holding herself back, just like Gladys. Gladys always keeps her light on for hours and hours in her room, so I asked what she did in there all day.

"I read," she said.

"You read for how long?" I asked, wondering if it was true.

"I get up at five every morning and read and spend time with God." She thinks she's spending time with God, but it certainly didn't show. If you give God an inch, God will work miles in your life without you knowing it. Looking at Gladys all I saw were delusions…ones that she uses for herself and ones that she saves for others.

"Every morning?" I asked again skeptically.

"Yup," she nodded a confirmation.

"Funny," I started, "you said that it woke you up in the mornings when I sang," I said, anger boiling up inside, "which is the truth or are they both lies?" her eyes got the same pleased look that Joan got when she made me repeat horrible things about myself back to her; one of dark pleasure.

"You lied so I would stop singing," I said out loud, "that's mean, why would you do that?" I was so angry!

"Why don't you write a song about it?" she sneered.

"I will…you're such a liar," I shook my head and watched the TV.

"Whatever," Gladys said, smiling maliciously and retreating to her room, "I'm not a liar, don't call me a liar!" and she slammed the door in my face; very mature. Later on she was in a huff because Gina had told her about the robberies and that I did not want to tell Gladys. "So you finally believe me about the robberies?" she derided.

"Yes, now I do, because they are actually happening," I said stepping around her in the kitchen. When she locked the door of the house with us inside it felt threatening, as if I was locked in even though I had my own keys. It just felt strange from the very beginning and she knew it, but it helped her own fears.

"Lucky Gina told me today…you didn't even want me to know. You would put us all in a dangerous situation, but when I lock the door it is for *your* safety. Your safety means more to me than my pride," Gladys said. Nothing means more to her than her pride; she was deliberately trying to me feel like shit. But then I thought about it and realized that in the same way I cling to my high guard for survival, is the same way Gladys clings to her pride. At that time I gave this no regard.

"Well it sure didn't concerning Frank," I snapped.

"Whatever, I don't know what you're talking about," she lied.

"And it was Gina who said not to tell you," I replayed it out loud – as it happened.

"Whatever makes you sleep at night, Karee, whatever makes you sleep," and Gladys went to her room to talk on the phone. I set a pot down angrily and looked at her, wanting to say a lot, but bit my tongue instead. *Self control*, I thought, it is one of the nine fruits of the spirit mentioned in the bible, well now I was tested and did not want to fail. Gina happened to walk right in at that moment, so I waited until she had come in and put her things in her room and taken her jacket off before I asked, right in front of Gladys, now seated at the kitchen table, "Did you tell Gladys that *I* didn't want to tell her about the robberies last night?"

Gina looked at me with a playful grin and then repeated the conversation of the night before – *as I had said it*, which showed me that Gladys had manipulated it to make me angry, and it worked. She was playing me for a fool and it made me hate her. When Gina admitted that she was the one who said "don't tell Gladys," I looked at Gladys and said "suck on that, fucker!" and flipped her the finger with both hands, grinning smartly, very much in the way that I used to do in high school.

"Did you just call me a fucker in my own house?" Gladys asked, looking at me from the kitchen chair where she was sitting.

"And she flipped you the finger," Gina added helpfully.

"And I would do it again," I pitched in for the benefit. I was so sick of her! Later I advised Gina to never do that again because it was sneaky and mean. She had just barely missed Gladys' little show, so when she walked in, my reaction looked like I was the antagonist; just the way Gladys liked it.

"You are a baby Joan," I said to Gladys. Sitting on the chair she looked downright evil to me. I know not giving in to anger is important, but I do have feelings that get hurt. That does not make it right by any means, but I was long past that.

"No, I'm not," she said, but the tone of her voice said that she did not believe herself, "stop it, Karee," she commanded.

"Are **you** going to stop it?" I came back with.

"*Stop* it," she insisted, not willing to back down, "**you** *stop* it!"

We repeated this a few times and then I said "we're just going in a circle now; I'll stop it if you will." We are both headstrong, so this was a dead end.

"You stop it or I'll throw you out by midnight tonight," she baited; so much for her little promises of not throwing me out without a place to go. I did stop then, but not until after I said "and you call yourself a Christian." Now my heart was growing cold and I found that I despised her. In my eyes she was evil, as proven by her words and actions.

"Whatever," she replied, "I'm not going to listen if you are just going to insult me all the time." I just thought *you wouldn't listen anyway.* The next day I told Helen what had happened because she could tell that I was down and out, so she asked what was wrong and I just dumped about things that took place at Gladys' house.

As I told her of these things and a few more, she grew angry herself and laughed when I said I called Gladys a fucker (which she was being one, and I had not apologized for it like she wanted, because I would not have meant it – still wouldn't have), and said maybe I shouldn't have said that. I owned up to that, but Helen said that the way Gladys threatened to kick me out my midnight was harassment. Just so you know, reader, I have not swayed these stories to be in my favor – I prefer honesty and so I tell it how it happened. I considered charging Gladys with harassment, but Helen was right when she said it was her word against mine and I couldn't prove it because Gladys always did these things when it was just the two of us. It shows that Gladys thought these things through.

I prayed to God, asking, **what am I doing wrong?** I prayed for a safe place to be – *I don't know where, but I just want to be safe for a while,* I told him. I also began to realize the extremity of grace. It was like Jesus had done something so grand for me and all I could do was stare and say "you didn't have to do that." I believe at that moment I accepted that Jesus died for my sins. Life was still a mess though, I felt like Gladys was suffocating me with a huge dark hand; that if she couldn't control me, then she was going to crush me. I knew that I needed to go to church.

I dragged myself there because Chloe had been asking if I was going and I hadn't been to church since Esther's house church on thanksgiving weekend with Alice, Norah, Megan and the whole family. That was about six weeks ago or so. I forced myself to go, walking fast as the day drew to a chilly close. I was so hurt that my body and soul was numb. As I stormed down the street, angry that God seemed to be forcing me to go to the church, and angry that Christians could be so dumb, I glared at the last remnants of sunlight and it slid behind the clouds. The clouds spread themselves out, matching the grim grey of my soul. I glared at the busy drivers as they drove by seemingly without a care and listened to the music in my ipod, desperately yearning to get out of this stupid world. Gladys had put me right where Joan had tried to keep me – and I didn't even see it coming. How foolish I was!

The sound of the electric guitar was soothing and then a song by Kirk Franklin came on that I did not know was on there. It says "help me believe" and it brought out the deep desperation inside as I found myself brushing tears away and then clenching my jaw as I stifled some more and stalked down the street even faster.

I stopped outside the church and turned to walk away many times; people were already inside, so God left it up to me to choose whether or not to enter. I paused, put my hand on the door, turned away, walked down the walkway a few times until I finally took a breath and just walked in. I felt like I did in high school – hurt and angry – and I let it show in my eyes as I walked in, but it was defiant. Righteous or not, I was angry and hurting and I *needed* **love.** To know that people care is not enough – I need LOVE. But then I realized that I did not know what that looked like, and it further broke my heart.

I went downstairs and waved away the program sheet, the lady was handing out – she offered it like five times until I just said "I don't want it," because I threw them out anyway. I ventured in and sat beside Chloe. Right away she knew something was wrong and asked if I was okay, I shook my head slightly.

"Do you want to talk?" she asked quietly, "are you sure you're fine?" I shook my head again and just stared up front. "Okay, well if you do, I'm here," she said and against my will big tears filled my sad eyes. I could tell that she felt bad, but when I get hurt like that, my guard is so high. "Karee," she said compassionately, "I like you a lot." She and Helen often said that because I do not accept the word "love" very lightly; a lot of people just throw it around, so this shows their care without too much cheesiness.

We sat down for announcements, and I just about had the strength to sit through the service, when the pastor came up to me and asked how I was doing.

"Oh, don't ask today," like I said, I am not a good liar, so I just say it how it is.

"Well it's good to see you, it's been a while, we missed you," he said. Something about his voice attested his honesty, and I found myself losing control. I looked away and clenched my jaw as tears welled up again. I had to get out of there, so I got up and left. I walked rapidly to the washroom and just held my head in my hands, the tension and heartache suddenly felt overwhelming, and I was realizing how weak I am.

When I exited the washrooms, the same lady who handed out the programs was there, pretending to care. "**Don't** say anything," I said firmly as I passed her quickly. She had opened her mouth to speak, and I just shut it for her as quickly as possible. I sat back down, but when the worship started, they sang songs about love and praise to God. I can praise and thank God, but I felt such a resistance to the word *love*. **Why don't I love God?** I thought, causing more despair to fill me.

I grabbed my jacket and scarf. "Where are you going?" Chloe whispered.

"For a walk."

"Do you want me to come?" she asked.

"Sure…no…if you want to," I hesitated. She had really pulled through for me with the whole Gladys and Frank situation. I just did not know what was going to happen. I walk fast when I'm angry, so she hurried to get her things and were out the door. I walked without knowing where I was going. I told her of things that Gladys had done and how it hurt. "I hate her!" I spat out angrily, "I hate her!"

I felt bad for saying so, but at that very moment, I did. "She is just like Joan – a baby Joan," I continued. Chloe walked quickly beside me, listening patiently. I was walking so quickly that she had to run a few steps to catch up and I was angry. The quick crunch of my footsteps on the cold pavement echoed that anger. I vented for a while and then came out with it *"I'm not okay,"* I bawled. All my strength and resolve and courage and facades faded with that statement. I had realized it a while back, but now I was driven to the point of saying it. "Why don't people want to help?" I wept bitterly, "Why must I be driven to the point where I have to ask for it?"

Poor Chloe; I think she was just praying the whole time. I was not this vulnerable since I ran away from Joan when I was thirteen to my friend Kylie's house, but I sure found myself feeling that same desperation. I did have to admit that Helen and Chloe were great, and I told her so, but *I needed help.* I did not do anything to warrant such treatment from Gladys and it was driving me crazy. We walked back to the church when I had calmed down and I was about to turn away to keep walking, but Chloe nudged me to go in. It was like a huge tug-of-war just to go into the church. It did look warm and inviting, a light in this dark and gloomy evening.

"That's why you wanted me to go with you!" she insisted, "because you knew you wouldn't come back if I didn't." she was right, so I went in. We sat at the top of the stairs to listen to the pastor speak. I think everyone in the church knew at that point that something was wrong with me. He spoke on encouraging one another with "brotherly love." "Some of us are hurting, right here in our midst," his powerful voice boomed out, "and we need to care for one another." I knew he was including me in that. The whole service was about pulling together as a church, helping the hurting, helping the needy and expressing the love of Jesus and he really said some encouraging words. "God loves you," he said, "and he wants to show you how much."

Then why doesn't he? I queried internally, *I am right here.* I went downstairs with Chloe at the end of the service and she again mentioned that I should speak with Sandra, so I set up a meeting time with her; every Saturday at four. I just knew that I needed help because I was in such distress that my body was not functioning well. I had constant diarrhea for a month solid, stomach problems, headaches, restless sleeps and moodiness. I was slowly fading from those around me and I knew that it was not good – time to do something about it. So I did. I prayed, I went to church that day, I asked for people to pray over me – lots of people.

Things were going wrong when I stopped desiring to sing, when I even skipped a few choral practices because I did not want to go out, missed the music nights and became angry with God. I could not be angry because of thinking that I was a mistake, because the documents from social services proved that untrue, so I wished to be a mistake. I was angry at God for not stopping the horrible things from happening – so many things…too many to cover – and I was angry with Him for showing me now what I missed. I was angry because I had no choice in the matter and He just let these things happen to me, even though I was innocent. Yes, the bible says, blessed are those who mourn, for the Lord will comfort them and wipe away every tear, and to bless those who abuse you, but how much longer must this go on? When was I going to be okay, *actually* okay? It just seems like life is this big long stupid fight – just to survive, and for what?

I resented going to the Johnson's house because it seemed to flaunt what I could have had, but then I realized that I had to start sucking the poison out of my life; like when you get bitten by a snake or a spider. I had to start with something, so I called Esther and expressed how I felt – just that it was hard for me to understand why she didn't help. I had talked to Drew about it and cried, making his eyes well up in tears. I thought it was best to talk to Esther, but it didn't quite sooth the depth of pain that it caused because she does not know how badly Joan treated me. I was trying to heal myself, but I did not want to do so by hurting anyone in the process.

She just went back to how much she had on her plate and that after a bit of time Joan shut the door on her and then opened and closed it frequently. Soon Joan closed the door permanently. I realized that I do not open and close the door quite so much, but I do widen it or shut it as well. However, if a door closes with me there has to be a very valid reason, and it usually closes permanently. Esther said that her son Lyle was bouncing on a bed and fell and broke his collar bone and when she and Wayne took the child to the hospital, they were accused of abusing him.

Of course, they were not doing that, and once it was proven, things were left well alone, but it was enough of a scare to keep her from interfering with Joan's situation. "There was nothing I could do but watch," she explained. Well it was good to know, the scare of having your kids taken away was great back then. Esther also spoke a little bit about her past, because one day I asked about it and she was about to tell me some, but since Alice didn't even know her mother's story, she had prepared to listen as well.

I did not mind her doing so, as this was her mother I was talking to; I just assumed that the kids knew her story already. Well Esther told me that was not the case – her kids did not even know, and I still don't understand why, even knowing what I know, but I do think that Esther and I have a lot more in common then she thinks. She is so kind and warm and welcoming and giving and bold and honest, and she probably had to work quite hard to get there. She did tell me of the supports that she had around her (like her mother and people she met) and how her increase of faith began, and I was left wondering how I turned out okay, because I did not have that support around me. But then I saw that I did have support far off in the Caribbean; from my grandpa.

These days I have many good friends who have my back, and right away when I told Alice and Helen and Chloe that Gladys had kicked me out, they immediately started to search the options within my price range. Helen actually offered to cover a damage deposit for the new place if one was needed, which was remarkable, because I had not thought to ask anyone for money; she offered it and said "and if you *don't* come to me, I will be very angry with you," but it was the fact that she was serious that shows that she has my back. I talked and friends searched places out along with me.

I knew that I would forgive Gladys once I was out of there, but right now I have to acknowledge the great amount of hurt that still resides deep inside, so I pray a lot more now. I pray that God does not let this little girl go unnoticed. I don't mean little in age; I mean little soul, broken little heart; little in stature and size. I am still broken and right now I wonder if I will ever be whole. God has children; we are all His children, but I was reading Matthew and in chapter eighteen, verse six it says *"But whosoever shall cause one of these little ones that believe on me to stumble, it is profitable for him that a great millstone should be hanged about his neck, and that he should be sunk in the depth of the sea."* Joan was always quick to make me read the verses on children obeying their parents (in the book of Ephesians), and I have always wanted to point this verse out as a retort. I am one of those "little children." So I prayed that God would not let this little child go unnoticed.

Thinking about this sucking of the poison, I also recalled the letters that I had written to Gladys. In my mind I was not harsh and my friends deemed them fair, but in Gladys' eyes they were probably cruel. I knew that the longer she held on to them, the longer she could keep her angst against me whether or not I knew it. In her mind whatever she had going on in her mind would be justified or worsened each time she even glanced at these letters, so for her own good I felt I should take the letters and destroy them, so I waited for an opportunity.

One day by fluke, I noticed that Gladys had stepped out for a while, so I locked the door and pulled my hair back into a ponytail and washed my hands clean. Then, tiptoeing to her bedroom door, I turned the knob while applying pressure to the door, creating a quiet opening. I knew she wasn't in the house, but it seems that I was in the sneaky mode. *Okay,* I thought to myself, *I want to touch as little as possible and get out of here as fast as possible.* I scanned the room, my eyes falling on her bedside table. I had a little flashlight since it was night it was quite dark and if I turned on the light to her room then she would be able to tell instantly that I was in there as soon as she pulled up. I had locked the door so that the unlocking would alert me for a quick exit. I crouched by the night table and flashed the light on the bottom shelf. I spied the latest letter I gave her about how she used her tongue to hurt me. Good, one down, two to go. I found another one that I had written, but could not find the one I wrote when she invited Frank over. Hearing a vehicle outside, I abandoned the mission and scurried out of her room, closing the door and stepping away just as Gladys came inside.

"Hi," she greeted me as per usual.

"Hi," I said curtly, curling my fingers around my mini flashlight and going into the kitchen. She looked extra long at my face; I'm guessing I had looked alarmed to see her in the house, but I knew that I was covered. Not for long, though, as I felt I ought to get the letters out of there. When I knew she was working, I went in her room again in the same fashion. I pulled out the two letters and slipped them into my room. I searched for any other letters, but did not find, so I let it go because I did not want to sift through her things. I don't know what Gladys was keeping them for, but I now possessed two of three letters – and one of them being the note that got me kicked out.

Considering my mission accomplished, I shredded them along with other papers of my own and stuffed the scraps of paper into envelopes and threw it all in the trash. Even doing that I felt a huge release and sighed with relief. I have no idea of the significance of it all, but I sure felt better having removed them from her grasp because they were no longer there for her to use as a physical reason to hold feelings against me.

When I started praying for a new place, a few options came up immediately and one place was quite affordable, but it was a single woman in her forties, much like Gladys, nice enough, but it looked to be a repeat of the current situation. This time when my flags went up, I heeded them. This lady was nice enough, but she also offered her place early free of charge and had two guys living there – one was a gamer and the other was a hermit. She said she disliked the fellow whose room I would be taking up and I took note of how she spoke about them behind their backs.

She had two cats of her own and said that I could have my lovely cat there if I moved in, but it felt like bait, so I put it to the side. When I looked into the room she offered, it was spitting image of Gladys' room that I rented – and I knew it was not the place to be. She works in cosmetology so there were fake nails allover and makeup and she herself was wearing these things…along with a red-haired wig; it creeped me out.

Nothing else was really coming up and time was ticking away, so I prayed to God and worried to Him well into the night. It was like I heard a thought in my head that was not my thought – it almost sounded audible – and it said *I will provide for you and you will be fine*. It felt like I had to trust that voice, so I laid my stresses aside and went ahead with plans for moving. Noella and Drew offered to help at the very end of the month, but I wanted out sooner – the sooner the better.

One night I was recalling a conversation I had with a girl named Rita. We had met a few times before – she was at the barbecue I went to this summer with Alice, and she was also with Shaun and Samantha at the pasta night, in fact she had sat at our table, I believe. I did not remember her name until later on, when Shaun and I were out and about, we randomly decided to stop at her house and watch a movie there with her.

She was quite welcoming and made us some lime popcorn – sounds gross, but it's not…well, it might be better if you don't burn it, but we ate it all anyway. We had talked about somehow if I had lived there what it would look like and she showed me the house and what the rooms looked like and everything. This was way back in September, when I thought I had the winter covered. I even said maybe not until the New Year, but now this conversation floated back now that I needed a place immediately. Now it was November and I had to be out in a few weeks. I took a chance and facebooked her, finding her on there through Shaun's friend list, but only after speaking to Alice about moving in with her. Alice said I would like her and that she thought we would get along.

Creepy I know, but I just had to see my options before I settled with the lady that reminded me so much of Gladys. I just threw prayers out left, right center, up, down and all around. Rita added me and then responded that she would ask her landlords – who are her parents – and get back to me soon. All this was taking quite some time, so I worried frequently. I decided to let God work and to not hound Him or to press Rita for time. Of course, God was at work anyway, but there is certain humility in just leaving life in His hands, especially in hard days like this when time is short.

I still had to go to work and force myself to act like I was happy for hundreds of people who don't give a damn. I still had friends who weren't friends…and did not want to hear about anything…I had joined a local choir to get some music in, despite Gladys' efforts to squash it. I count this as a HUGE blessing! I *loved* being in the choir and singing and blending my voice – a lady with a very sweet soprano voice sang right behind me, so I followed what she did because she knew the songs better. ☺

I was warmly welcomed into the choir and the director told me that she auditioned everyone first, but because I joined late, she let me sneak in. "Do you want to audition now?" I asked, gesturing politely to the piano.

"It's okay," she said in her friendly, quirky way, "I think you have a good ear because usually when people sing off I have to pull them aside and see where their voices fit in. I haven't had to talk to you yet!" she made me smile because it was so pleasing to sing for somebody who loves what they do. She was a sweet lady. I ended up agreeing to dance to one of the songs that the choir was singing – because it is a Spanish lullaby and I have the Hispanic look. This was a little stretch because even though I have been in a few musicals, I have never danced a solo and do not consider myself special in that art.

I also joined a band that was by fluke…I was talking to a girl I knew in a store about music and a young lady overheard. "You're a musician?" she asked after we were introduced…she is an author as well; in fact she had advised me to go with her publishing company since Noella's publisher friend had my book for two years and it was still sitting. I followed her advice and my first book went into production.

"Well, I've been called that once or twice," I answered modestly.

"Sweet, what do you play?" she asked.

"I play guitar, piano and sing," I said, "and a bit of drums." She said that she and her friend were starting a band asked if I would like to be in it. "Sure," I said, quite pleased. I have wanted to be in a band for a long time. Well I went to her house and we sang, and I played guitar and the singer sang and she played drums and it was fun!

It is a lot of hard effort to work with other musicians – I think the singer is alright, I mean, she can sing on key and stuff, but I don't *feel* anything when I listen to her sing. We all sing different genres, too, but I think as long as we are flexible we could figure something out. The drummer and I get along better – she is also good friends with the singer (that is what I will call them for now), but we each have to realize where we stand and how to work with it.

Example: the singer wants to be all sexy and things like that, but I don't because I know how something innocent can turn downright wrong in the blink of an eye. Actually the singer and I know each other from high school – when I was in San Frisco for grade nine – but we did not know each other well. The singer sang a song she wrote and I right away began to figure out chords to it to put it to music and the drummer drummed along. It was awesome because for a while we were actually playing together – I like it when there is less talk and more play, but I think that talk is important because we need to know who we are working with. I am also so glad that the drummer is an author as well because without her I think my book would be still sitting.

The drummer and I both write poetry, and she said she planned to write a novel. We kind of motivate each other to write. Even though she is not a Christian, she is one of the nicest people I know. The singer is married and with two kids of her own, so I suppose I don't see any long term commitment when it comes to her – it is not to be held against her, but the drummer and I talk as if we'll be a long term band.

Life gets busy and sweeps you away with all kinds of things, so we have not had many practices together, but the singer smokes – like a chimney – and I do not like that because although it givers her the breathy sound she's after, it ruins my own clear sound. Being in a band is trickier than I thought and it requires more practice – each member must know the music and be able to work together.

One day at the end of practice we were all going upstairs to hang out when the drummer's huge dog went ballistic. We tried to stretch out our hands for him to sniff but he snapped. He took to the singer more quickly than to me, but in time we worked together, tossing him treats and getting him to do tricks and then he let us up. As a band we need to agree on the songs we do – I am more of a belting Broadway type of person, but the singer likes softer pop and mushy love songs. The drummer is the most flexible, but she has the most creative ideas to get us to work together.

The drummer and I met again and talked – she spoke of her sickness and then I understood that each person goes through their trials. She is a little bit like a woman in the bible who bled for thirty years. This biblical woman touched the hem on Jesus' cloak and was healed instantly because she believed. The drummer is not a Christian, but a very kind person, so I pray for her because I believe that Jesus can heal in the same way today. She did change her diet and cutting out meats have helped a lot but she is due for a surgery sometime in the New Year, so I hope things work out alright.

I told her a bit of my story and she said she had a new respect for me "not that I didn't respect you before," she said, "but no wonder you don't want to sing mushy love songs!" I told her that was why I don't want to become a sex symbol – good looking or not, it is not my desire. She understood and then we fooled around and came up with a cool little doo-dad by just jamming. It was fun and a great distraction from Gladys.

As the middle of the month came and went, I fretted because I still did not have a definite answer from Rita because she had not approached her parents yet. She asked to meet for wings and so we visited and she appeared to be quite level headed, but when she said she was a Christian as well, my guard went up instinctively. I shared a bit about my distresses with Gladys and we both agreed that it was not right. I had a good feeling, but was so uncertain about moving in with her! When we finished up the wings, she invited me over for a movie so we hung out and chatted and I left wondering how it all went.

I had been downright honest, but not rude…just blunt about everything that happened. "If you can communicate, I think we'll get along," I had told her. Was that too much? "I just need a safe place to be. I need to be safe for a while," I had said earnestly. She had looked at me with her clear brown eyes and I saw care. She said that even if it didn't work out to move in with her that she would help me find a safe place. However, I was rapidly running out of time with no where to go because I was waiting for an answer.

In my remaining time with Gladys, I expressed great frustration about her stupid little games and my friends reached out. "You can come over here any time you like," Helen offered. I did go there *several* times for supper or to vent; Helen always listened.

"You could come over and we could hang out," Chloe offered. I went there.

"I'll be there soon, will you see me?" Alice asked.

"Of course I will!" I replied and began counting down the days – a whole month...it felt like too far away. Lily even chatted with me on Skype as did Uncle Tim.

"You should come visit me in Richmond," Norah suggested. I perked up at the idea and off I went. I intended on being there for two days besides the day I left, and did not tell Gladys where I was going – she did not need to know. I did tell Gina so that she would ensure that the doors were not locked when I got back. Gladys had several locks on the door and we only had keys for the deadbolt. That is part of the reason why it creeped me out when she locked the door when we were inside – because we didn't need that many locks when we were home!

Anyway, Gina agreed and I went on my days off of work. It was my first time driving in a large city, much bigger than Portland which used to be big to me. I was surprisingly less nervous than I thought – even when I took the wrong exit and ended up in the center circle drive during the rush hour. I just hummed happily and kept my eyes open and alert. Eventually I pulled into a store lot after waiting at a red light for *forever,* I ended up turning at the red light because once the light was green, there was no chance of me getting enough room to go, as there was no green arrow at this stop. It was fine, but the drivers in Richmond were a lot more courteous than the drivers in San Frisco or Portland! It was snowing and blowing, but for some reason I was so cheery that even getting lost did not faze me.

I called Norah and told her what happened. "There are about four signs that say to turn off, so I took one and then saw the right one as I was on the ring road," I said lightly, "gosh, these signs lie!" but I was just kidding, I wasn't really mad at the signs.

"Well, that happens all the time, I'll come to get you," Norah answered back. We exchanged information and she left to find me. While I waited, I marveled at how chipper I was and then turned the radio up to sing along with it. I had prepared for the trip, a few hours away and everything went well thus far. Norah found me and I followed her to her house – I felt like a little lost lamb led back home in a silly way.

chapter 11:

Well the trip to Richmond was great – just the break I needed. Now if you ever want to meet someone truly on fire for the Lord…go meet Norah! I had no idea she was so passionate about her faith. When we met and played games at thanksgiving, I laughed a lot and knew she was a Christian, but she goes to church or prayer groups or potlucks or devotions or worship services *every day of the week!* She has no obligations to go; it is what she likes to do – crazy because I **definitely** drag my feet to go to church.

We cooked and ate and talked and shared a room. She was very welcoming and fun to tease because of her great sense of humor and quick wit. She reminded me of a friend from college – I see that friend once in a blue moon but we have drifted so far apart that we are not friends anymore. Norah is a massage therapist, so while she was out giving massages, I cooked for the potluck and sang in her little digital recorder thing.

It was cool because you could record up to eight tracks and so I played piano and sang, then I sang a song, harmonizing with myself. I was just trying it out and while there are many areas that need doctoring…there is some good stuff too. When she listened to the song of me harmonizing with myself, she said I was singing the right notes but I was mixing genres, which is kind of a talent. I was pleased and am after getting one of those little digital studios myself. They are handy and I have so many songs in my head and if I got one then I could go into the studio better prepared to work with Dylan. Well Norah got ready and off we went to potluck and I met many Christian people close to my age.

I was baffled to see so many young people gather together for the name of our Lord of their own accord in a city as big as this one. This city also has the highest crime rate per capita in the country, so this gathering of good people was something new to see. In Portland even the Christians who gathered were cold and distant, but here they were welcoming and open. I chatted with a few and was approached by a few more and was soon bouncing around from person to person.

I had invited Ephraim because he grew up in the church and has been so buried in his books that I thought he could use a little break, so on our way over to the potluck Norah and I picked him up. It was good to see him, but he was a little bit distant maybe because of our last phone conversation where I hung up on him. When we were in the house chatting, he met someone he knew and talked away so I actually didn't see much of him.

The food was great and everyone was polite, letting people go ahead of them, offering assistance and figuring things out. I felt oddly comfortable among these strangers, I think because of the familiarity with parties back in high school. The parties I used to go to were filled with people I knew and people I didn't – the houses were usually overflowing onto the lawn; yep, big parties. This house was not overflowing, but it was full enough to bring back the familiarity of those parties – instead of booze we had a good wholesome meal where they prayed before eating and then carried on normally.

Later we drove around and dropped Ephraim off because he was behind on schoolwork and then Norah and I went to another house to meet even more people. At this house there was a guitar and so I sat across from the fellow playing it and listened.

"Do you want to play?" he asked, glancing at my peering face.

"Uh no, that's okay," I declined politely, "whose guitar is it?"

"Kevin's," he answered, pointing at the man who had let us in. I watched him pick at it a little and realized that I had not played guitar or piano for quite some time! How could I let myself go without for so long? That's probably why everything has been feeling like the end of the world lately…not much expression. "Here," he said, passing the guitar to me, "you obviously want to play it." I blushed because I hadn't realized that my face was so obvious, and took the instrument.

It felt *so* good to hold a guitar and I played some simple chords, first picking them loosely and then strumming them. Then I did a few bar chords to go up the neck and a few harmonics. I didn't do anything showy; just tinkered around, making little musical noises while some people talked and some people listened.

"You should sing," someone suggested.

"Oh no, that's okay," I declined again, "not today."

They tried to get me to sing and I wanted to badly, but I had grown somewhat ashamed of the way I sound; I do not think I am a very good singer, especially with so much recent criticism from the music nights. I know that criticism is good when it is constructive but it was at the point where they were nitpicking *everything* so I was quite surprised when Norah said she thought I sounded like a more skilled singer than her. She has a good voice and recorded a worship song (that got stuck in my head) just before I came. I also tend to play and sing songs that most people don't know, so in a Christian circle it was hard to pull something out of my head because I do not know worship songs. Eventually I gave the guitar back to the fellow and listened in on a busy conversation.

Through the evening they talked about many interesting things – about God in the world, spiritual events, conferences that they knew about (I had no idea about any of them or what they were for), people they knew and I was happy to just listen. A little later on a girl was struggling with some chords and I helped to teach them to her, bringing back my teaching days. It was fun, but then the group decided to pray.

Like a child, my eyes were opened wide while theirs were closed; my head was up and looking around while theirs were lowered. It was not a matter of disrespect for Jesus, but I just had to observe these current events because it was all new to me. I thought it was a bible study set up through a church or something, but Norah later conferred that most of the people there did not go to her church and some of them were Christians but did not attend a regular Sunday service.

It rather baffled my mind to see so many young adults get together of their own choice to discuss God, read scriptures and pray for one another, and in this city of high crime rate, nonetheless. It snowed and flurried and huffed and puffed flakes everywhere, so I actually stayed an extra day because apparently a woman was stuck in her car overnight on the highway and my phone had died, so I thought it wise to leave during daylight. I texted my boss on Friday and she reluctantly gave me the next day off.

Friday night was my last night there and Norah had invited a friend named Dustin for a tea. We talked about God and it was quite intriguing. This man said that he had experiences of angels before.

"Like what?" I asked as if skeptical…but secretly quite interested. He described a situation that he had in his home country of how a security guard was coming back that night to shoot him and he was not allowed to leave his job, so he was scared. He prayed and two men came to him, knowing things about him that not many other people knew and they said that they would take care of this threatening guard. Later that night Dustin was at work and the same guard came up to him and apologized – an *extreme* rarity. I believed him. I told him of my story how I was caught in a snow storm when I was young and was not dressed appropriately.

When I called the foster parents to pick me up, they declined, saying that I walked everywhere anyway, but the snow was mixed with ice and they lived far across town. I had called a friend and she said as long as I could get there I could stay the night. I had braced myself to walk far in this miserable storm and pushing the store door open, I was surprised to see a bus pull up directly in front of me. The bus driver opened the door and motioned me in. I had no money to pay, but he said not to worry about it.

The buses were not supposed to be running, that is how bad the weather was – I have no idea how this man drove because when I looked out the window all I saw was white with hints of brown close by. The bus driver took me right to my friend's house – which there was a bus stop near by, but he dropped me off across the street from her house. This was alright since no one else was riding it. Dustin believes that the bus driver was an angel and I have been told that by Lily, my good friend. I began to believe it myself. I also told of my vision that I had in college and how I did not know what it meant. I was told to use my voice for God, but having no idea how, I am starting to feel that I am like the man who buried his master's talent in the ground.

The biblical story is that a master trusted a servant with ten talents (money) and that servant went and invested, doubling the amount. The same master trusted another servant with five talents and that servant went and invested it, increasing the amount and earning himself a great reward. The third servant was trusted with one talent and he put it in the ground to keep it safe. When the master got back, he punished the servant, saying "you could have put it in the bank to let it grow interest."

I always thought the story is harsh because from the servant's perspective, maybe he hid the talent to keep it safe because he was afraid it would get stolen. People don't always know things about investing – I sure don't! When I mentioned this to Dustin he said maybe I ought to be seeking ways to invest the talent; a thought that never occurred to me. We talked well into the night, the three of us and it was very eye opening – I quite enjoy having conversations where people bring new perspectives and one can argue or debate respectfully. I like being stretched in a healthy way, and I liked that I walked away with things to think about.

Well, lo and behold, the time had come for me to drive back to the house of doom, but I felt nourished and ready for the two weeks that lay ahead. The roads were actually in decent condition – the internet exaggerated – so I made good time driving back. As soon as I was back I emailed Rita and we set up a time to meet with her parents. I thought this was peculiar because I would not be living with them, but I guess since they own the house they just want to know who is going to be living in it.

Her mother was sick so it was Rita's father who showed up. He is a quirky man with a good heart. I think he has good discernment and might be a little set in his old ways. We started talking and it was all nice and friendly at first but I was apt to be honest about everything and completely direct to just keep things in the open.

"Yup, if you have any alcohol, you're out," he said observing me. Gladys had the same rule, but I tested the limits. The thing about Gladys is she had *too many* rules – even for people who like things orderly, so I stretched her boundaries by being myself. It was a stretch for her to even have a fish in the house! I played hockey in the house to relive some high school days – and to show Gladys that things like that are fun and harmless. When Gladys found and emptied my bottle of coconut rum that I had brought back from the Caribbean, I could not be angry with her because she had strictly said "no alcohol in the house," so what she did was fair. I even told her that in a nice way and she was fine.

I lifted an eyebrow and looked at Rita's dad and said, "Even just a sip?" He was adamant about it because he said he had never had a drink in his life and never wanted to. "Not even one drink," I asked skeptically, "you've never had one drink your whole life?"

"Not even one drink," he stated seriously, "no, I don't want any of it. I have seen how it makes people act stupid and say things and do things to other people and I want no part of it." He went on to explain that his workers drank and were not always kind when they did, and I saw that he was serious and also speaking from his personal experiences.

"Well, most of my friends are Christians," I assured him, "except for one but she is in Portland." I was talking about Emma. He did not like that and thought that I should not have my friends over and kept saying that if I struggled with drinking then maybe this wasn't the right place or maybe I shouldn't have my friends over because he also did not want his daughter around that. I understood what the man was saying, but I would not disallow *all* friends because of the one or two that drink. "I don't think I should punish my friends for another person's sins," I explained calmly, "if my friends want to see where I have moved to, I expect to be allowed to let them see the place."

"Oh yeah, yeah," he consented, "but at the same time I don't want your friends to be staying over night all the time either." Understandable. We agreed that if I had a friend from out of town coming then it would be alright for them to stay but he was just being cautious because Rita usually knew the other roommates she's had very well; I am a stranger, so I let it all go and soon enough our issues seemed to resolve itself.

We had it out and Rita kind of kept her nose clean, stepping in to clarify what I was saying for her dad or visa versa and eventually we figured things out and became quite agreeable. When he heard that I was looking for a safe place he said "I will never hurt you as a man, I would never come into your room even if you're not here." I looked at him directly and I think he could see that I had been hurt recently.

"You know how you feel about my friends' coming here," I began, "that's how I feel when you say that." I did not say it in a mean way, but I wanted to give him perspective as to what I thought as well as to let him know that I got where he was at about my friends. He understood and all of a sudden our icy beginning melted away and we figured things out in a jiffy and I signed a renter's agreement of basic courtesy.

"So you think I might be too stingy on the friend side of things?" he said with a slow and friendly grin. I nodded shyly and suggested that we allow some time to work the friends in and to give us a trial period to see if living with Rita would work out. We all three agreed, much to my relief, that I was moving in on the twenty-fifth!

All of a sudden I had to come up with four hundred dollars off the top of my head because of the damage deposit! I had budgeted and gauged my finances to get by the winter at the rate that Gladys had set – which was cheaper because she had graciously lowered it for Alana back in the day when being nice was cool.

I did not fret over the money, though, but sternly told myself that I would figure it out. I had a credit card and if worse came to worse then I could put it on there, seeing as I keep it paid off all the time (I only use it for groceries or gas or sales or the odd purchase online). I was talking to Helen about it because we had discussed finances before and she promised to cover everything if I needed it.

"Oh I can pay the rent, it's just the damage deposit," I explained.

"Okay, how much is it?" she asked. Holy crap, I did not mean for this to happen!

"Four hundred."

"Okay, I will write you a check for four hundred dollars." Just like that. I thanked her and asked if there was anything I could do and she said "no, you give me rides all the time to and from work and I need those rides as much as you need rent." It is true; I give her rides when she asks for them if I can because her job is way on the outskirts of town and winters are chilly here, especially at night.

"I wish I could do more than just say thank you all the time," I protested.

"Well, you could come over for supper more often," Helen said. I had to smile at that because Helen hates cooking so once in a while I'll go cook and eat her food – it is a trade-off we have. It makes me smile even right now. Well I had a place and thankfully so because Gladys was starting to hound me about people coming in to see the room.

"Just show them; it's gonna be messy because I have to pack," I explained firmly with a careless shrug. She tried to see what days I was working, but I was evasive. A lady came on Sunday and Gladys said "I thought you work Sundays," which I usually do.

For some reason I wanted to meet this next person who moved in, so I said "well, not today," and stuck around. The lady's name is Wanda and she is *the sweetest* person ever! Gladys was in the bathroom noisily blow drying her hair as she did every single day even though she was still on her stupid holidays and not going anywhere…and she had the bathroom door open so that the noise wafted into the living room to where I was.

When Wanda came Gina opened the door and we greeted her warmly. I was not going to sabotage anything, that is what Gladys would do, but I just wanted to meet her. That is all…partially because I knew Gladys didn't want me to. Gina went back into her room to focus on school work and Gladys was still being noisy in the bathroom so I went over, shut the door in her face with a little smirk and showed Wanda the room, displaying the shelves in the closet and above the bed, pointing out the mirrors on the closet doors. I pointed out that everything was within walking distance – stores, post office and bank, and that the neighbors were nice. I could see curiosity on the woman's face so I just said "I'm leaving because we have irresolvable issues," and left it at that;

the same thing Gina said Gladys had told her. Well as soon as Gladys came out of the washroom she said "I assume she showed you the room," and went about pretending to be super cheery.

Wanda and Gladys had a nice little chat which I left soon but I felt bad for this new lady. Gladys' kindness, her smile and her laugh looked and sounded like one big deception. Now that I had figured out her game, she kicked me out and was ready to prey on another sweet and innocent bystander. I wanted to caution this lady to be careful, but what could I say? Nothing, so I left and when I returned Gladys left the lady's check on the table, a small victory. I am so glad that I already had a place to go to because once again her promise of "I won't throw you out with nowhere to go," was smashed at my feet. She prided herself on her word, but it seems all her words were easily broken.

I know that it seems like I am being dramatic and overreacting, but reader, you need to meet this lady in order to know what I am talking about. On second thought, maybe not because she will rake you, too, over the coals. I had been played for a fool and I *felt* like a fool for giving her benefit of the doubt, for forgiving her so easily so many times, and also for being so easily swayed by her fake Christianity. I no longer hated her because I realized that I was the fool – I have never told her these things because how do you call a bully a bully? She would not have listened or she would have twisted it, so the point was lost before it began. I have never seen anyone with such a hard heart to lie and deceive only to destroy – and to do so as joyfully as a child eating sweets.

Gladys enjoyed watching me hurt. She only said she loved me because she knew it irritated and bothered me because I knew in my heart that those words were phony. People these days throw around the word *love* so carelessly and it is a true shame because it makes it oh-so-hard to even believe in the meaning of the word. I also saw that Gladys had waited until she placed herself in a good position financially before throwing me into a poor one. She knew that I am not made of money and that I budgeted for the winter, she waited for my next rent check and then latched onto the first person who showed interest. I feel terrible because I have this strange feeling that Wanda is going to walk out of that place not quite as kindly as when she walked in, but who am I to judge?

God knows what is really going on and I had no choice but to let it go; to stand up for rights would have been futile, to express feelings would have been useless. Well I did not tell Gina or Gladys that I was moving out five days early; I aimed for a peaceful exit, but life had other things in mind. I started to pack happily on Tuesday, humming and singing to the radio, and washing and drying all the clothes before folding them into my suitcases. I had a scarf and one mitten for a long time and had considered giving the mitten away or tossing it out because although I looked and searched and even called for it (just kidding, I didn't call for it), it was nowhere to be found.

For some odd reason, I held onto that single mitten for over a year. When I washed my clothes and packed them, lo and behold, in my seemingly empty suitcase lay the little lost mitten!! Now my mittens and scarf match! It is so small and trivial, but it just tickled me pink – to think that I held onto it for so long for some strange reason! Anyway, Tuesday night sailed by and I was anxious to finish packing on Wednesday. Now Gladys was being a little sneaky, using the front door and locking her bedroom door (her bedroom was the porch, so we always used the back door), just to keep me guessing if she was in or out. There were no windows to look outside, but I have good ears and eyesight, so I could tell when the light was on, or hear when the door opened, no matter how softly she tried to close it. Perhaps Gladys was doing this because she noticed and resented the absence of the letters as well, but it was always a mind game with her.

I feel that she was doing this to be sneaky because she closed all the doors around the house quite loudly and when she would suddenly burst out of her room, she would watch my face for reaction, often opening the bedroom door loudly to try to startle me. Funny how she closed the front door so quietly that if I hadn't figured out what was going on, I wouldn't have heard it at all...sometimes I would think she was in and then go outside to see her car was gone; she liked to keep me guessing. I knew that Gladys worked on Wednesday, but was not sure when, or even what Gina was up to; I was just relieved that it was my final night there! *Thank you God, for releasing from here,* I prayed happily as I skipped off to work on Wednesday morning.

I had felt that I could not walk away before, but now even if Gladys were to withdraw her notice, I would still be free to walk out. I was anxious to walk away for good, and miraculously, the day sped by cheerfully. I had forgotten my cell phone, so calling Derek about moving arrangements was…well, it didn't happen. I had told Noella that plans to move were covered because I wanted out as soon as possible, and Drew said he was in town on Thursday and could help for a bit. I appreciated it, but now I could not call either party because I had forgotten the phone. I did not want to call in the house because Gladys was playing her guessing game and I did not want her to overhear.

As I rushed to my car, started it and tried to drive off, I realized that it was stuck in the snow. You have got to be kidding! I unstuck myself and then got stuck again…and then unstuck myself again. Finally at the house, seeing no other cars there – meaning both roommates were out – I was delighted because that would be the most efficient for packing. However, my smile soon dropped when I could not find the house keys. I checked the pockets, checked the car…nothing came up. "Where did I put them?" I wondered aloud, researching the jacket and car. I even drove back to the lot and looked, but there was another car parked right where I would have dropped my keys – if I did drop them. I drove around for a little while, pondering my plight. I could not call Helen – or *anyone* for that matter – because I had forgotten my cell; the *one* time I forget it, this happens. Well, there was nothing to do but wait. I considered breaking a window, but did not have the money to repair it and the back door was dead bolted, so I could not just pick it – it was an older bolt with the key for getting in from outside, but no key hole inside.

I drove back to the lot and the orange car was gone, so I left my car running, turned the lights on bright and raked through the snow. No luck, and the work place was locked up as everyone had gone home. I did not have anyone's numbers memorized, as I just click their names on the phone to call, so even if I could borrow a phone it did no good. I went back to the house and no one was there yet. I went to the neighbor's house and no one was home yet. I sat in the car to warm up – it was freezing outside and snowing and blowing and I began to feel desperate again. *I just want to get out of here,* I thought sadly, but even that seemed too much to ask.

I drove over to Chloe's house and got there just as she was heading out. She was waiting for a ride and I vented about how life seemed to be a stupid fight all the time "just to survive – what's the point?" I cried out angrily. I beat a pillow against the couch, feeling on the brink of a break down. There was so much desperation and angst and no way to express it. Luckily Chloe is the most patient person I know, so she just let me vent without saying anything. She gave me an apple and some oatmeal bars because I had not eaten all day and then the girl who was giving Chloe a ride out arrived out of breath.

"My car is stuck," she panicked urgently.

"Where is it?" we asked.

"It's over there, not too far," she pointed, breathing heavily, "Oh gosh, I'm so scared!" we got on our jackets and boots and went to pull this young girl out of the ditch. There was snow blowing everywhere and the wind bit anything that it touched and I found that I was shivering even with layers under the winter jacket.

"Don't worry," I assured her goofily, "this happens all the time."

"Really?" she asked dubiously. Chloe went back to her place to look for my car keys because I had misplaced them and needed to go when she left. I walked with this young girl who was very worried about her car.

"Why are you so worried?" I asked.

"I've never been stuck before," she explained, "this is my first winter driving by myself." I was empathetic so I told her about how I got stuck twice that very same day, only a couple hours ago. I looked at the car and tried to direct the wheels while she drove, but she was so nervous and uncertain that she drove the car further into the snow.

"Okay, get out," I said lightly, "I'm going to drive, is that okay?"

"Okay," she got out and let me take the wheel. I had almost got us completely out when she said "I think you're making this worse!" I got out and she went in while I calmly and firmly told her which way to turn the wheel. I even walked up to the window to turn the steering wheel to straighten them out, but she was gunning the gas so the wheels spun, creating little ruts.

"Okay, let me drive," I said when we got a little bit of leeway. She did and then I pulled us forward and then we swung out.

"Yay, we're free!" we celebrated; at least we did until…she got us stuck again. Luckily some people in a van stop by to help this time, because she really did a number! She got behind the wheel and I sat in the passenger seat – when I opened the door to get in, the snow was right level with the floor of the car; the door scraped snow away as it opened. I chuckled at the situation and then tried to steady her nerves. Eventually she let one of the boys that stopped drive the car and we were out in no time. I found my own car keys at Chloe's house when they took off I drove away to do…nothing.

God was with me, though and soon the next door neighbors came home. I had hung out with Stephanie a few times and we got along well. She is a very nice young lady, renting the house by herself with her two cats. She is very pretty with thick dark hair and nice true-brown eyes with long eyelashes. She had shared some of her toughest things with me and I thought she was sweet and caring with a genuinely kind smile. I knocked on her back door and she was happy to invite me in. When I told her what happened with my day, she got concerned.

"What time did you get locked out?" she asked.

"After work at five," I answered, keeping my jacket on to stay warm. Her black and white cat came and nuzzled against me kindly; the other one was given away.

"Do you know Gladys' number?" she asked, "I can't believe you've been out there that long, it's like minus thirty two outside." Her boyfriend even admitted that it was crazy to be outside for so long in the cold.

"Well, I stayed in my car for a bit," I explained, "I don't know anyone's number because it is in my phone and I forgot my phone today of course," I added with a little hint of sarcasm directed at the irony of the current situation. I had forgotten to eat breakfast as well, so now my stomach grumbled unhappily. Stephanie heard and offered some chips. I felt bad for intruding, but what could I do?

"Well where does Gladys work?" she asked and we tracked her down and then Gladys said she was at a bible study. It was only seven thirty, so her story seemed plausible. Stephanie did all the talking with Gladys, as both she and I felt she would be better received than I would be. We tracked down Gina who was an hour out of town at an event with her family and said she would get me from next door if she did not find me when she came. I was relieved at that because I knew that Gladys was enjoying this way too much. Ten came and went and then the clock hands slid to eleven. We went outside to see about prying a window open and even to unscrew the dead bolt, but no luck.

"Yeah, she's not at bible study," Steph voiced, quoting my thoughts exactly, "what bible study goes this late?" I dunno, but the ones Gladys attends end at ten the latest. I told her that Gladys was probably enjoying the situation.

"She's not that bad, is she?" Stephanie asked carefully.

"Well, she can make good first impressions, but she is not a very nice person to me," I said, trying to be fair.

"What did she do? Why are you leaving?" Steph asked. I told them a little bit about the things that were going on and they both thought it was crazy. "So she gets room and borders and then she bullies them," Steph said with distaste. She knew I wasn't lying and I knew that I had not considered it bullying until that very point.

"She sounds messed," her boyfriend said, tapping his cigarette into the ashtray.

"Yeah, all the things you say and the way she acted when I came in and the fact that she hangs out with twenty year old boys…it just doesn't line up," Steph said thinking out loud. She wants to be a social worker, (I think she would be quite good because she cares about people), so she has the psychology background. We talked a little bit about it and they agreed that it was best that I was moving out. We watched a movie and chatted about general things and they snuggled together on the couch while I…pet the fluffy cat when he came purring by.

Steph and her boyfriend were getting tired, as she had to work at seven in the morning, so she offered her place for the night and began to get ready for bed. I was at a loss for what to do because the plan was to start moving things over to Rita's house in the morning and my simple goal of being moved out of Gladys' by four in the afternoon was now looking to be impossible. *Oh, but this time, Lord, you gave me a mountain, a mountain that I may never climb* the words of a song sung by Elvis Presley, very fitting to this moment, floated around repeatedly in my head.

At midnight I looked over and saw that Gladys' car was parked there and had gathered snow. How long had she been home? She knew I was at the neighbor's house and still didn't get me? Steph had told her that I forgot my phone…I grew angry, then. What the hell?! I said goodbye and thanked Steph and her boyfriend for letting me interrupt their night, and then walked over, singing the words of the Elvis song under my breath. I was out tomorrow – that was all that mattered…at least that's what I told myself.

I tried the door and it was locked. I knocked at it, humiliated, until Gladys answered. I brushed past her, abruptly thanked her for opening the door and firmly told her that the key was lost – I had searched for it and did not find. I used a direct tone of voice to let her know not to mess with me; thankfully she took the hint and went to chat online in her bedroom. I was exhausted and she had to know by this point that I was packing to be out the next day, since she told me herself each time we had a huge scene that she always looked inside my room to see if I was packing to leave like Alana did.

I had planned on things being difficult just for me to leave, and I had hoped for a peaceful exit, a few days early to give Wanda a few days to settle in, but I never imagined that it would be this humiliating. Seconds after Gladys went to her room, Gina came in and we had a chat. I made arrangements to borrow her key the next day. She had to work at four, and while I was hoping to be out before then, it seemed unlikely. The weather was not being very kind these past few days, so I shot a quick prayer request for good weather for me to move the next day. Packing was useless so late at night, so I just went to bed tired and angry and feeling discouraged.

While I was clearing the bed off, my cell phone was dead, so I plugged it into the charger and received a text from Gladys saying *I'm home now* but Stephanie had told her plainly that I had forgotten it at the house…whatever, I texted her back saying that I just got the text and that it had been a very long, hard day. **I'm sorry** she texted back, but I did not think she was – she was enjoying this and knowing that she was gloating over my present misery just added to it. I fell into a troubled sleep, feeling very disheartened.

The next morning I arose quite chipper and hopeful. Even though it was not as early as I would have liked, I was efficient in packing, and was soon piling full bags and boxes onto the living room furniture. Gladys made sure to get in and out of my way a few times and kept her bedroom door open and was suddenly asking questions about my church – questions that I **knew** she did not need me to answer, so I was very curt and kept packing, getting quite anxious to leave for good.

Rita texted and I caught her up on the present happenings and she offered to come by for a load of stuff with her car. I was not sure if she was actually going to come, but she did and we had fun loading the car and off she went to get things ready. Gina said she would help me load the car, but she had to focus on school work because she was lagging behind, but Gladys ignored me when I asked if she wanted to help. She had told me this tall tale when I first came of how when she was moving into her house with two roommates right away, she was bringing things in – heavy stuff, she said – and the two girls at the time looked at her and said "this is boring." Gladys said that the two girls watched with disdain and did not offer help and that was part of the reason why Gladys appreciated me so much – because I offered help constantly. Sure, I had my grumpy days, but even then if Gladys asked for help I gave it because that is what I do.

Well on this Thursday, the twenty-fifth of November, I doubted that story's validity. Even though Gladys knew how it felt to be loading with two people watching and not helping when asked, she put me in the same position – *knowing how it felt*. I did not let it faze me for too long, as there was a lot to do. I had reached Derek and he was coming around one o'clock, as was Drew. Now Drew and Noella have helped me move so many times! I was glad that he was coming into town soon. When Gladys left I was able to work more efficiently and soon my bed was taken apart, everything was cleared out, I swept the floor and filled my car with suitcases and bags and boxes. Gina was true to her word, helping me load up, but on our first trip to the car, Gladys waited until

I looked over and then she looked right at me, got into her car and drove off.

What the heck? I thought she had left half an hour ago because she had slammed the front door from her room this time. Why did she wait until I looked before driving off? Her car did not need to idle for twenty minutes! And then I shook my head as I realized that in the one year and two months that I had stayed with this woman, she had tried to recreate **everything** I told her about my past.

Everything from placing blame for things I didn't do to favoritism between the roommates, to constantly bossing me around and snooping, to unsafe situations with men, to consistent battery, to being locked outside for hours in unfavorable weather, to the ultimate rejection. It was angering at first, but took only minutes to see that it did not hurt like it did with Joan because Gladys did not mean that much to me. I did not consider her a friend, but it was irksome that she would be intentional about placing me right where I came from with the knowledge of how hard I had worked to come away safely. Why did she want to destroy all that? What was it about me that set her off in such a manner? What Gladys doesn't know is that I am strong through the Lord **my** God. He has brought me out of the darkest pits of despair and her little games are only little pictures of those valleys – not the real thing.

I am stronger than she realizes because even though she pulled out the stops to try to crush my spirit, all she did was open my eyes to her deceptions. I am not invincible or anything like that, but I can say that even though I was brought down and faced with many new challenges all at once, Gladys should have realized the coldness in her heart to try to bring me down further. One might be able to knock me down for a while, but it is only a matter of time before I spring up again. God has ways of doing that – very much like the music in my life that *I* try to squash; it keeps coming back.

God has an undeniable persistency. Gladys resides in my eyes as a very wicked and manipulative lady. Her tongue is of poison and her heart is of cold black stone. She is the one who is hurting gravely and I think I have seen a lot of vulnerability on her side, so she feels that she must act out to survive. She had asked me to not make her pay for other people's sins, but in reality that is what she was making **me** do. There is no way I could make anyone pay for the things that happened in my life – it was out of my control and the people that should pay will pay one day at the hand of someone greater.

Gladys had nailed me to the cross instead of Jesus; a very foolish and dangerous thing to do. This was not my choice – I just listened and offered advice when she came; I just offered help when she needed it. *I* was the one who paid for how hurt Gladys was when Alana left without paying or telling her; *I* was the one who paid for the ups and downs of Gladys' relationship with Frank and *I* was the one who paid for choosing to be there for her. It made me pity her because I feel that it is not smart to make a person pay – sure, the pain on my face is more evident than a God whose face you cannot see, but I am not Jesus; not even close. I have never claimed to be.

To even *try* to put me in that spot is the mark of a fool – I am a human being, nothing supernatural, in fact I tend to be a fool sometimes as well, so I *will* **let** you **down**. I also felt like a fool for constantly giving her the benefit of the doubt, for brushing things off and for entrusting her with pieces of my story. Gladys knows of God and has the theological background and the books and videos and songs, but what good is knowledge when it is not applied? These things flashed through my mind in the blink of an eye…or two, and then I forced myself to keep up with the tasks at hand. No time to dwell when people were coming to help move; there would be time for thinking and processing later on. When the guys came over we loaded up all our vehicles to take everything in one load, but we ended up coming back because I kept forgetting things.

Drew had to leave for work soon, so he helped transport the big stuff and then Derek and I went back for the smaller things. I hadn't planned this, but Gladys had a printer that she said did not work on her computer – she claims to have searched for the software but could not find it. I got the printer working on my computer and had bought new ink for it beforehand. At the last moment – partially because of need and partially out of spite, I grabbed the printer and loaded it with my belongings.

The three of us had fun moving and then I invited Derek over for a supper in a few days. With Drew's blessing and a new roommate to get to know, I felt there was a lot on my plate. Right away I started unpacking and Rita would poke her head in to say "how's it going?" or "you getting set up?" or just to say "hi." She seemed nice, really, she did. I wanted to believe that she was, but I had to keep a careful eye. I am not ready to dive into anything to quickly as my heart had been lacerated and I need time to heal and get my feet on the ground.

Luckily she knows this and gives me space. One evening we were talking and I told her of some things that went on with Gladys. "I can see why you needed a safe place!" she said. She also said that after the meeting with her dad when I had left she had said "calm down, dad, we don't want to scare her away," and although Rita said that in passing during the conversation, I liked it because it showed me that she cared. She was not looking for a roommate when I asked to move in, so I told myself to be on my best behavior and we get along just fine. She can be outgoing and knows when is too much and said she knew I wasn't lying when I needed a safe place. "You will be safe here," she said, "I will not invite random strangers over without letting you know," she said with a laugh. She has a good laugh – nice and loud and clear, straight from the belly.

She also says she is a Christian, but I think with her it is true because we had a conversation about God and it was intriguing. She also explained that when I spoke of needing a safe place something inside her was already fighting for me and that's partially why she let me come in. I thanked her because when I had no place to go she had definitely opened the door. She welcomed me and also shared some food in the beginning to help me out, all the while just saying "I am merely a vessel." Well, vessel or not, I am glad to have ended up here, and it is only at this time that I realized that God had indeed provided like he said he would – but would I be fine?

chapter 12:

With Christmas lurking around the corner I felt myself wanting to burry into the rush of the season. Rita and I got along swell – we both sing and play piano and she really appreciates music. She is on a worship team and according to her actions and words that I've seen; I feel it's safe to say that her faith in Jesus Christ is (for her), a matter of heart. I will admit to a high uncertainty upon first entering the house, but I had invited Derek, Chloe and Helen over for a potluck supper and Rita joined in. By the end of the night the mutual decree was of good stature.

Well, I tell you – I have *never* laughed so hard at one meal! I have laughed hard and with the same people, but we were all laughing all together and so hard that our sides were slitting, our eyes were watering and our throats were getting sore from speaking and laughing so loudly. We teased each other mercilessly – all in good fun, knowing one another quite well – and I had almost made it through without being teased, but my turn was sure to follow the many witty comments I had made for the others. One of my first mornings in this new house, I was still sleeping internally, so when I plugged in the electric kettle, placing it on the stove top, I came back a minute later to turn on the burner, forgetting that it was plugged in. happily and very sleepily brushing my teeth, I hummed as I prepared for work – pulling my hair back, putting the makeup on (this is the only time I wear the stuff – for performances), and sticking some earrings in so that the pierces wouldn't grow in; I had a good start to the day.

As I dipped between my room and the bathroom, I noticed a funny smell. Thinking it was nothing; I wandered into the kitchen and was horrified to see the kettle on the red hot burner! Even typing it now, I feel so silly, but at the time I felt horrible! I figured Rita would be upset about it, so I vowed (and forgot) to buy another kettle at the end of my shift that day. Luckily, Rita just let it go and boy, did my friends ever tease me about that! Still do, sometimes! I am so glad Rita was able to laugh at it!

Shaun came over a few times as well and we had a jolly good time, with Rita joining later on. I tease her and her boyfriend – much in the humorous way I teased Chloe and her friend Ben when he came for a visit. Chloe had asked me to be an accountability person – so I did, keeping it as light and funny as possible because I know how awkward things like that can be. Chloe and I had a few conversations before about where she stood and where he stood and all kinds of things, so I was quite honored that she had asked. I also kept it funny to let her know subtly that I was there, keeping a careful eye out and would be there for either of them if they needed.

Rita thought this group of friends was great and I am glad that her boyfriend thinks I'm hilarious because I give the two of them quite the hard time! Actually Rita told me when a previous roommate of hers was dating she teased them a lot, so what comes around, goes around! ☺ As long as it is all in good fun – I am careful to keep myself in check because I know sometimes it can be quite easy to get carried away, and I check with both Chloe and Rita to see if they mind.

Surprisingly, neither party does. Both Rita's boyfriend and Chloe's friend Ben think I am funny and that is good. Rita is laid back in the fact that she knows that I write and is quite willing to let me do my thing. She does not watch TV which is fine with me as I grew up without watching it and so we watch movies sometimes, but mostly it is music or shows on our laptops. I feel more liberated here, as I can write at any time and not be bombarded with imposing questions. I told her about my book and was delighted when she said "not you've got me pumped to read this book… you have such a fire…" when we were discussing the situation with Gladys. I only told her of these things to bring awareness of this girl that she was allowing into her house – but her reaction along with my friends showed me that the recent happenings with Gladys were indeed abnormal.

It is to my utter suprise and complete amazement to find that Rita makes funny voices like I do! It is hilarious! I think her funny voice is better than mine and I feel that it would suit an anime character of some sort! The best thing is that although we get along so well, there is no control, no answering to or dependency. Her house is right close to the school that I will be attending soon, and it really is the perfect house for two people – *and* my car is now parked off the street, so no more hits…hopefully!

Well soon I was able to relax and really sleep well. I could feel my body returning to normal after all the present stresses and then I began to focus on choir. I was picked to dance a solo while the choir sang a lovely Spanish lullaby behind me. I practiced with a girl who dances for her living and it was fun to be in the studio again! I hadn't danced since I was in musicals, so it had been quite a while…but absence makes the heart grow fonder as in this case. I had a ball.

Still not seeing myself as much of a dancer, I planned on looking nice and innocent so that if I messed up then I could just smile sweetly and hopefully no one would notice. Funny, right? It was my plan, but I did not mess up. I wore a nice flowing red dress and pulled my hair back into a long playful ponytail, letting the natural wisps come out because it seemed to portray a more youthful appearance. I darkened my eyes and put a white flower in my hair that Mrs. Krieger had sent me from a trip to Mexico.

I had practiced the dance for a little bit – one brief run through with a dance teacher and then a few times on my own. Once I had practiced with the choir, I was appalled to realize that I had been dancing way too fast!! I had been practicing on my own on empty tours at work and did not carry a copy of the song, so timing was hard. I altered the simple dance to make it a little trickier and soon I had to find a similar version of the song on youtube. Thank goodness I did because I practiced it the night before a few times and then only once with the choir and that was it!

I loved being in the choir! Singing in there was fabulous and I am hoping to join again next fall because school scheduling will not allow me to join in the spring. I invited some people to attend, but not all were able to come. Drew came but Noella couldn't because she worked until ten and was by herself at the dairy barn, milking, so she couldn't get out of it. Shaun and Ruby came as did Rita with her boyfriend and Chloe who sat by herself near the back, sadly.

I had met up with Pat from elementary school – my best friend of grade three - and we talked about hanging out, but it never happened because we were busy, but it was a delight that she was also in the choir, as an alto. We started the evening by filing down the isles of the big church and singing lined up in between the full pews. I could see and feel tonnes of people looking at me and listening when I sang, but for some reason it spurred me to give more; to sing more loudly, to concentrate and listen more, to smile wider. During a musical interlude, I looked around to smile at people behind me – to make sure everyone was acknowledged in the audience – and saw Rita right away.

When the first song was finished, we all continued on our way forward to the stage. I heard a voice say something about a "lovely smile" and turned to see Ruby looking right at me with Shaun smiling beside her. I waved quickly, but had to go as we were getting ready to sing! I had tried to invite Esther and Wayne Johnson, but I don't know if they had alternate plans or didn't get the messages or what. Performing is always so grand and it is a true shame when it seems to slide so far back that I don't remember what it feels like. We sang Christmas songs seated within the audience for part of the evening, and it was then that I spotted Chloe sitting in the back by herself, so I strode toward her gallantly offering a bright smile.

"May I sit here?" I asked jokingly.

"Yes, you may," Chloe answered with a sweet little smile and moved her jacket. Then we sang our choir songs together and soon it was time for the dance. I changed into the dress (the wearing the second costume under the first one trick – works every time) in the blink of an eye and stood by the tall elaborately decorated tree on the stage. As the choir sang a lovely rendition of *Duermete mi Nino,* I could feel my arms wanting to shake, but I firmly told myself not to and danced right close to the people in the front row. I kept myself firm and used the space around me, accenting my long arms and legs.

I was nervous but confident at the same time. I am less familiar with dancing, but I know that when I sing or act, I go right close to people at times, as if they draw it out of me, or as if I could speak to their souls through the music or words. Dancing was different, but here I was not in an ensemble so I couldn't just blend in with others or mimic what they did. Here at this moment I learned that dancing is also an expression. I listened to the music and the movements seemed to fit right in with the melody.

Even though this dance was made up and only one girl was dancing, there are a lot of people that I attribute to the success of it. A lady in the choir by the name of Dina provided me with the quick dance lesson through her daughter and the lovely red dress. Another lady, the one with the fine soprano voice that I followed at the start of choir practices, named Martina, also used to dance and had a daughter who danced as well. She stayed to watch me practice with the music and said I had "good lines" and it was a nice little dance. "Just relax and have fun. Don't hop in, just sort of float in," she demonstrated, lifting her hands about her and looking around in a very theatrical way, saying "you don't want to wake the baby, but take a look as it sleeps."

The song *Duermete mi Nino* means "sleep my child" in Spanish. Pat also kindly told me of her figure skating days, that she used to "stick her chest out" and keep her shoulders "open to everyone." I liked the input and taking their advice, was able to better the dance overnight. I had thanked each one liberally for their input as any advice at this point was great! The dance was wonderful and people thought it was good and I looked very sweet with the lily in my hair. The choir had been featured in the local paper and so the pews and balconies were quite full in this nice big old church.

The church has a highly raised stained glass roof and so the sound was amazing. There were a few soloists and quartets and things like that, as well as a variety of Christmas songs – different genres, so it was fun. At the very end we invited people from the audience to come sing with us and then sang the mighty "Hallelujah" chorus by from Handel's Messiah. I think that one song is my truly favorite piece of music of all times. I wore a huge grin on my face the whole time we sang it (I didn't know it was there, but Chloe told me she could see it from the back of the room) because I loved it **that much.**

The funny thing about this is that I always sing the Hallelujah chorus with my friends, say if I won a battle of the wits or had a smart comment that got a good reaction…or even if I just won a hand in a game. Because the choir was singing it that night, I now learned to sing it on key (but I actually learned that I hadn't been too far off the mark before). I just thought that was pretty funny.

The night went well, and as it always is in every show, all the work was over by the end of the night and I was quite sad about it. Everyone pooled downstairs for cookies and hot chocolate and visits. I met up with Chloe and managed to see everyone that I knew that had come as well as a few acquaintances that I didn't know were coming. Many people complimented the dance and said it was very well done and that I looked confident, which was good, because I did not feel overly so! It was a bright and cheerful atmosphere with kind hearts and lovely music and outside it was snowing, but the sky still looked bright. While I walked to my car with Chloe, I felt for a moment like I was in a Christmas post card.

While driving back to the house and watching the snow swirl towards my windshield, I felt that finally life was going to be alright for a while. I just felt that I would be safe like God promised and I was grateful that He had provided like He said He would. *Everything is gonna be alright,* was the thought as I drove carefully, *I am gonna be just fine,* but this time I believed it. Well as Christmas time drew nearer, I all of a sudden had many options for what to do and where to go and who to spend the day with. Drew and Noella were going away for the weekend – which I couldn't do because I had to work on Boxing Day – sounds petty, but winter is always tight financially, and I was set up for a ten day run of work, which would completely cover all the bills for February and would allow some rest in January…and maybe some focus on music.

I had ordered a portable studio (much like the one Norah had) online – a reluctant purchase because I don't have much faith in online buying. Ephraim had paid twelve hundred dollars for a laptop once and got…nothing. I gambled and bought this portable studio from a seller who had extremely high ratings. Well, a month later, I am sad to report that the studio still had not arrived, but it was Christmas time and things do get a little bit crazy in the mail side of the world. At least, that is what I told myself, but I had ordered and paid for it a month ago with US priority mail; maybe it was stuck in customs.

Something lovely did come in the mail, though, a package from Mrs. Krieger! I told myself to wait until Christmas to open it – as I had done in previous years, but got so excited that I tore open the package a few days ahead. Luckily Mrs. Krieger knows me and had wrapped a few of the things inside as well, so I ate the Carmel peanut butter popcorn and waited before opening the other gifts.

Life was not too boring in the mean time, though, as Rita and I set up the tree that Noella and Drew bought me (now three years ago) and a few decorations. Rita also had a tree…well, more of a skinny bush. It was a tiny tree, not far from a foot or two tall, with decorations, and although it was fun to mock, it suddenly turned quite cute when plugged in. Rita also had a girl's night party and it was fun as a coworker by the name of Simone came over with me at the end of our shifts. Chloe and Helen were busy and Rita invited some of her other friends.

It was alright – a bit of a new thing for me because of the all girls' thing, but we played games and Simone made us all laugh with her outrageous jokes. I went to bed happy and tired while Rita stayed up to visit with her pals. Now here is one *wonderful* thing that I adore about Rita. I do not hear her when she wakes up in the mornings or comes in late at night! A miracle! Once again, life has offered me the bedroom right next to the bathroom, but with Rita I usually don't even hear a peep! I make sure to praise her about it, but she's not the only person I have got to praise.

Drew and Noella were going away to a Fairmont gathering for the weekend and decided to come over on the twenty second for supper. It was good! Steak and pasta and vegetables and Rita also joined us for the meal. We had fun and teased each other and visited for a short while. They liked my new homestead, agreeing that it has "good character" and they got along swimmingly with Rita.

Helen insisted on making me create a list of things I wanted. I didn't write it; I just spoke to her on the phone about it. "Well, I need some warm socks because mine have holes and…I like food," I suggested, thinking that was asking a lot.

"Okay, those are things you need, what do you *want?*" Helen pressed. I racked my brain and could not think of anything. Later I told Helen that I had my eye on a book by Julie Andrews called *Home* and a few other knick-knacks. "That's better," Helen said with a snicker, "you suck at writing lists!" Mrs. Krieger sent a package as well and it contained the book itself – I was excited to dig in – and it had some very fuzzy warm stripy socks. On Christmas day I was going out of town with Chloe, so I decided to have the gift opening day on the twenty-third instead because that was Christmas with Helen.

In the mean time there was a Christmas party at work and I used to hang out with a lot of the workers outside of work. As things got tough with Gladys I pushed most of them away, but they had no idea that I was going through anything (most of them still don't know), so they thought I was a big snob. Well anyway, among the workers were Derek, Simone and Chloe. I sat at a table with Johnny and Simone and a few other people I knew. We ate a nice Christmas meal and then had a scavenger hunt in the underground tunnels, below where we work.

There were nine clues placed allover these tunnels, hidden in the various rooms down there. The tunnels are swept up and well lit so running around was quite easy. At first I was uncertain for how I would be able to keep up with the young high school student guests that were on my team, but I was running the whole time…by young, I mean only a few years difference in age. ☺ Sometimes we would just scream at the people running by or shout back and then laugh at the ones who were already hollering to try to scare us. Of course, my team did come in last place, but we were also the last ones to start and there were prizes for everyone all around.

On the twenty third, I visited with Rita and we sang in our funny voices to Christmas music while dabbling around on our computers. When one o'clock came close I peered out the wide front window wistfully waiting for the mail truck to drive by. I was *still* waiting for the port studio to come in! It had been a month now since the seller received my payment and every time I emailed her she just typed *"give them some more time."* As frustrating as it was, I kept waiting – getting hopeful when there was mail, and drooping when the package notice failed to show up. I heaved a wistful sigh when I realized that the studio was not coming that day and kept looking out the window anyway. My friends were constantly checking up to see if it came in.

All of a sudden I felt a little bump on my back. I looked over and Rita had filled my stocking and laid it next to me on the couch, wearing the sweetest little smile ever! I think the best present was the look on her lovely little face! It was a great distraction – again she also had some handy things in there – a gift card for some clothes, good quality lip balms...and some fun stuff too like sour rockets, a bath thing that dissolved in the water (and smelled great). After opening the stocking I was in much better spirits. I had some running around town to do yet, and Helen had called saying to come over whenever I wanted to. I drove to her house first and she wanted to wait to open the gifts. I was pretty excited – partially because I knew *she* was thrilled to give them to me, and partially because of the effort she put for my Christmas to be good. Last year was a busy blur of preparing for the big trip to the Caribbean, so there weren't many gifts, but there had been the roommate Christmas and supper with Noella and Drew as well.

This year Helen waited until I got excited...a tact that actually worked! I made food and then bugged her until we opened gifts by her lopsided tree. She and her lovely roommates got a real Christmas tree and the smell is just divine! Helen is an <u>awesome</u> gift shopper! I had things that I needed like razors, toothpaste, toothbrushes, the *warmest* socks ever...and I **love** getting things like that (call me weird, but they are always handy). I design clothes and things with little rhinestones and studs, and because she couldn't find them, she gave me the money to buy it with. She also got me new running shoes – very good quality – and studio headphones! I was thrilled. I had bought her a few presents as well – one was a box of *Pot of Gold* chocolates, and I informed her that she must have this box for herself because she tends to share things.

Yes, it is great to share, but I wanted her to have something delightful for herself, so I also provided another bag of treats that she could share. Helen had told Chloe that she had written a letter for herself to read for when she gets really sad or angry or overwhelmed, and I was there too, so I thought it might be neat to write her a letter myself. This way she could remind herself of the good things she sees in herself, as well as have some of the good things that another person sees. It was funny because we thought alike – she had also written me a letter; it said that even though the bad memories couldn't be erased, she hoped her efforts would create some better ones and it did.

The package from Mrs. Krieger contained the book *Home* by Julie Andrews and I was thrilled to begin reading it right away. I read during the slow times at work and it is a very well written book, reminiscent of her earlier days on stage and then into her Broadway and film careers. There are many things in there that one would not expect her to have gone through as well as a strong and persistent characteristic that one would not have perceived, having only seen her in the movies as a polite well mannered babysitter (with a lovely voice). One part of the book was particularly hard for me to read, though, and that was when she was describing how her alcoholic stepfather would use the strap on one of her half brothers named Donald. She said that he would lead the boy into a separate room because Julie's mother would become distraught and then the whole house could hear the strap hitting her brother while he cried. Julie says in her book that she did not interfere because she was afraid that the stepfather would turn on her. [1]

I had to set the book down and walk away for a while to soothe the burning in my chest. Yes, her words hit a nerve. Those words were almost *exactly* what Susie had said to me a few years ago when she apologized for the way Joan treated me. She had said that she felt terrible and I had coolly asked "well then why didn't you do anything?"

"Because I was scared that they would turn on me," Susie had said honestly. Although I never show it, those words have never left me. Julie

---

1 Home Julie Andrews; end of pg 107, pg 108

would know exactly how my sister felt. Except that Susie did not have as open relationship with me as Julie did with her brothers, but she was the kindest of the family, since she was nicer when no else one was around because she would "get into trouble" if they saw. From reading about her, I have decided that I would love to meet Julie Andrews for coffee one day. The rest of Julie's book is a great peek into a lifetime of performances, tossed in with a few nuggets of humor; it was what I had asked for this Christmas.

I do not understand why people get so anxious about buying or opening gifts – or why there is one day designated for it, but this Christmas was packed full new stuff for me to experience. There was **no way** I could walk away without feeling special. I know that I've got friends in high and low places. Alice came to town but I hadn't heard from her at all except a call to take some shifts at the resort – which I couldn't take because I worked at the other job on those days. It kind of showed me where I stood, which was good to know.

I knew that the Johnson's would be calling about Christmas Day at their house and that Esther would be looking forward to it, but I just couldn't bring myself to go. I debated for a really long time and then Chloe asked me to go to Jade's house for Christmas with her, I knew if I didn't have anywhere to go then Rita would invite me and all of a sudden it seemed that everyone wanted me to be at their house this year. I suppose it ought to have been flattering, but it just wasn't.

I have been down this road many times – people always try to take me in or "adopt" me or "take care" of me or "love" me for their own reasons. They want it to be shown that I went to *their* house for Christmas. Often times a person will say things to try to get me to come – offering empty promises or sudden friendships that I never saw before. However, contrary to their beliefs, these words are not what I need. I don't need to hear nice things – I need to *see* it and **feel** it. With the Johnson's it did not feel this way, however, it seems like they don't want to think of the perspective of pain – not that they hide it, but that they turn a blind eye, or they don't want to look at the depth of it. I had started to tell Norah and some of her friends (when I visited) some of the things I went through because they had shared during my visit to

Redcliff, but when I started speaking, they interrupted to leave. Such is life, but still…

People do not want to hear of these things (or probably read them, ha, ha), but they are a fact of life, and I am upfront about it because I believe in honesty. Although…I do kind of cheat, having written about it, I don't have to talk about it as much. Alice is great to talk to because she listens and then she relates and shares tough things within her own life to show that she also grew up with difficulties. It is often a good chat and perhaps it brings awareness to me of what trials happen even within a good life – things that I would never think about.

I had told Alice before thanksgiving that I might not go to her house for Christmas because it is hard. I can do dinners and gifts with friends – Noella and Drew don't really celebrate Christmas although they have made more of an effort since I've lived with them, so suppers are fine. Friends are great. Gifts are fun. The season decorations and music and baking and cheer are all wonderful. Even the cold, murky and blanched white snow can be festive with their postcard views of every house.

Don't put me in front of a family. Christmas was the *one* time of year that Joan was at least sure to be civil in her contempt; the food was *excellent* and the house was transformed. Going into foster care took all the majestic festivities away. The Swazies were great about buying gifts and what not, but they lacked in empathy – when I was moody and sad, they were slightly like "all these things we bought are getting to your head," but they were by far the most considerate as other places made me do all the cleaning and cooking and sit at a different table while they acted like a happy family or they would send me away so that they could have their family times. Pain goes deep. I am not explaining it very well, but I make myself put these feelings on a shelf for most of the year, busying myself with ideas and projects. Christmas is the **one** time that I do not pretend to not be hurting because it just doesn't help; I prefer to be by myself on that day, but I suppose it is good that my pals are boisterous.

Luckily this year my friends really came through for me and lifted my spirits. I always knew they liked me! Yes, Alice texted me closer to Christmas day, inviting me over, yes her cousin Shaun asked if I was going and they seemed excited, but there was just too much pain for me to pretend otherwise. Last year was a great turning point of recovery when Ephraim and Jonas and I met our family in the Caribbean, but this year was not nearly so hectic and the truth always comes out – it is better to acknowledge these feelings before facing them head on, and expressing them is a quicker start.

I knew that if I went I would leave angry and to give Esther credit, I think she was feeling uncertain as to how to proceed because I just suddenly pushed everyone away. Alice was quite empathetic when I later explained these things to her in the New Year. I have decided to maybe just be more friends with her and Shaun as they are indeed closer to my age, and I do enjoy their company so very much, and I still sing with Esther at music nights once in a while.

Even though it happens to everyone on the planet, I find that one still fears the bomb especially if they don't know where it will drop. I felt that I was in "unfamiliar territory," (a term Noella used once). Family is something that I am not accustomed to, or fit into, and experience has taught (and continues to teach) that often times when a person extends an invitation to "be a part of the family" it does not mean literally. However, I do believe the Johnsons meant well.

To pull myself away from myself, I volunteered at a community dinner held at Prairie Winds – not just to dine and dash. I shuffled in with my big clunky boots and offered to help, instantly put to work. At first I was to bring the meals out on big trays but they needed someone serving, so we set up a system and away we all went, dishing big dollops of steamy food onto the plates. A much more comfortable arrangement, for things big and awkward have been known to fall out of my hands! Pastor Russell was there, wearing a little hat that looked kind of like a cop or a marine's hat, but I told him he looked official and he said he was the captain.

"Captain of the cooks," we agreed and it was fun helping out. Many people dined and I sat with two girls in the church closer to my age that I don't usually mingle with. It was alright. The food was delicious and then I learned that it was the birthday of a lady at our table. Since I was nominated as probably the most gutsy one at the table, I went up to the mic at the front and said "excuse me folks, can I get your attention?" about half the heads turned my way, but I was not satisfied, so Russell bellowed "ATTENTION!" in his big booming voice. "It's this lady's birthday today," I explained, pointing as the woman stood up excitedly, "and I think for everyone whose birthday is in December we should sing happy birthday on the count of three. Ready? One, two, three," I counted firmly, putting that number of fingers in the air with each count.

I was going to sing happy birthday into the mic but then I realized that I didn't know the lady's name, so I held the mic down and sang with everyone else, not singing for her name, and I thought it was funny. Actually one of the elders of the church approached me and said he would like to do that at each community dinner as he thought it was a fine idea. I appreciated that. I helped clean up and a lady from the church – the same one who saw me crying when she was handing out pamphlets at the door – was seated at our table and she gradually spoke more and more to me.

I realized that she is much kinder than I had perceived and since desert was dark chocolate cake I refused to avoid hives (allergic to cocoa powder), she generously offered an alternative. "I know a place where there are cookies without chocolate," she offered, "would you like some?"

"Sure," I accepted, "maybe after we clean up."

"Okay," she said with a twinkle in her eye, "just look me up – I could even give you some to take home if you want." I was pleasantly surprised so I accepted the offer again. She found me after the cleaning was done and handed me a tin, saying "as you eat these, remember that," she whispered this next part "you are loved."

"Okay," I said lightheartedly, "I'll also remember that when I eat cheese." Of course I was insinuating that it was cheesy, but she paid no mind.

"A lot of love went into the making of these," she continued with a smile. I thanked her and offered them to Shaun, Chloe and Derek whom I was visiting with. I also decided to get a grocery bag from the church…to give to Jade. Having had a nice meal and offered some time (something I wanted to do last year), I felt better by the end of the day. Shaun, Derek, Chloe and I chatted for a while and then it was off to bed.

The next day was Christmas Eve and I actually ended up going to Chloe's house for a visit after my first vigil candlelight service. It was a modern one with glow sticks instead of candles (lame, but safer I suppose), and it was nice. There was a bit of a service and then some families sang together. Pastor Harry had made a point of finding me and shaking my hand at the end of the service and I realized that when I received his greeting, that somewhere in my heart I had truly forgiven him for everything. It must have been tough in his situation as he had Joan's word against mine; his friend versus a small child whom he'd heard terrible things about. I think that was an issue that has reconciled itself inside of me and there is no point in keeping a grudge **and** being a pastor is hard business! The couple that remembered me at Samantha's pasta night were also there; the gentleman had passed me a glow stick when I searched for one. They had run out of them, so he had given me his unbroken yet; a kind gesture. Chloe and the girl whose car I had unstuck (when I was locked out of Gladys' house) were there and then I met up with Shaun and Alice after the service.

It was awkward because I think Alice may have wanted me to go to her house for Christmas and I had frozen her out, albeit unfairly. In truth, I felt that we did not know each other well, so I didn't feel too terrible at the time, although not proud of my actions. She had sent texts and facebook messages, saying "what about the presents under the tree for you?" but I didn't care; it was not enough to lure me out of that dark shell. Credits go to Alice for trying, but sometimes I am unreachable. I just couldn't do it and at that point I had to allow time to grow. I did feel slightly guilty for being cold so abruptly, though.

Chloe and I ran into Simone at the church and right away she was talking very cheerily about her family and their traditions. "What traditions does your family have?" Simone had asked brightly, turning to me with a wide grin. I just bit my lip and blushed and Chloe interjected with something subtle to take the moment away and I was glad for her discernment and tact.

I visited with Chloe after the service – actually later than I intended and then ventured off to bed. It had been many late nights in a row combined with long days at work between both jobs calling and staffing for the holidays. Rita was off with her family for a few days, but she did text to ask how I was doing and I thought it was kind. A call to the Kriegers to thank them for the package and a small chat with Jonas ended the day well. I rather enjoyed the time to myself because it allowed me to hurt but the business forbade time to sink deeply into the rawness of the wound. I feel it went well.

The next day I received a call from my favorite twin as well as from Jonas. I had agreed to pick Chloe up at three and we were off to Jade's house for Christmas supper. I was quite reluctant to go, but Chloe had insisted, saying "I told everyone that wherever I go you're coming with me."

"I can just be by myself," I had interjected.

"No – you are not being by yourself for Christmas!" she sure sounded like Helen at this point. I did not argue because of many thoughts at that point. One was that this might be Chloe's last Christmas in San Frisco because when she moves away, she will be with her family hours and hours away – I think a three days' drive away. The other thought was *do I want to hang onto this pain forever?* True, I have just come out of many messes seemingly all at once, and not too long ago, so the pain is still deep and rather fresh, but I have to take steps towards healing and part of that is by letting go of the pain and substituting it for something better – sometimes by stepping out of your nice little shell. In this one instance I cannot just leap, though, I have to fight my way just to crawl to the opening because it is such a quick retreat.

I had prayed many things and for many people over the holidays – same as I do regularly, but I do not recall asking specifically for my own Christmas to be good this year, God just planned it. I woke up after a decent sleep and sang for a while and then chatted with Ephraim, making plans to visit grandpa together sometime soon. On the way to Jade's house I wanted to stop by the farm where the elderly ladies took in my cat. It is uncertain that they get many visitors, so I thought a bunch of chocolates and maybe a few candy canes mixed with some smiles would be nice. They were not home so sadly I did not get any snuggles and buggles from my kitty, and we went straight to Jade's house.

I wanted to leave as soon as we pulled up to Jade's house, but with Chloe there, that was hard to do. A few days ago I had told Chloe that I get angry around Christmas time and quite bitter. "I can be quite rude," I had explained to still protest her offer of going to Jade's house, "I push people away and it's not nice, you don't want to see it."

"But I am willing to," she answered and that was the clincher that swayed my decision to go. If I went with Chloe then I knew I would be safe to express, and she also offered to mention this to Jade so that if I left then they would understand. I chose to go to Jade's because Chloe and I would have been by ourselves this year and I knew I was with a true friend. It is not too often that a person says that they are willing to see the worst side of you. I knew that if I went to the Johnson's house I would have left angry and thinking *yeah, I can't do this,* but I think it is okay to allow time to heal, but not okay to dawdle.

Christmas dinner was fine – her sons were there and it was not awkward at all – I did have a bit of alcohol (which I enjoy every now and then) and it helped me to relax. We played games and ate a very tasty meal and then enjoyed Chloe's delicious homemade pumpkin pie and then relaxed to watch the nativity story. I actually felt that this Christmas had more of Christ in it, probably from all the church followed by the nativity, but also because of my own unintentional generosities as well as that of my friends. I know it is sounding like a big ball of cheesy right now, but it really did feel like that. I also did not regret postponing the Johnson's house – I felt bad that they were looking forward to it, but I thought they may have been offended if I had went and then left angrily. Of course there was the pounding question *if you turned away once, how easy would it be for you to turn away again?*

I actually was telling Alice most of these things when we were having a nice chat – I missed her a lot – and she said "actually I don't think anyone would have cared," so I may have underestimated everyone just a tad bit.

"Maybe next year," I offered genuinely, "I need some time to get to know everyone better and thanksgiving was good because it was new, but it was still hard."

"No, I understand," Alice said and I believed it. Her mom was nice about it too, saying "it might have ruined your Christmas to come here," in a slight joking matter, "because everything was so chaotic." All in all it passed over well, despite my rapid judgments and lack of honest communication for all parties involved.

As fun as the day was, I was relieved when Christmas was finally over. I think I was worn out from all the late nights and just looking forward to some time alone. However, Chloe and I drove back from Jade's house a bit late and, the moon was hard to miss. It was huge! Clouds tried to cover it, but their futile attempts could barely conceal the base of the moon – it was unusually large. I later heard from Shaun that a few days before there had been a lunar eclipse – and a meteor shower, but it was cloudy all week long, so everyone in town missed it, sadly. I went to bed that night thanking God for a nice Christmas and actually quite happy that I had not freaked out like I thought I would because that presented hope that letting go will get easier in time.

Immediately following Christmas day was a long stream of work days all in a row along with a few more gifts and a lot more thoughts and realizations to ponder. I thought about Esther and how I felt about the Johnson family. I realized that there is an immense amount of distrust on my part because I did not know them well and part of my frostiness was because I could not allow myself to be so vulnerable around them. It almost had nothing to do with the actual family at all, except the new awareness of the "abandonment" when I was a small child. I thought about how Joan had taken a great many things away from me whether intentional or not. I think she knew exactly what she was doing because she went so far out of her way to lie about everything, showing a full conscious choice in the matter. For example; when Ephraim and I had recently tried to call Aunty Rosa, Joan's younger sister, (the one who sent me a music box in my younger days), we were shut down pretty hard… and we both have the same idea as to why.

First we had to get the number from Joan, so Ephraim made me call to get it. I was very direct and to the point, skipping the formalities and politely asking for the number. At first Joan tried to play us; "I don't remember the number, it's on my phone," she lied. Even her vocal tone said she was lying.

I rolled my eyes and repeated it back to Ephraim. "Yeah right!" he scoffed aloud, "she dials that number every day!" I was glad that he said it clear enough for Joan to hear on the line because it left no room for games.

"Just a second," she said, a little more formally, "let me call you back with it." I knew something was up because I knew that Rosa had lived in the same place for a number of years, so she had the number memorized.

I hung up and repeated what she said. "She doesn't need to call us back," Ephraim said, echoing my thoughts directly, "she has it memorized!" Joan called back several minutes later with the number and was a great deal frostier. We called our aunty anyway, half thinking Joan gave us the wrong number on purpose – something I would not put past her.

"Is this Rosa?" I had asked politely when a lady had answered the phone.

"Yes it is," she said coldly, "your *aunty* Rosa. Do not call me by name because that is rude," she went on, knowing who I was without introduction. "Your cousin did that one time and I kicked her out and have not spoken to her since."

"Okay, well I apologize, I just wanted to be sure I had the right number," I explained. Wow, this woman had issues! To kick your own daughter out for that?! I happen to know that my cousin has two kids so Rosa is missing out on being a grandparent because of an argument she had with her daughter. Knowing what I do of my cousin, she is headstrong and so these two probably clashed quite often, but still, it seemed a petty reason to expel a child from your life for so long.

"Oh, you did," she said knowingly, "you know you did." Whatever; when I asked about visiting, she replied that she did not want "strange people in my house" is how she worded it – and she is the one who insists I call her aunty? She blatantly said that our uncle Vinny (the musician) and she did not speak because "I want nothing to do with those people!" I could not fathom this – she was so *insistent* about how it was disrespectful to call family by just their first name, but here she was calling her own family "strangers" and "those people" because they had offended her years ago (at least if talk about Joan, I call her by her first name – which is what she said to do on the day I ran away). Rosa gave no regard to the fact that Ephraim and I had sought her out and were being kind…or to the fact that the girl she was behaving this way to is indeed her niece. I feel really bad for her, though, as she still seems to be hurting – worse than I am.

As she jabbered for a while, I just passed the phone to Ephraim because he is way better at handling people and getting them to calm down. He had a hard time swallowing that pill! We both agreed that Joan had not hung up with me to "get the number" but to call Rosa; a sneaky, underhanded trick to deprive us – or more so, me – of knowing our own family. However, nothing more can be done – we gave it a shot, even if in the dark. When I typed to Uncle Tim about it on the computer later on, he was comforting in the fact that he filled me in on why Rosa had spoken so harshly.

Rosa had been hurt tremendously and it may have stemmed from her first marriage where she was beaten by her husband and then her daughter was a wild child with way too much attitude (I know this to be true) and when my uncle Vinny and his kids came from the Caribbean to stay with her, they treated her **very** badly, so she wanted nothing more to do with them. All of a sudden I found myself empathizing for the woman who had just lashed out. The way she talked of Vinny and his sons is similar to how I feel about Joan and Daniel and my two sisters. I am more receptive to the sisters, but I would not say that other than DNA they are *family* or even friends and (for now) I'm alright with that.

Rosa shuts herself inside her house as much as she locked away her heart to stop the bleeding; kind of like I do at Christmas time. She said she never went out – just to the grocery store and that was it. Perhaps I am not quite as bitter as our aunty, but it seems that now I have chosen to bend toward the light; towards life. Here is a woman who holds no hope and as little as I know of her, I do believe that Joan may be the only good thing in Rosa's life right now. Perhaps God was showing me something through that brief acquaintance.

As uncle Tim and I chatted online, he typed something that caught my attention **I must tell you something.** *Ok,* I typed back, somehow sensing that it was serious. **And it should not need an explanation,** he continued. Now I was worried, so I typed *ok* again and waited. The next words infuriated me; **the consensus was that you should not be allowed to stay here**. Instantly I knew what he was saying. Joan had tried to convince him not to let me stay there.

Anger boiled inside and I did not respond. **But we decided to go against that,** uncle typed, **and I was honored to have you stay here.** I thanked him and then responded that if I ever had kids I would love for him and aunty to be a part of their lives and he said they would love to. I am blessed to have an aunty and uncle like them – to take a chance despite all the terrors that Joan had crooned about and to let me stay anyway. I am sure that it was because of Joan's adoration for Ephraim that she did not pursue this to the full extent. Whenever I think of this a dull anger burns in my chest toward Joan. Not hatred, but anger – and rightfully so.

See, the Caribbean is a very dangerous place – many brutal murders, so if I was on my own in a hotel or anything, I would have been toast. Especially because I am a girl and I look different and sound American. Joan knows this very well as she grew up there and "cautioned" Ephraim and me to be careful. How funny it is that she tried to arrange it so that we weren't going or would not be safe...or come out alive. I think the objective was that we would not go.

I had thought about calling her on it and just hashing things out, but then it dawned on me that honesty is something this woman does not know. She has no idea how to tell the truth when it comes to me because it would allow a conscience to bloom and then she would have to face many things. So from the first strike – since birth – Joan has been lying to herself and everyone around to cover things up. I have become a symbol of all the horrible things she's ever done and her distance and coldness towards me marks the same reason as mine toward the Johnson's; vulnerability, or perhaps for Joan, fear.

I am strictly guessing that Joan's issues are not to do with pain and moving on, but with guilt for various reasons. Noella was right; Joan carries a big guilt on her conscience. This Christmas was a reminder of things that I don't have. I knew that the Johnson's would have been an even greater reminder – I have wondered what my life would be like if Esther had just taken me in. I wonder what it would have been like to grow up with love in a big family like I have always wanted to, but this Christmas showed me that I will never ever get to have that, ever. My days of being "raised" are over as I am an adult now; parenting is too late – I have been my own parent at a young age. Perhaps God will redeem it all, but I have no idea how...or when or if.

Talking with Alice and a few friends recently, I have been so encouraged because even though my "issues" are more dramatic and stuff, each family has their own problems. Alice shared personal things about how she felt with her family and I realized that if I had been taken in by them or adopted in a good home I could probably be worse off than I am today. See, there is a defiant nature inside that enables me to "rebel" against conformity, so the tables would probably have switched – I would probably be in the same boat I was at sixteen instead of the other way around.

So although I think that a gallon of progress was made this year, it feels like it hurt the most, too. Even at work when families bounced in and resembled each other unintentionally while they listened, it was hard to act cheery with these things thrown in my face every minute of every hour of every day – there was no break! See, even though Chloe was also by herself this Christmas, she still had packages and phone calls and cards from her family and when she moves back, they will be there with open arms. I feel like I missed out on a whole pile of life that people take for granted, but here I am on the outside wishing to be inside. However, all I can do is pray in this instance, and even that seems fairly barren most times.

Of course, I am lucky in the regards that I did not miss out one thousand million percent. Even though they seem like an illusion, I still had the Christmases from my childhood to remember even though they were always a bit dim; they were the best times of my years with the Stardens. The Kriegers are far in distance, but they have kept close by sending cards and letters throughout the year and emails and packages, so although she tried, Joan did not completely rob this house of everything good. Joan did try to prevent me from having friends at school when I was young, but now I got friends that stood by me through a very rough time. Realizing these things sure helps to lesson the pity party!

chapter 13: _____

Overall this year had been a great one – the first real good one of my life, I think, as I have lived the most in it. I call it the year of the "first times" because I went from meeting more long lost family to holding deadly jelly fish and petting sting rays and raccoons to roller coasters to facing new challenges and all kinds of people I had never dealt with before.

True, the year was not a billion shards of pure joy, but it was most certainly the best year of my life. I bonded with my brothers in a way that I don't think can be erased too quickly; I learned to asses situations and have seen God's providence in ways that most people read about, but it is the little things to look for – not the big ones.

I've had to reunite with absolutely everything from my past in some way or another and while there was much resolution, there leaves the fresh pain and the need to face these monsters from the grave with swords of hope and truth and real friends. Everything seemed like great closure – going to the Caribbean with my brothers, reading the files... now I do not wonder if Joan hates me; I know it and it is enough "whys" answered that the "how's" can be left alone. Even calling Aunt Rosa was closure in the fact that it was indeed her choice to stave off the feeble attempts at a relationship.

Mixed in with the closures, I got to see resolutions in other people's lives, too. Our uncles have probably wondered about us for the twenty years that we "disappeared" for, and I wonder if I had not tried to find Jonas or Ephraim, how different my life would be. Jonas would still be questioning his identity and I would still be vowing to reconnect with four people who do not care. I have decided that the Johnson's are good people and so I will allow them into my life because I think that they are welcoming and they *want* to give. Esther had bought me a jacket one day because my old one was stained and well worn. I had thought it was fine at the time, but she said she would look around for another. I forgot all about it until…

One day she came over with a big bag of three winter jackets! I took one, but declined the rest because she said she would take them back. She was so great about it! I was reluctant to go out that day because I was recovering from the flu – quite sick to my stomach – so she had said "why don't I bring them to you?" little things like that just tickle me pink. We had tea and she tried to hug me, laughing and saying "I'll get a hug out of you someday," but honestly, she is one of very few people whom I don't mind doing that, (but don't tell her I said so!) and now Wayne has joined in the teasing, but it all remains in good fun. It is all a learning experience right now.

I have seen ultimately that my impulse to shut them out is strictly because of the past. It is so hard to know how to deal with things like that, but I am writing songs and poems and expressing things that way. Luckily for me, the Johnsons have seen the struggle, I'm sure, so they are patient and fairly open. Little by little all the garbage is coming out and (I believe) in a healthy way because I am allowing time for expression and healing.

I have decided that if I do end up hurt, I will be able to handle it and get through it – plus friends hurt each other all the time; it is the ability to get through it that makes the relationship work. Sometimes people let fear run their lives and I have decided that jumping in with both feet or flying over your head is way better than just sitting in a circle of what you know. This whole year has been of taking chances – going to the Caribbean, recording in the studio, singing in the competition… sometimes when you jump you stumble or fall flat on your face, kind of like I did in April with Joe, but then you learn to not jump so high in certain things...kind of like jumping rope, versus a trampoline. That is what time is all about - to teach you to live; where to jump and how high and when to stay on the safe side of the tracks.

What's true now is that I don't necessarily need a boyfriend or popularity or anything like that to get by, but I do *need* family and I **need** parenting. Although...a nice man in my life wouldn't be so bad...I have realized so much this year about people – free will, the way people work...and myself. I have learned that free will often means that someone else does not have a choice, for instance, in abuse or rape or violence or vandalism.

It was Joan's choice to strike me and to hold my head underwater when I was a kid. It is her choice and Jocelyn's choice now to hate me because of things that happened years ago, and because of their own free will; there is *nothing* I can do to mend the chasm between us. I have learned the extremely hard way that Joan will constantly choose to meddle in my life if there is a way to knock me down. Upon realizing this; I have also seen that it is up to me to split that circle for good.

I have seen that I need to disallow her in my life because if I don't then it will become a constant and steady pilgrimage of my happiness and well being. Rita said she was open to letting me stay at her house because she could see that I have taken drastic steps to not only stay safe, but "to become a better person." I have grasped now that that is what I am doing, although I never knew it until that point. Part of the reason why I have come out "on top" of all these terrible things is the fact that I **chose** to get better. There is something within that does not allow me to be truly wicked, or to desire to be so, and I ought to attribute it to God because it is just *no* conscious effort on my part.

I have learned that people often choose to stay in the ruts they create for themselves – Gladys chooses to be mean, she chooses to eat unhealthy and stay inside and to not exercise. People often long for what they don't have without realizing that with a little bit of determination and hard work that thing they yearn for could be theirs. Like Gladys and her reluctance to work out or eat healthy. Some people do not love themselves enough to put forth an effort and people limit themselves so much by being afraid of change. Gladys was so set in her ways that she was afraid to try new foods! Or she would try a tiny smidgen of it and choose to not like it because it was something new. Man, to live in that fear!

Gladys chose to hold on to the bitterness inside and in the end it has cost her great amounts, but the sad thing is that it may keep costing until there is nothing but a crumbly shell left. In her case, as in Joan's and Rachel's, Gladys knows better. Loving who you are and arrogance or selfishness are separate things because a person can be quite cocky and still hate themselves – that's where imagery comes in. When I get insecure I present an image as if I am not, like many millions of trillions of people out there, pretending to be tough, but I find that it grows wearisome very rapidly because I know the truth...I'm secretly a wimp!

I have watched people thrash around for help, only to try to drown those who do try to help. I do that sometimes. It's called pushing people away. Rachel chose to do the things that she did and she chooses to put herself into horrible situations while always knowing better. Rachel and Gladys and Joan are all **very** smart people, to name a few, and they all have the right answers if you want them to, so they are not truly ignorant of the consequences of their actions. Gladys and Joan know better because they can play the nice card when they are being manipulative and it just shows that they are both fully aware of the choices they are making and most of their choices are intentional - learned behavior or not. That just reflects their characters...or lack thereof.

However, what people fail to realize is that there are consequences to actions – **every** single action has consequences of some sort. Right away when I think of that word "consequence" I go back to the teenage years and think it means "punishment" (i.e. detention). It is not a bad word – it means more of the "outcome" or the "result" of a situation. For example, I went to the Caribbean half way across the world without knowing the people whose house we were staying at. Our consequence was great – a nice aunty and uncle who lovingly welcomed us in and treated us (and fed us) very well the entire time.

This might seem like hullabaloo to you, but free will is a huge deal!

God cannot even mess with it...because it is His choice not to! But He *can* knock you on the head so many times that you change your mind, or he can punish/reward you for what you do, and He works within other people's wills and I am living proof of that. God *is* invincible. We are not. I **HATE** when people think I am strong or invincible because I am really very weak. I have risen out of the ashes and grown into a decent young adult in spite of the dramatic life I have lived, but I *cannot claim it in any strength of mine*. God has raised me up for whatever reason and I am glad (sometimes). I was chatting on the phone with a pal recently and telling her some miracles in my life and she said "when God picks His children He never lets them go."

Of course, the small, defiant part of me wants to fight and test and run from that, but a little bigger piece of me is intrigued. I have not given myself time to grieve or to process or to move on or to heal because I have not actually been out of anything for too long, but knowing that, I have decided that time is what I need. I also need to go with my instincts more often because they have yet to fail me.

So what to do with all this new knowledge? I don't know, write a book? I do count it as wisdom of sorts. There is so much but it is hard to explain and if I try anymore, then it will surely appear as mad ramblings and quite frankly there is enough of that in this world! Speaking of madness...so, about politics...just kidding! That, I will keep to myself. ☺ But where do I go from here? I think this is a good place to close off with what I would like to do.

I would like to have a family of my own one day, I would love to travel more; I would love to do music for my job, every single day for the rest of my life, but let's be realistic. Music is a hobby – and a fantastic one at that – family is far off in the future as I do not see anyone overly trustworthy nearby and traveling is quite expensive. Something within grins a little as I type this: *where there's a will, there's a way*. Well, who knows? So this Christmas was a good conclusion to a great year.

I have many blessings to be always counting and have not been able to take anything for granted because of where I come from. This might sound over the top, but I am actually glad to have traveled this road as dark as it may have been because having realized the freedom that people have, I can now choose to be my own person. Joan and Daniel are the ones who have befallen a curse in the fact that their lineage dies with us children, leaving us the sole deciders of what we pass down. There are no more children to carry on the generation of the Stardens because Jonas and Ephraim are both adopted and so will all be carrying on someone else's generation. That also brings peace of mind – how we can choose what to pass down.

I feel for Daniel, I really do, but he consciously chose to stand beside, join in and hide what his wife was doing; ever the loyal husband. Joan chose to take no matter the costs of the people involved - as did Gladys, but there will always be consequences for their actions even if I don't live to see it. This keeps me in check, too, because the same applies to every single person that is and was and ever will exist on this murky but sometimes lovely little planet, and I have definitely done some things that I am ashamed of, but sometimes that is how you learn.

While I vandalized as a teen, Esther chose to turn a blind eye on a child that needed help – under respectable circumstances – but look at the cost of my life. Look at the cost of the person whose house I broke into. I *could* choose to hold this over Esther's head in my mind, but I don't really want to. I could choose to forgive and still get to know the family in due time. I had talked about these feelings with Alice and Rita way back when, but I almost felt…worse. Afterwards, when I was struggling with the bitterness, I talked to God about it for maybe five minutes – mostly just "this is what's going on, but I *don't want to feel this way anymore! – how do I not feel like this?"* – And shortly afterwards I felt so much better! I couldn't believe it! Seeing the Johnson's since then, there has been absolutely no tension or bitterness or resentment or jealousy or…anything. For real. I love it!!

I think talking with Alice and other friends with family issues going on was quite encouraging – and it helped me to look away from myself – which I also love!! The Johnson's did not have to change anything in order for me to be alright; I just need time and answers that a person couldn't give. I have hung out with the Johnsons since then and it has been so fun! Yes, there was a time when everyone was praying for everyone and I was just watching and I saw the favor on their side…and of course, I started to think "I could have grown up…" but then I realized that I *was* in the moment. Ruby is still as funny as ever, Esther still loves to feed me, Alice still teases me and Wayne still likes to listen to me play piano. So I am glad with the decision to get to know the Johnsons although my first choice would have been to slam the door and forget the whole thing. It's far too easy to run – but to stay and face things does not always mean a fight. It means learning and working and increasing wisdom and tact.

Publishing my first book was new but hard because right away there was talk of splashing this "great story" on TV and stuff. Right away I shied away from that idea because I want people to be more focused on the actual story and the encouragements of choosing to be strong and moving on. I see how people take others that they think are "great" and build them up only to smash them into the ground. All I have to say is Britney Spears. But sensibly now she is stronger than most people because she has sat on top of the world and has also been crushed by the weight of it and has gotten back on her feet. So kudos, Britney Spears!

When I started receiving calls for my first book by the company to market it (before the book was printed, which I thought was too soon), one of the first questions asked was "so is this true? Did this really happen to you?" *of course it did!* I felt like saying, *I didn't just lie about it!* Perhaps they mean well, but it is so offensive! Where would I come up with this junk? Why would I lie about it? I know different ways of making money or attracting attention. Man, if people think I am lying about these small details, they need to open their eyes to world around them! There is so much worse than this going on and to younger children nonetheless! My story is way super better than tonnes of people out there, but also worse than too many right here.

The second thing is for people to say "I'm so sorry," with a condescending nurse-like tone, to which I would like to reply *"why?"* or *"you didn't hit me,"* (or jokingly, *"you didn't tell Joan to hit me, did you?"* good thing I've not actually said these things!) but I know they would say because of all the horrible things and blah, blah, blah. Truthfully, I have been robbed of a terrific amount of life, but I have also reached up to the sky in a few years of actual life. Because this reach keeps surpassing my grasp of the years of hell on earth, I have done some pretty awesome things and have come a long way (because of the Lord above). Don't think of my story as a sad one – it **is** tragic at times – a prisoner in my own home, unloved, abandoned, used…but think of it as eye opening. Think of the turn around! I'm not even done turning around, yet! Reflecting on this right now, I see that the one worst thing is to be either the one who denied the help or to be the offender. I am so grateful that my conscience is clear in this respect. I <u>cannot</u> express the strength of God's hand in my life, now that I see it years later. It is amazing! And I have only been alive for about five years!

Another thing is that although I have been in many dating relationships, I chose specifically to not write about them because I know what kind of dirt people dig for. The marketing consultant who called proceeded to ask for photos of me and tried to dig around my personal life – asking questions about relationships with men (saying it was a work survey). He kept saying "I will take care of you," but that was irritating because he thought that he was getting somewhere by saying that! He would ask questions like "so you and your boyfriend are together, and what does he say to you?"

To which I would reply "I don't have a boyfriend," because I didn't want to say *I love you,* which is what that man was rooting for.

And then he would laugh or say "why not?" or similar things. I knew it was a game, to see if I was in a relationship, so I willingly gave in to stop more games. He made up some dramatic life story that apparently was his friend's life to try to get me to say what I would say to a person in those events and right away I knew that it was not his story, so I grew distant and told him so very bluntly. I was at Chloe's house when I took the call and she thought it was funny when I told him I could tell he was lying. I actually switched workers because he was queer and very unprofessional – I was not seeing his face, so why did he want to see mine? How do my relationships with men affect the professional marketing of a book? They don't.

That man's actions were enough to tell me that my choice was right. Don't folks realize that people who go through tough stuff can see through facades more clearly? This is part of life; there are sharks everywhere. I do not want my face to be splashed all over because that is how I prefer it…and…when I say I don't have money – I meant it literally. I will not bend over backwards for fake glory. Maybe most people would relish the glory, but quite frankly, right now I choose different…just like God chose different for me.

I actually sold some books to my social workers – all three of them – Jasmine, Bertha and Lexi. It was amazing to see their support and that they are actually kind of proud of me. The looks on their faces were exactly what I needed to know that it was a good thing to have written the book. Lexi had walked me to the car to get her copy of my book and she was reminiscing… and some of the things she spoke of are things that I wrote about! She manages the place now and wants to read the book to see how things could be done better – which is so cool!! I hope it helps! It is moments like these that let me know that I am the lucky one. Lexi had looked at me and said "you are shining" and she meant it. I have never been told that, but it was so good to hear! My last childhood dream is now fulfilled!

I wonder if God could truly have stopped everything from happening – I know He is God who can do anything, but I wonder if He could have swung it so that people would have chosen to behave better. I wonder why He didn't. I try hard to motivate or encourage people around me to do well, but it is just words because most people don't **want** to be better because they don't believe in themselves enough to work hard. I can yak all I want, but in the end it is the person's choice. Not everyone is a survivor and Helen helped me realize that in regards to Gladys.

Sadly enough it is also my choice to slack off of practicing music when I am tired or not feeling well or just being lazy or busy, and so the improvements are coming very slowly. It is so hard without a direct motivation, though! I am not taking lessons because I can learn by myself, but it is hard without a person there to kick my butt. I know now that I do have musical talent, but without practice…sometimes love of music just is not enough.

These are the things that I wish to see for the New Year coming up. I wish to keep growing in faith in God. I am seeing the extent of grace, reaching to the lowliest to meet me in the darkness, and I have experienced God's providence from rainbows to dirt. The credit card coming the day before I left for the Caribbean was definite providence as were my bills being covered despite the money I gave away this year. I always give away and then calculate it in my head somewhat remorseful of the amount I chose to give because I seem to always find that it has cut me short of just getting by. True enough, the finances pull together so that I am always, *always* getting by with just a little extra on top. I have no idea how it works but it's awesome! I think there is merit in generosity and also in being gutsy.

This coming year I would like to know God's love. I know that Jesus died on the cross, but I am talking about His fatherly love. I think it stems from my needing a parent – true, there is Noella and Drew, but I need someone who will fight for me and who knows me well and while I believe they do know me, God just knows me better. I need Him to be the parent that motivates me to learn music, to practice and perform and also to raise me with love. I need love. This is the first year of my life that I have experienced love from humans…or admitted that I need it. I know that Noella and Drew have proclaimed it and shown it, so to rephrase I will say this is the first time I have **seen or accepted** love from people.

The next thing I desire is self control and discipline; to be on time for work, to really grow in music and performance, to focus on studies at school. I know that people seem to think there is this great rush to get a degree when you're young, but I see no hurry. I barely scraped through grade twelve with hardly the classes I needed – I am not sure if I should have graduated at all because I went as far as grade ten in some classes, and it is biting me in the butt now. I have decided to go for a medical degree, but in order to do so I need to upgrade five or six high school classes (good times; I still look young enough to go to high school!).

Medicine has always been interesting – how they work and what works for which parts of the body, so I thought that this would make a fine plan B and still allow music in my life because lets face it; if I was meant to be famous and sing for the rest of my life I'm sure it would have happened by now. Someone was trying to get me into the pre-med years without upgrading grade twelve classes because it would be quicker, but there is no way I would be able to maintain higher grades in that case, so I am going to take my time and do this right; there is no big hurry.

I would also like to be more encouraging – I just want to be a nice person because it is something that I am choosing to aspire for myself. I like nice people and so am working at it and am starting deep first so that it is not a shallow thing. I will not be a floor mat though, as I had been recently for Gladys, but wisdom shows that kindness goes further than arrogance or anger and even though I am not a meanie, there is plenty of work to be done.

This year I would like to publish my second and third books and would also like to have a few more songs under my belt – recorded on my own or not. I strive to be a better performer so I am determined to go back to music nights. Last year my goal was church – for some odd reason it just felt like something God wanted to happen, so I reluctantly followed (kind of without knowing it). This year my goal is music nights. I want to become a good singer and entertainer – just because I want to - and the way to do that is to get out there and do it, so I will. I like that Esther gives good and honest input in this regard.

This year is probably going to be one of business what with the books and music and school and work and all that, but I think it will also be a year of movement. I cannot sit still for long, and it is time for me to stop floundering in this little hut. Earlier on I had said that life seems like one big fight and for what? Well now I know that we all fight for the same thing: sunlight. Like the trees and plants in the rain forest, we all wait for the giant trees to fall so that we can struggle and push our way up to the sky. We will strangle each other and trample around and battle all the way uphill for a brief second in the light.

These two years have been of great character development and boundary expansion. I feel like the closure will enable me to grow more quickly now, and as it is, I go out of my way to stretch my boundaries in a healthy way.

Living with Rita, keeps revealing that there are basic things that I just do not know about – that I should care about, but don't (like taking pride in hard earned material things) – and so I have to remind her that I come from a different life. She gets it, but she also has to adjust to having someone in the house because she was by herself and now she cannot do everything the way she used to. When we see each other, we get along and she is fine at communicating, but I that ole wall of mine sure goes up quickly. She is tolerant and I am trying to remain on my best behavior. I like it because she has taken a genuine interest in my writing and she is very considerate and good hearted…and enjoys my humor most of the time; even when I wake her up by playing the trumpet at seven thirty in the morning. ☺ She said I could!

One time Shaun and I were visiting before supper and a movie and I did the dishes while we waited for Rita to come home after work. Seeing her car in the back alley, I turned to Shaun quickly and said "hey, do you know any good pranks?"

"Not really," he said good-naturedly, sitting at the table.

"Hm," I schemed while I opened the oven to clean a dirty pan from there. All of a sudden I had a stroke of genius. "Would you be able to fix the oven door if I took it off?" I asked with a mischievous grin. He shrugged and said "probably."

"Ah, she's coming!" I squealed delightedly. He grabbed the oven door and ran to put it in my room. I quickly turned back to the dishes and he slid into his seat at the table just as Rita unlocked the door and walked in.

"Hello," she greeted cheerily. We chatted for a short while and then as Rita turned to exit the kitchen to put her things away, she froze. I could tell by her stance that she had noticed the oven door. Shaun and I killed ourselves, laughing so hard, but when Rita was less than amused, we put the oven door back on. "How do you even **think** of things like that?" she had said later.

"Oh, quite quickly," I had answered, still giggling. A sense of humor is always great as long as it is used in good measure. The trials of this year had not squashed that out – I was still myself.

Rita has shown me things, too, like how sometimes people do things in a caring way, but I am totally oblivious even to their efforts. This is not intentional, but it is because of total ignorance – I just don't know certain things, but I am learning. This also comes with knowing a person and time allows that. Rita and I do not chat to get to know each other or really want to, so even if she does something to try to look out for me, I will not see it as such because we do not know each other at all. Of course I will react more harshly with her than with someone I see regularly. But I keep in mind that she is a good person and it helps plenty.

Sometimes I do not know what is "normal" and what is not, so oftentimes things happen and I think it is a huge deal, while other things happen that are huge deals to other people that I give no regard to. For example some people take pride in material things – or money – Gladys bent over backwards for money – but I hate working for it, so I don't have much of it. Some people take pride in their material things – for whatever reasons – but I do not understand that because it is all temporary. I worked hard for my keyboard to buy it straight out, but would not say that I take pride in it…I like it and I use it and let other people play on it. But I know that if I worked hard for it once, I could do it again if necessary. When we die, all of our material things are not going to be with us.

Well Rita and I discuss our differences and she is usually (if not always) the one to start the talks, but we both recognize things about each other and I think that for once I really am in a good place where I can rest and grow and hopefully heal.

One thing sticks out the most when it comes to Rita; some words that she spoke that have not left me as of yet. When I had first moved in and we were chatting, she had said "I *want* to be a good person in your life." Not often one hears that, hey? Speaking of life…

I wonder what song my life would be if it were one song – I feel that it would be unpredictable with some nice chord progressions, but it would start with tri-tones and then play in a minor key with sevenths and suspend fourths for some dissonance, but the words could be almost anything from sorrow to bitterness to anger to longing to laughter. It is hard to guess as I am not the one writing it, but I do have input – very much like in the studio where I bring ideas to show Dylan, and he puts it together and tweaks it here and there. I wonder if God is tweaking my life to allow my own ideas…who knows, but I do know one thing: there is no choice but to go on because even giving up has been impossible for me to do!

It is **so** hard when I look at other people's lives – like my roommate and her family – and see bountiful blessings. Everyone has their struggles – the grass always looks greener – but here is someone who has *never* had to fight for her life, or even to get by, but then it dawned on me that the blessings in their lives is because they have done right by God. Someone down the line really pleased God, so the generations are blessed, just like David's sons were allowed to reign over Israel or Judah if even for a short time "for the sake of their father, David." It is crazy. If you do something right in the eyes of God, it will carry on for years. Perhaps it is my turn to try to do so. For some reason – maybe to start a lineage of blessings – the pen has been placed in my hand – to write my own sonnets. I have sought death and it would not meet me, so I have to keep living and listening. The unspun sonnets teach more than the generic ballads because they are so predictable! As the saying goes, "experience is the best teacher!"

An unspun sonnet is beautiful because it is untouched, so I am at the point where I can choose the next keys or lyrics or melodies or musical phrases to put in. As time goes on, my musicality in more than one way will get so much better. Right now my hand is wobbly and the pen is heavy and I keep spilling the ink and tearing the paper, but my song is not completely new. Maybe I have come to the time to write something different. The bridge is the most unpredictable part of the song, as it is to be the most unique section. Here you can change keys, go atonal if you want and either repeat words with a different melody or harmony… you can be very generic OR turn the meaning of the whole song right around! It is so exciting! Perhaps some bright, happy, major chords will float here to stay - or better yet- maybe the whole song will end in a major key. Perhaps one day I will look at my own life and tell my own kids of my many blessings.

I think this past year was a series of unplanned chords that sounded good. It seems that everything had to happen this way all at once to draw out the poison. There were so many leaps as I jumped from stone to stone, and I feel that I almost fell into the rushing waters head first, but somehow I always regained balance. I hopped a few stones in this one year, and hopefully one day I will make it safely to the other side, to finish my unspun sonnets under a tree on a blissfully sunny day. As Jesus said when he died: "it is finished," (John 19:30).

Epilogue

Well this brand new year opened up slowly, but it was nice. With a good night's sleep under my belt, I felt ready for a new start. I went to church and took communion to symbolize a new commitment to God and then Pastor Russell prayed that I would experience the love of God - something I had been asking for in secret; a great confirmation that I am seeking the right things. Actually *everything* he prayed echoed my own quiet prayers (never discussed with anyone) of dealing with knowing God's love.

When my book finally came out, it was very peculiar to hold it because although it was new, I never need to read it to know its contents. It is almost weird to look at the words – my words – printed in the pages of a book. A book that I designed and wrote and edited...I think it is a good weird. At first I kept flipping the pages just to flip the pages. It is even more peculiar to sign it as the author because I am so detached from it; it feels like someone else could have written it, which maybe spares me from an ego?

Maybe now I will just publish poetry; I enjoy writing poems much better than autobiography or long pieces and it is at the point where I can either leave this as is or continue the series as my life progresses. People insist that this is such a big accomplishment, but I just don't see it. However, the word "author" rolls quite nicely off the tongue; another childhood dream fulfilled in this very instant! I had a surprising amount of support and people were anxious to buy the thing to read and things are fine for now. I was pleased to see that Marie, Noella's daughter was the first to buy a copy of the book! Ephraim and Jonas actually seemed quite excited about it, too. Not gonna lie, but I was quite surprised to receive their support.

I told Pastor Russell that I wrote about his brother and when he asked why I didn't change it, I said "because that's not the way things happened, but I do not feel the same anymore." And at first he was displeased but I think it's all good now, since I was fair about what I wrote. That scared me about the whole thing because I did not want Joan to get a hold of my book, so I told that to the family in the Caribbean and they just said "I'll leave that for you to decide." Then I decided to not care about it anymore because everyone knows that I wrote the book and she will probably not even read it. I still pray that this book will be a good thing somehow, but I think it already has been in the fact that I have never really expressed feelings about things and through writing, that has changed. If Joan and Daniel ever *do* read it then they will know exactly how I saw things and how I feel. The ball is in their court and it will probably stay there; game over is what I suspect. Unlikely, but I could be wrong.

I recognize from sharing my testimony in Portland that not everyone will believe the contents of these books and the fact of the matter is that some people *do* deny the bad things happening right in their midst. Even people I know refuse to buy it or read it because they know it will make them sad. But I don't care if people don't believe it; I care if **one** person out of five million is truly encouraged to try again or to do something wonderfully great for somebody else. I myself have been doing little good deeds – far more than used to be – giving rides to strangers, lending money, donating if I can (sometimes when I can't, but always pulling through), helping with groceries if someone needs it, checking up on elderly folks of the church, giving things away, helping load or unload things, letting the drivers cut me off and go ahead, giving directions…even smiling or listening for a few minutes *or* sharing back when a person confides and it all makes a huge difference. At this point I know I have found a good church, but the band...well...sadly...

When visiting with Alice around Christmas time, we ran into the drummer and we had a chat and found a few things to work out between the lead singer and myself (such as no smoking for her), but it was nice because the drummer let me know that I was not just a commodity in the band – I was a fundamental part of it. The singer and I made more of an effort to stand each other and I see now that she really is not so terrible. We got along well and with a lead guitarist I had a lot more flexibility within the band – to sing back up, or play guitar or piano... and it was great to jam with other people like that because it increases musicality. We had great fun and I am learning that I can do what I do within songs that I don't believe in, and it is good to just relax with music and be goofy.

I did get the boot from the band even though the drummer vouched for me, but the singer knew that I didn't quite appreciate her lyrics, so she had issues with that, and the fact that I had pretty much ceased going to practices did not help my case at all. The drummer said that the singer had said "I don't want her playing my music," but the thing is - I had written the music for some of her songs! Without me she wouldn't have the music to sing with, but she wanted to go solo and it all kind of fell flat. The band actually broke up, but it is fine because the business of life swept me away and so I was removed from that whole scene.

I actually didn't know about any of this until months later when the drummer texted to ask if I still wanted to jam with her. I did and she said the whole band broke up after I left and she still wanted to learn guitar, so I started teaching her casually and it was great fun to goof off. Who says you can't have musical humor? Cuz we sure do!

A worker from a café knows this drummer lady well and we had interesting conversations about God and then (when Alice left) music. His name is Paul and he is very knowledgeable of music – he told me of modal changes and playing atonal within certain keys...we spoke of various scales and sounds and I walked away with my head spinning – but I loved it! I played piano on my breaks at the resort and am now known as "the girl who plays piano" but I was still surprised when workers informed me that a position to play at banquets was offered. I took the hint and went to apply.

I got the job, to my complete surprise and utter delight! It is the best job ever – to play and learn a skill – how great that they gave me the chance! I feel it was very God ordained because of how it all played out and there has never been a time in my life when I actually felt triumphant – like I had accomplished something, but the first day on the job, I walked away thanking God and grinning from ear to ear because *I did it!! I finally did it! Music is my job and I LOVE IT!!* How lucky am I that God allows me to do this?

The portable studio came in – just a small "pocket studio," but I have already experimented with it, aiming for just two songs per month – one cover song and one originally written song...but many more than that keep pouring out. Maybe through this little gadget I will spin many sonnets. I am experimenting and finding my own voice and sounds to match the mood of the words. Life is not just one song for everybody, but many books of it, placed into chapters with brilliant, fanatical, electric, dreamy or dismal pictures. I am living through the eyes of a painter, with the ears and hands of a musician, with the voice of a speaker and the words of a poet. I love being creative! I am glad that God has picked me for this!

Even now I see my free will *within* His will for my life – people say that we have no choice because God is going to do what He wants to anyway. Well IF that were the case, He still allows you to choose what to do within His will – for example I feel that He chose creativity for me...like writing, but I can cross-assimilate that creativity and choose to do music too...or painting, or pottery, or photography, or acting... It is not working outside of God's will if I pray for His will and use what He gave me. Even if He chooses music (which is hard because it does not come easily) then I still have a choice as to where or which way I use the songs...or what to instruments to learn. Or I could say no and be miserable like I was in Portland.

I can choose which colors to paint with, which chords or modes to use, which story to tell and this has been the one I have chosen to share with my writing. My own story told in two parts – one of overcoming hardships and the other of great conclusion. The first book, *One Life* is about hope and overcoming trials. This second book *Unspun Sonnets* is about resolution and joy in stretching and resting. So let's dissect the title. Why *Unspun Sonnets*? Because that is where the best music comes from – the new songs that are not planned. When I sing into the studio, I lay a beat track through the keyboard and then sing, often not knowing what key or words follow which notes. I find that I am singing a lot about things that are deep (to me) and so music is also becoming quite an outlet…but my songs seem to revolve around the dating relationships… the boys that I chose not to write about in here.

The music comes out is best when it is unprepared. Of course no practice is the wrong way to go – heaven knows that I have learned the hard way that preparation is good! When walking across town this winter, I bundled up good and took care of myself only to find that I could go long distances with more endurance **and** I quite enjoyed being outside. But not planning every single dot and line allows time to live and grow. Perhaps the next picture I paint with be of a burnt bridge, or the next song I'll listen to will be *Bridge over Troubled Waters,* or *Walk On* or *Blue.* Perhaps the next song to write will be one of hope or love, or the next chords to hear will be major lifts. So in music also, God is saying that I am not finished yet. Not even close. The title *Unspun Sonnets* could be translated as *You'll Never Know if You Don't Try,* but that is a rather long title, don't you think?

Sometimes I am glad to have lived this life the way it has spiraled down. There are many things that I will always struggle with – example being school; example being people who manipulate; example being people who did things; people who didn't do anything…the feeling of missing out on life. Another example is how I feel about Joan and Daniel and the Stardens. True, I did receive a vast amount of closure in the fact that I no longer have to wonder what is true or why we were given up, but the deceits have left my heart hardened towards them. God has this fickle way of making people face the worst things in their life (if they truly want change) and for me right now that is Joan, so I wait for the day since I have not seen or talked to them since reading the files. Hopefully by that time I will be less calloused, but right now I prefer to keep my distance. These past years include the fulfillments of all my childhood dreams – reuniting with my family, meeting Paul Brandt, becoming an author…acting in movies. These are all things that kids dream about, things that I never dwelled on (except for being an author), and it is crazy how they have ALL come true in some crazy God-schemed way!

Back to winter this year my, how attitude makes a huge difference! Whether known or not, each person can choose to like or dislike or learn from each bump. People whine and whimper about winter, how cold it is; how they hate shoveling; how long the season is; how the roads are slippery how long snow removal is taking…it gets on my nerves! I used to dislike winter too, but now am so chipper that I find myself quite enjoying the season. I also do not find it as terribly chilly as I used to and shoveling is a *tremendously* great work out! People complain and gripe and mope, but it's so easy to find cheery ways to cope and that's why people say things like "*you inspire me*," or "**you're too positive**," or "*it was a pleasure to meet you*," (with a nice firm handshake), or "**you have such a fire** (a funny one for the winter)…" and on and on it goes.

People say these things and while I smile and accept with a courteous nod or a polite "thank you," but it is not flattering in the least and I'll tell you why. Every single person on mars (kidding! on earth) could be just as "amazing" if they chose to not let little things bother them; if they chose to like winter or to be cheerful and try again when the moment calls for misery and defeat. Of course I am a bit of a hypocrite because when things get down and ugly, the last thing I think about is smiling. At work I had a little time on my hands, so I was reading *Chicken Soup for the Kid's Soul* because that was the only book available.

I came across a quote that seems cheesier than cheetos but fits right into the theme of this book, and it goes like this: *Attitudes are self-created. You are free to choose to be victimized by circumstance or people, or you can choose to look at life with an open mind and be victorious. No one else can choose your attitude for you. Your perspective and choice of attitude gives you the power to be in control. That is the essence of true freedom.*[2] Note the words *power to be in control.*

2 Chicken Soup for the Kid's Soul; pg 127; quote credited to Irene Dunlap.

Power is what everyone seeks – from people to animals to plants to microbiotic cells. Irene Dunlap is very right in this quote because although people can force ideals or brain wash you, at some point in time you become brainwashed because of your consent of being controlled by someone else. Someone once said to me "you cannot refuse my prayers," and it bears the same manner of this quote. Joan did hit me and lock me away and made me believe terrible things that were untrue, but instead of submitting to that forever, I chose to know truth.

While these truths have been very hurtful, and hard to obtain, I also chose to let them help me grow. Sometimes I hold onto anger because it feels like there is nothing left without it, but I choose to not harness it toward anyone since they cannot pay for their own sins by my hand. It is not my job to judge or punish anyone. Joan does not care if I know the contents of the files, nor do I have intentions of telling her, as it will make no difference. Sandy at the church described me as "beauty from ashes" and "a joyful mourner," but I am wondering when do I truly become beautiful? When do I stop grieving? What is honestly true in the world?

Gladys had convinced her "best" friend Denise to divorce her husband in one short month from when I left and all for petty reasons. Now Denise is living with her and Gina. I was relieved to find out that Wanda had indeed been spared from Gladys' daggers. It is known that I am blessed to have found Rita at the time that I did – which proves that God provided ahead of time because He knew what was going to happen at the house of Gladys.

Poor Denise has fallen into the games and I see that Gladys is recreating herself in this young so-called friend of hers. Not good, because although I pray for her, it seems that Gladys just hashes out more poison. Thankfully Gina has strong resilience and good support around her constantly, although one could still see certain influences seeping into her. We still chat every once in a while. I now pray for both Joan and Gladys because although there is nothing I can do *physically* to help them or to change them for the better, I **can** pray for both of them freely. Perhaps one day I may see the difference it made just like grandpa in the Caribbean.

Of course, attitude also works within what you believe. For me the Christian faith works well, so I pray to God and choose to believe that He hears and answers in His way (although many times I still question and doubt), and then I see or experience definite results. Just because I choose to be positive and like winter does not mean that winter is always nice to me. Sometimes the roads are terribly slippery and some days I have to drive twenty everywhere, or walk in minus forty-two degree weather. Other times I have to walk all the way across the city in a blizzard, or in thigh high snow. But to mope about winter, I just sit in the grumpiness and then will find things to complain about in spring, and then in summer, and then in fall, and then nothing makes me happy at all anymore ever again. Ah, the life of a moper!

Every situation has something good in it, but you have to work to see it, and if you can't see anything good then you have to choose to be safe. If I were to stay inside all day and not go outside ever in the winter, then that would make it more unbearable; the same happens when I do not dress appropriately or eat right. Preparation goes a long way.

It has all been very eye opening but now the time has come to work towards my latest dreams and to give from what I have learned. It feels good to have some of these things come out in different ways and I cannot wait until it all comes out and then I can start sucking the poison out of the snake bites and then apply the healing salve. I am still just sucking and spitting poison, but I know that it will end for real someday soon. I must admit before closing that I was surprised at the amount hardness and hurt and anger still inside, especially after writing the first book because I was so sure that I had moved on and was doing okay. God obviously knew better and chose to show me because I had sincerely asked Him to reveal what wasn't right so that it could be fixed. What a long but definitely not boring road ahead!

Speaking of roads…I had wondered how I was going to top off last year, you know, with excitement because I had went to the Caribbean and rollercoaster and sea animals…but boy, oh boy! This year is a topper! I randomly decided to go with a friend to stay with her family for a couple weeks this summer – and her family is from the same place as my uncle Vinny who claims to be a musician. We are also going to drive to see

Niagara Falls and Marine Land and a musical and maybe even busk! I want to busk so badly! Just for fun…

Oh, you think that's exciting? Check this out – I am also going on a cruise expenses paid (except for the flight ticket) because that is what Drew's family is doing for Christmas this year and I can actually go because I will have the holidays off from school! How crazy is that? At first they were not going to cover my cruise expenses (including meals) but they decided that I *am* family and so they are! I have always wanted to go on a cruise or a ship! And *then* Drew wants to stay longer in LA to go to Sea World and Universal Studios and Disneyland. I am going to see if there are auditions to work at Disneyland as a character. Why not?

Years ago, Drew had promised to take me to Disneyland when I told him and Noella of how Joan got tickets for the whole family to Universal studios and Marine Land. Joan had rubbed it in my face just before terrifying me about foster care for the last time. Drew's promise was made out of compassion, and many other people have made similar promises, like the Swazie's, but lo and behold, that ship's about to sail!

Also, I tried out for a musical and a medical job at the same time… uh, okay…in the same week. The pharmacist hiring said I had the job, but then I tried out for the musical and told the doctor about it and then because the trip with my friend in the summer for two weeks was already booked, she said it just wouldn't work out. I was sad because it would have been great experience in the medical field, but I wanted to live a little before settling down to smell some old textooks.

I chose on the last day of auditions to try out for a local musical and so did not have a song prepared, but I winged it and the try-out was rather fun. I was told that I now have a "beautiful voice" with a "rich tone." And I thought I had sung horribly! Talk about encouraging! When discussing rehearsal schedules, I mentioned that the new job needed required evenings and then it didn't look like it would work out, so I left without being asked for a callback. I thought I didn't make it, so I was put out because I lost both opportunities because of each other.

Instead of moping about it, I sat back and thought, *now what, God?* Well the "now what" answered itself soon enough. I wrote a placer exam for schooling, so that took care of the fall, and was notified that I was in the musical! I don't know how, because I was told that everyone was required to attend callbacks, but I wasn't asked to! Oh, well. I am more proud of it this time because I did it on my own – no voice teachers vouching, no friends swinging around – it was on my own; no strings attached.

Also, Paul (the musician who works at the café below my workplace) and I were talking and he suggested that I teach music through the local music store on Main Street. I chatted to the owner of the store and because I am hired to play piano at the resort, I do not need an official grade, but I think I may study up for grade eight piano and voice anyway. So that was a window that opened up and I think I may be teaching on the side of schooling in the fall – and also I will join choir again in the winter! AND my boss just mentioned a Christmas production that will be going on soon and said to hand in a performance resume because she thought I could get in! It is so crazy how one can seek something so badly, and they yearn for it **so** hard, but as soon as they let it go, the thing just comes their way like a boomerang. Aaand…I just started another part time job playing music for disabled people! I was kind of tossed into it, but I think I will like it in time…this is part of my stretching my boundaries thing. I had applied as a health care attendant.

Uhh…I think God wants me to do music – maybe because I love it or perhaps for the people I will meet, but I am glad that He chose me to live this life. Talk about living! It is all so crazy. And it is cool how God **really does** take care of things. Shortly before try-outs for the musical I had prayed specifically for encouragement for direction. I have not given up on medicine, but right now I intend to relax before going to school for that.

Of course, not everything is perfect, as I am facing things I have never dealt with before, but I know it will get better – I just don't know when. And in the mean time I am trying to keep moving forward. I had prayed for a time to rest when I was at Gladys' chaotic house and now God has answered, so if it means loneliness for a while, then so be it. I was granted a request so now is time to heal and learn…and grow…and try…and…Yeah, that's all I got for now. Well, this is where I have been and where I am at and sort of where I am heading, so I hope there was at least one word that made you smile or think something good! Keep yer chin up and just know that things are NOT impossible! And don't be a jerk because someone else will be a jerk to you and then it will start a vicious biting and barking circle with rabies. Life is what you make of it.

This Easter was different in the fact that I gave Jesus more regard. At church it was shown how severe the crucifixion was. The pastor speaking had made a short version of the whips they would have used and hit a solid bag of flour five times, (not very hard), and after five strikes the bag was open and flour flew everywhere. He said that Jesus was cursed for our sins (as he was sinless) and I realized that it was so that we could live. People focus on laying down your life for Jesus, kind of like "he died for you, so can you die for him?" which is fine, in the measure of self sacrifice, but when I think of Jesus' back being whipped for me, I picture it being for my freedom. What if Jesus died so that I could *live?* But now also, Jesus owns our lives because of this and so he could place us into whatever situations he chooses – good or bad – but only when we allow him to have dominion. Maybe I am just crazy, but in reality Jesus owns us all, even if we don't want him to, but he lets it be our choice because of the significance of free will.

The thought kind of freaks me out and my heart tends to harden, but the odd time I will ask "what kind of master are you?" and then hope for an answer. But I don't know if realizing this really changes anything…I am still me, but I just have to listen more to his voice. This is where living **for** Jesus comes in.

Like Hagar in the wilderness, after running away, I have also named God, not as the one who sees – but as the One who Hears. God listens and Jesus has good ears and these past years and my little zests for life keep proving that. It's just hilarious that God is *so* gigantic, he can roar and shake and crash and blast and boom and bang as loud as possibly possible, yet he chooses to speak in a small, tiny, barely audible whisper. That's being modest!

Okay, one final thing – I promise – because it has brought about the most extreme closure possible! First of all, this part is written months after the actual book was done – I am just editing now ☺ but I hope that you will find this interesting. I went to Esther's house church where Alice showed up later on. The Johnson's are firm believers in prophesy and payer and the laying on of hands… they had some guest speakers speaking about "divine appointments" and perhaps my being there *was* once such meeting!

At the end of the service was a prayer session where everyone prayed over people one at a time (since it was such a small group, this was not too tedious) and as per usual, I stood further back and observed. I am used to seeing charismatic things like prophesy and tongues and all that, but I am not used to being a direct part of it…

So this couple prayed over everyone and I was the very last person they came to (of course), and I reluctantly consented to their prayer "but don't touch my face," I had said. The lady wanted to hold my hand, but I was shy – I don't know why, but I tend to get defiant (probably an indicator of fright) – so I said if she absolutely needed contact, then the elbow or shoulder was fine. I just remember thinking that I needed "a gentle hand" (whatever that means) and so this woman paused for a second or two and her eyes welled up with tears and she said "Jesus loves you," to which my head responded *Jesus loves everyone.* "He died for your sins," she continued, and I thought *he died for everyone's sins.*

"God has a purpose for you," the pastor continued…the game in my mind continued with *God has a purpose for everyone,* and she continued with "He has a future designed just for you," and my brain continued with *God has a future designed for everyone!* It was a mixture of defiance as well as a strong overdose of cliché's. I am beyond sick of people saying things like that without meaning them…or when you least want to hear it…or as if those words make everything better! Like "Jesus will take your troubles away," when I'm down and I hear that I think – *well where is he **now**?* I was getting to that same mood by this point, but then she said "God takes those tears of yours, and he just bottles them. He bottles them and keeps them because they are so precious to Him."

My head started to say *God bottles* – but then I realized that I couldn't even think that! God does not bottle everyone's tears! This woman also said other things that hit close to home and they were things about what happened when I was a little girl and I think the only way she could have known was if the Johnsons spoke to her previously, but what she said went deeper than what they know...like about God hearing me when I was a child crying in the dark. Her saying that was strange, but it captured my attention! So I got all emotional and instead of singing afterward, I played the baby grand piano, partially to soothe my soul and partially because tears were literally falling out of my eyes – not running down my cheeks, but falling **out** of my eyes – so I played for a while and tears fell while I played. It was surprising to get so emotional.

Later that week while preparing for that trip with my friend, I was about to facebook someone some details, but I typed into google instead: *why would God bottle my tears?* And the answer was surprising! First of all Psalm 56:8 is a direct reference to God bottling the tears and it's pretty fancy how not only what the lady said was scripture (which she might have known, but I hadn't), but it was also from a song! Pretty cool...and from exploring the results on the infamous internet, I learned that the Romans had used little bottles called lachrymatories to catch the tears of suffering or sick loved ones. These bottles are tiny fine glass or pottery and once they were full of the tears, they would be sealed and kept in remembrance of either the event or the person if they passed away. How cool is that? Don't believe me? Google it yourself! ☺ And there were essays written by people who were hurting in different ways – welcome to the world – so they seemed to come from good places and they were based on scripture and the messages said (summarized)...

The vials of tears that God keeps will one day turn to vials of blood for Him to pour out on judgment day...which is pretty severe. And awesome! So no matter where I go in life until judgment day, those tears will be present. How strange that God is interested in our tears... or collects them, nonetheless. You see, I have always thought that I was invented to be a garbage can – to hold trash and to make people feel better about themselves – "that Karee, always good for a laugh!" but God's purpose was so much bigger! And I had *just* asked Him to tell me why everything had to happen – that if I was a garbage can to tell me so that I could know. My "why" is finally answered!

It makes me feel small, actually, and a bit amazed because His purpose is so much better than the one I had assumed for myself. It really means something and that is all I know to say to describe how it feels. It is really humbling…which I like. So all the tears that I cried because of Joan, Daniel, Susie, Jocelyn, foster parents, boys…they are all there, in jars, probably cool little jars since I'm an artist in various ways…and on a shelf with a purpose. The cool thing about this is that it takes away the pressure to cry – people are always telling me that I should cry – but I don't like to or really want to. I do think it is good every now and then, but I certainly don't make a habit of it, but this way, there is no *need* to because all the tears I couldn't cry are in bottles, too, and all the tears I **want** to cry are there and they will all pour out someday.

Now the weird thing is these things I say that I had been asking God for have all been in the silence of the house when Rita is out. I do not discuss prayers and things very often – if at all – because people cannot be trusted with deep things like that. People cast so much judgment and make up stories when they don't know the facts. Such prayers are so personal that it ought to be between God and my heart. So these were answers to things that I had *never* spoken of to people!

I knew for a while that I was "flipping the dead leaf" (as I wrote in one of my poems for my third book), but this bottling of the tears thing just wraps these two books up so nicely that it seemed fitting to slip it right in! I like to say that I am at the "now what?" stage because I don't know what is to come, but hopefully it will be great! I have a feeling that the greener side will be this one – or to paraphrase, the best is yet to come. This year has been terrific so far, and I know that it will keep getting better!

Well, these are my personal experiences typed out for you to read in hopes that you might one day find a reason to share them with someone else or maybe relate to them yourself. Even though not every dream has turned out the way I imagined as a child, some prayers are better answered with a "no." But God is not completely heartless, for he gave me more resolution and closure and family than I ever dreamed of. If He can do all this in two tiny years, imagine what He could do with a whole lifetime! Let it be well with you and blessings on you, reader, for seeing my story. Lastly, the traditional clean joke… ☺

God's Left Hand

Little Bobby was spending the weekend with his grandmother.
His grandmother decided to take him to
the park on Saturday morning.
It had been snowing all night and everything was beautiful.

His grandmother remarked... "Doesn't it look
like an artist painted this scenery?
Did you know God painted this just for you?"

Bobby said, "Yes, God did it and he did it left handed."

This confused his grandmother a bit, and she asked him
"What makes you say God did this with his left hand?"

"Well," said Bobby, "we learned at Sunday School
last week that Jesus sits on God's right hand!" [3]

---

3 http://www.Christian-Jokes.Org/jokes37.html

About the Author

Karee Stardens began writing One Life in grade twelve and decided to publish it a few years later. Unspun Sonnets is the concluding sequel and was written as the events took place - while the first book was being published. There were so many unexpected events that allowed such great closure that she could not leave the first book unfinished. Unspun Sonnets adds a nice close to the burnt bridges and leaves an open door of better things to come. As a child, Karee dreamed of becoming an author, and she quite enjoys writing poetry, so keep an eye for the next books!